SEERS OF GOD

DATE DUE

april 22, 2014

Early America
History, Context, Culture

Jack P. Greene and J. R. Pole
SERIES EDITORS

✳ ✳ ✳ ✳

SEERS OF GOD

PURITAN PROVIDENTIALISM IN THE RESTORATION AND EARLY ENLIGHTENMENT

✳

MICHAEL P. WINSHIP

THE JOHNS HOPKINS UNIVERSITY PRESS

BALTIMORE, MARYLAND

© 1996 The Johns Hopkins University Press
All rights reserved. Published 1996
Printed in the United States of America on acid-free paper
05 04 03 02 01 00 99 98 97 96   5 4 3 2 1

The Johns Hopkins University Press
2715 North Charles Street
Baltimore, Maryland 21218-4319

Frontispiece:
Illustration was taken from the title page of
John Foxe, *Acts and Monuments* (London, 1563).

Library of Congress Cataloging-in-Publication Data
will be found at the end of this book.

A catalog record for this book is available from the British Library.

ISBN 0-8018-5137-8

ISBN 0-8018-6376-7 (pbk)
paperback edition, 1999

For Eleanor, Eva, and Milton

The people of New-England were of a grave cast,
and had long been disposed to give a serious solemn construction
even to common events in Providence.

—THOMAS HUTCHINSON

No man knoweth either love or hatred by all that is before them.
All things come alike to all.

—ECCLESIASTES 9:1–2

Contents

✳

Acknowledgments xiii

Introduction 1

1
The Providence of the Massachusetts Puritans 9

2
Providence Besieged 29

3
Israel Strikes Back 53

4
Cotton Mather and the Hand of God 74

5
Cotton Mather and the Perils of Natural Philosophy 93

6
Cotton Mather and the True Power of Devils 111

7
Cotton Mather and the Decline of the Demonic 124

8
A Farewell to Wonders 138

Notes 153
Index 219

Acknowledgments

✳

Drafts of the manuscript, in whole or in part, were read by Patrick Curry, Michael F. Gibson, David D. Hall, Peter Lake, David Levin, Susan McMichaels, Laura Mason, R. Laurence Moore, Mary Beth Norton, and John Winship, and by Charles L. Cohen, the reader for the Johns Hopkins University Press. Peter Charles Hoffer read the manuscript and helped the project in numerous other ways. I am grateful for their advice and suggestions, saving me from factual errors and strengthening the arguments of the book. Responsibility for the end product, of course, rests entirely with me. My editor at Johns Hopkins, Robert J. Brugger, improved the manuscript's structure, and my copyeditor, David E. Anderson, improved its prose. Librarians and staff at the American Antiquarian Society, Cambridge University Library, Doctor Williams Library, Houghton Library of Harvard University, the Massachusetts Historical Society, Olin Library of Cornell University, and the University of Georgia Libraries facilitated research. The University of Georgia awarded me several grants for travel and writing. I tried out ideas in articles in *Early American Literature*, the *Essex Institute Historical Collections*, the *New England Quarterly*, and the *William and Mary Quarterly*. Anna and Nathaniel Winship ensured a larger perspective and listened with enthusiasm to bedtime tales spun off from seventeenth-century "wonders." Eleanor Fruchtman Winship and Milton and Eva Fruchtman provided unstinting moral and material support without which the book never would have emerged. My thanks and appreciation to all.

All quotations have been reproduced as found in their source, except for obvious errors and where the original might be misleading. Thus, *i*, *u*, and *vv* have been replaced when they stood for *j*, *v*, and *w*, and "ye" has been replaced with "the."

Introduction

✳

The Puritans were gifted—or cursed—with an
overwhelming realization of an inexorable power at
work not only in nature but in themselves.
PERRY MILLER, *The New England Mind*

uritans had a term for the inexorable power they felt to be working within them and without them. They called it Providence. Providence served many purposes for the Puritans. It functioned as a learned theological term, and learned Puritans joined other theologians in dividing it into a myriad of subcomponents—common providence, special providence, first causes, second causes, governation, and conservation, among others. But Providence was far from being simply an abstract doctrine. It had a formative effect on the experience of these devout Calvinists, and its overarching presence gave it a great breadth of explanatory power. It offered consolation by assuring believers that all that befell them came from a loving, if often angry, God. It explained and organized the shifts in a believer's mental states in terms of the manipulations and comings and goings of supernatural agents involved in a great drama of redemption or damnation. It served no less as an explanatory and organizing principle for the external events in a person's life, as well as for the sweep of history. Providence provided a constant communication of God's intentions and commentaries to the Puritans, and Puritans scrutinized Providence for help in decision making and predicting the future.

Belief in Providence was scarcely limited to Puritans. It formed a fundamental aspect of religion in seventeenth-century England, although certainly not everyone matched the Puritans' intensity of belief. However, despite, or perhaps because of, its ubiquity, it remains relatively unexplored by historians.[1] Providentialism is a rich and wide field; the present study focuses on the her-

1

meneutics of the Massachusetts Puritans' providentialism. It is set within a
context of the suppression of Puritanism and the Puritans' providentialism
within English learned culture in the second half of the seventeenth century.
How did Massachusetts Puritans understand and react to those changes? How
and to what extent did they distinguish between hostile political impulses and
new, normative cultural standards? How did they transform their own assumptions and practices in the light of these?

✳

The Puritans' Providence thrived in the culture of wonders (to use David
D. Hall's term) that pervaded early-seventeenth-century English society. In
that culture the world seemed unpredictable and communicative. Natural disruptions like storms and earthquakes might be messages from God, and certainly strange sights like armies in the sky and rains of blood carried significance. A member of Parliament fainting on the House floor triggered earnest
discussion about the meaning of the omen. The press of semiotic significance
did not confine itself to events external to the psyche; a depressed person might
not know whether to attribute his or her state to God, Satan, witchcraft, or
simple melancholy.[2] The world bubbled forth a rich semiotic stew of intentions,
which all could freely taste. If a culture of wonders united all classes, until the
mid-1620s an unofficial Calvinist orthodoxy united the religious establishment
of the country. Calvinism fitted easily into a culture of wonders, and the Puritans' providentialism differed little from Calvin's.

The culture of wonders was a united one insofar as it grew out of widely
shared assumptions about the pervasiveness and effective material agency of
supernatural beings and the capacity of the natural world to offer commentaries
on human affairs. But wonders generated knowledge, and given the intertwining of knowledge, politics, and power, the issues of exactly how knowledge
could be generated within these assumptions and what constituted legitimate
knowledge produced heated dispute. Protestant reformers in general, and Puritans in particular, attacked a host of practices that today we would be likely to
subsume under the rubric of "magic," including many forms of divination and
astrology, as wicked and impious. But their vigorous attacks should not obscure
the fact that they had their own array of pious techniques for divining the hidden patterns of the world.

The discursive practices of the culture of wonders never more fully displayed their protean political potential in England than in the 1640s and
1650s, the time of the English Civil Wars and Interregnum. Puritans saw God's

arm constantly stretched out in their favor and raised against their enemies. On the Puritans' fringe, strange new sects emerged, inspired by the power of the Holy Spirit and by their understanding of the intentions of Providence. It has long been a historical commonplace that the "moderation" of Restoration Anglicanism constructed itself against the perceived excesses of the previous period. Similarly, historians of science recently have been exploring the way in which natural philosophers at this time consciously began to delegitimate the culture of wonders and the discursive practices that sustained it.[3] Historians of science have focused on the process as a reaction to occultism, political radicalism, and fringe sectarian groups, but the process they outline was directed no less deliberately at Puritanism and its form of providentialism.

Those existing strands of historiography, the religious and the scientific, form the starting point from which this book traces the development of providentialism in Restoration England. As a result of perceived Puritan political interpretive excesses, Anglicans deliberately redefined the nature and hermeneutics of Providence, in both the areas of religion and natural philosophy. These efforts formed part of the larger movement to redefine and exclude "enthusiasm" in the name of "reason" and "rational religion" for the furthering of social stability, a movement largely constituting the proto-form of the early English Enlightenment. Anglicans made it perfectly clear that Puritanism and its discursive practices, anchored in the assumptions of an earlier learned culture, fell decidedly on the wrong side of the newly expanded boundaries of enthusiasm.

By the end of the century, the landscape of English learned culture had settled down into a form in which one can discern something like a modern distinction acknowledged between religion and magic, with "occult" information largely inaccessible to humans through religious practices and magic mostly an affair of the "vulgar." In the context of this new division, the Puritans found themselves on the wrong side, the magic side. With a hundred years of fighting "superstition" behind them, Puritans discovered their own wonder-working Providence deemed superstitious and enthusiastic. While Protestantism has often been taken as responsible for the decline of magic, this expansion of the categories of superstition and enthusiasm did not result from Protestantism's teleological drive, but from a political and cultural struggle that the Puritans lost.[4]

As a result of being on the losing side, from the 1660s onwards the Puritans found themselves in a position of increasing intellectual marginalization, paralleling their political marginalization. Puritans, however, did not simply beat a retreat before these new standards. They actively resisted them on both sides of the Atlantic and reasserted their own, as they clung to categorizations of experience and interpretation that many Anglican thinkers were trying to render unacceptable.

That resistance is important for understanding English religious and intellectual history, but it is no less important for understanding the early intellectual and religious history of New England. This book accounts for intellectual change in Massachusetts in an English context, only occasionally evoking social, political, and economic change within Massachusetts, considered in an internalistic fashion, as explanatory factors. That focusing of attention, while not meant to minimize the complexities of Massachusetts Puritanism's internal development, is quite deliberate. The standard scholarly model of New England in the Restoration period is one of isolation.[5] One of the contentions in this book, however, is that changes within Puritan culture in Massachusetts closely paralleled changes within Puritan culture in England, for the same forces were at work on and within each, and given that parallel, those changes in Massachusetts can be studied as a part of, and indeed to a certain extent as a way of helping to understand, changes within English culture.

That parallel development was no coincidence. Ministers in Massachusetts were well aware of their transatlantic position. Members of New England's elite unquestionably felt themselves at the geographical periphery of intellectual discourse in England and expressed their frustration and concern with their remoteness. But they were also at a religious periphery with regard to English learned culture, and that religious periphery, relatively neglected by scholars, had no geographical basis. The cultural isolation of Massachusetts was not only geographical but also a reflection of the "isolation" of the Dissenters in England, and that isolation in large part is due to the fact that history tends to be written from the winners' perspective.[6] With the English Dissenters, Massachusetts consciously shared a lively, if beleaguered, providential culture, and the orthodox ministers of Massachusetts felt much the same inducements and pressures to modify that culture as did their English brethren.

Locating Massachusetts orthodoxy within this transatlantic context provides a perspective on it different from that of much recent scholarship. Quakers, Anabaptists, Gortonists, and other religious radicals have all been studied against a background of an at best only very grudgingly tolerant Puritan orthodoxy. That framework is certainly a valid one within the Massachusetts context; marginal religious groups had to construct themselves against the cultural domination of Massachusetts orthodoxy. But Massachusetts orthodoxy derived much of its cultural authority from its anchoring in English learned culture.[7] Within the larger transatlantic context, the orthodoxy of Massachusetts itself struggled in the second half of the seventeenth century, with varying degrees of intensity and duration, against domination, as part of a losing side in English learned cultural politics.

By the end of the century, however, Puritan resistance to new cultural imperatives on both sides of the Atlantic had significantly abated. While an older generation resisted efforts whose political origins were still visible, a younger generation experienced those efforts as cultural norms to which one adapted. What were the pressures that led from the one to the other? How, and to what extent, were the imperatives of the early Enlightenment absorbed into Massachusetts culture?

Those questions are dealt with here through a study of the providentialism of the best-known third-generation Massachusetts minister, Cotton Mather. Mather produced a large body of writings covering the spectrum of providential issues debated between Puritans and Anglicans in the Restoration as well as other topics that were often pulled into the politics of wonders, like witchcraft and the demonic. Besides their breadth, his writings have an idiosyncratic quality that makes them especially useful for this study. They are often unashamedly derivative and highly eclectic, while being intensely self-conscious. The effect is to evoke an imagined audience assessing the cultural worth of the different discursive materials Mather offered and assessing him as the provider of those materials. These qualities make Mather's writings a valuable record of his own appraisal of cultural politics in Massachusetts and abroad, and the way that politics affected traditional Massachusetts providentialism. While Mather's publications are unusual in their range and sociological transparency, ample evidence exists confirming that his assessments were not idiosyncratic; Mather made visible in his writings cultural pressures and dilemmas that others worked out tacitly. Although it would be a mistake simply to equate Mather with the "New England Mind," it would be equally a mistake, given his prominence and his concern both for tradition and for contemporaneous trends, to discount the exemplary quality of his development or his value as a barometer of cultural change.

The issue of changes in providentialism touches on themes that reach beyond changes within learned culture itself. David D. Hall, in *Worlds of Wonder, Days of Judgment*, has recently made a powerful argument that seventeenth-century Massachusetts had a unified religious culture, that "ministers and people worked uneasily together within a framework that empowered both."[8] While Hall was more interested in re-creating Massachusetts's religious culture than in explaining why and how it changed, he correctly noted in passing that its unity was broken when the clergy began withdrawing from the shared culture at the turn of the eighteenth century. However, he left largely unexplored the rough and incomplete process of that withdrawal.[9] If the withdrawal of the ministers, along with other educated people, was responsible for the breakup of that culture, then a study specifically of the ministers and their internalization of new cultural imperatives antithetical to the earlier shared framework is critical for understanding cultural change in Massachusetts.

The usefulness of such a study is not limited to Massachusetts. Hall's typology derives from Peter Burke's model of cultural change in seventeenth-century Europe.[10] If Burke's model can be applied to an American situation, and if orthodoxy in New England was more closely synchronized to orthodoxy in England than is usually assumed, then the American situation can be helpful for understanding cultural changes within the broad English cultural world.

Mather himself is particularly appropriate for such an application because he was remarkably successful at projecting himself onto a transatlantic stage. A study of his providentialism therefore suggests the pressures that helped transform the Puritanism of England of the seventeenth century, embedded in a world of wonders and resisting the post–Civil Wars readjustments of learned culture, into the Dissent of the eighteenth, embedded in the regularities of the Newtonian universe and accepting the new parameters of discussion within English learned culture. In a similar fashion, Mather can also help redress a lacuna in Keith Thomas's classic *Religion and the Decline of Magic*. Thomas documented the abandonment of a wide range of magical and prophetic practices and beliefs by England's learned elite in the seventeenth century, while lamenting that "contemporary literature . . . throws little light on how people came to change their minds."[11] The progression of Mather's providentialism in the eighteenth century provides as detailed an opportunity to observe that intellectual transition as perhaps is afforded by any figure within the English "nation." In so doing, it reveals the cultural negotiations involved in the diffusion of the early Enlightenment.

✳

This book is concerned with the construction and negotiation of meanings. It assumes that reality is, to an indeterminable degree, provisional and consensual, and that terms like "Providence," "God," "human nature," and so on, are themselves to an indeterminable degree contingent and socially created, even while they help to determine the reality within which their creation takes place.

The term "Providence" I use more broadly than was the usual practice in the seventeenth century. Preachers commonly distinguished between the domains of Providence and Grace, with the former roughly applying to the supernatural manipulation of a person's external life, and the later the manipulation of a person's internal process of salvation. But on occasion, they ignored the distinctions entirely, making the term "Providence" cover all those operations, and I do likewise consistently. The *Oxford English Dictionary* (1989) defines "divination" as "the foretelling of future events or discovery of what is hidden or obscure by supernatural or magical means." The problem with that definition is that it dodges, understandably enough, the question of how the categories of supernatural and magical come to be determined. For the purposes of the present study, the prepositional phrase at the end is changed to "by means not practiced in modern research universities."

The definition of Puritanism has been a matter of much debate among historians, as they attempt to give a positive content to what in the seventeenth century was usually a loose term of abuse.[12] For the purposes of this book, in the first half of the seventeenth century, Puritans were English Protestants who were intensely concerned with their salvation, involved in the larger community of the "godly," and likely to find too many "dregs of Popery" remaining in the English Church without being inclined to jettison that Church altogether. After Charles II returned to the throne in 1660, I use the term "Puritan" to mean someone who was alienated from the reestablished Church of England and who retained allegiance to orthodox Reformed theology in the shape hammered out by the second and third generations of Reformed theologians. From the Restoration period onward in this book, the term is often replaced by "orthodox Dissenter." Use of the term "Dissenter" for the period before the Toleration Act of 1689 is somewhat anachronistic (the contemporary term was far more likely to be "Nonconformist"); I employ it only for the sake of stylistic simplicity.[13]

If "Puritan" is not a term that lends itself easily to analytical use, at least it has the virtue of being a contemporaneous term. That virtue is not shared by "early Enlightenment," but by it, I mean, with no attempt at fine precision, the Restoration campaign against enthusiasm, shading imperceptibly into the normative cultural values of Addisonian England.[14] The terms "natural philosophy" and "science" I use interchangeably; that interchangeability is anachronistic, however, and the reader should keep in mind the former's contemporary interdisciplinary richness when encountering the latter.

The book does not examine, except in passing, eschatological and millennial predictions. Eschatological prophecy involved once-and-for-all events, whereas providentialism dealt with recurring patterns. Providentialism and eschatological prophecy were closely related but separate topics, formally at least, in the seventeenth century, and I treat them as such, focusing on the first.[15] Nor does my book deal with the theme of a glorious providential errand into the wilderness (usually discussed by historians as occurring within a framework of millennial fervor). The idea that the first generation of settlers had an exalted conception of their journey, or that the second and third generations read such conscious intentions into their journey into the wilderness, was first propounded in the scholarly literature by Perry Miller and given a new lease of life by Sacvan Bercovitch and his followers. It has been convincingly refuted by Andrew Delbanco and Theodore Dwight Bozeman.[16] While books continue to come out reiterating the claims of an errand into the wilderness, that literature either does not engage the arguments of Delbanco and Bozeman or else portrays the errand in highly chastened terms.[17]

No millennial errand into the wilderness, no city on a hill, no origin of the American self, no soil for the roots of American involvement in Vietnam— my Massachusetts is constructed as an English backwater, if a singular one. However, it is no less interesting in that purely provincial role. I hope that the reader will be able to see critical long-range intellectual and cultural changes thrown into a sharp relief by the strategies of resistance and accommodation those changes encountered in an obscure corner of the world.

CHAPTER ONE

‗✳‗

The Providence
of the
Massachusetts
Puritans

One spring morning in seventeenth-century Ipswich, Massachusetts, John Dane's wife told him that the family was out of food. Dane dutifully headed into the marshes, gun in hand, to hunt waterfowl. Unexpectedly, his prize pig followed him; what could this mean? Dane had undoubtedly heard his minister, John Norton, many times call upon his listeners to "Concure with God in the Scope of his Providence to you; he is fitting you to walk with God." Like all good Puritans, Dane did just that, and he scrutinized his mortal pilgrimage for signs of messages from the Almighty. The unexpected behavior on the pig's part could only be such a message, and Dane interpreted it as meaning he was to turn back home. He did so "and when I cam within les then forty Rod of my house, a cumpany of great grey geese cam over me, and I shot and brout down a galant goose in the very nick of time." The hunger of Dane's family was assuaged and the reality of Providence reaffirmed.[1]

Dane's story illustrates an important point. Providence was a highly learned and technical doctrine, and John Norton, Dane's minister, was among the most prominent of the first generation of New England Puritan divines, renowned for his "scholastick eminencies."[2] Whether Dane had any interest in Norton's elaborate definition of Providence as "that transient acting of God, whereby he upholdeth, & infallibly governeth all things, and the several natures of things according to the immutable Counsel of his own Will unto their best end, namely the Manifestation of his own Glory,"[3] we do not know. Likewise, we cannot determine if he dwelled upon Norton's subtle scholastic attempt to both affirm and deny the Creation's autonomy: "God causeth the burning of the fire, yet we do not say God burneth, but the fire burneth. God worketh repentence in the Soul, yet it is not a truth to say God repenteth, but man repenteth; God is the next efficient Cause, but not the next formal Cause."[4]

What Dane did learn from Norton and the other ministers he heard in both old and New England was to interpret his life in terms of utter reliance on the Providence of an actively engaged Calvinist deity. As Thomas Allen told his Charlestown listeners in 1649, "Jesus supports our being as the Beams of the sonn have being from the sonn . . . Providence is all . . . God disposeth Tymes Thoughts Words Causalities Synfull Acts." Such providential dependency led Allen's audience effortlessly into orthodox doctrine: "All our worth must be received. Its not in our own hands."[5]

Dane learned his providential doctrine well. He asserted that "God hath all along presarvd and cept me, all my daies." However, as seen above, Dane's providentialism was more than simply doctrine. It was also a system of hermeneutics. God communicated with Dane either through the "mercies" and "afflictions" of Dane's life, or more overtly through dreams, storms, bibliomancy, the actions of animals, and the "motions of gods spiret."[6] While Norton would have had reservations about some of Dane's distinctly loose providential interpretations and overreliance on techniques like dreams and bibliomancy, and while Dane probably would not have been interested in the farthest flights of Norton's scholastic eminencies, Dane learned from him a providential frame of reference. That frame of reference grew out of the Reformed orthodox tradition, and it did not differ significantly from the providentialism of John Calvin himself. It offered the Massachusetts Puritans a rich variety of providential divination techniques, and it remained unchanged up to the last years of the seventeenth century.

✳

Contingency presented a great mystery to sixteenth- and early-seventeenth-century learned culture. That culture enjoyed "no means of understanding the process of transition from one particular situation to another." Learned culture confronted the mystery of contingency through divinatory means, through a search for the hidden purposeful patterns that lay behind and tied together the visible marks of the world, be those patterns strands of astral influence, the cycle of fortune, or the eternal intentions of God.[7] Such analysis was unsurprising, since, as scholars have frequently pointed out, Renaissance knowledge in general was analogical, and in it meaning was often generated by divining "the reciprocal cross-reference of signs and similitudes."[8] The providentialism that orthodox ministers in Massachusetts believed and taught was a form of Renaissance knowledge, and it bore the stamp of its origin. Both as an intellectual resolution of the problem of life's randomness and as a means of divination, it satisfied the needs of people as diverse as Norton and Dane. Thus, there was nothing new or particularly English in the deterministic and divinatory nature of Providence. Indeed, those characteristics intertwine in the providentialism of John Calvin himself, primary founder of the Reformed tradition.

To Calvin, contingency itself proved that God's providential attention was ongoing: why was one couple barren and another fertile, why the harvest good one year and lean another, why storms and hail? Why any of these disorderly and unpredictable contingencies except that God was continually at work manipulating phenomena for His own ends? "Nothing is more natural than for spring to follow winter; summer, spring; and fall, summer—each in turn. Yet in this series one sees such great and uneven diversity that it readily appears each year, month, and day is governed by a new, a special, providence of God."[9] Phenomena were the tools of special providence: they were "nothing but instruments to which God continually imparts as much effectiveness as he will, and according to his own purpose bends and turns them to either one action or another."[10] The sun, for instance, brought forth the herbs and fruits of the earth, but the "godly man" knew that it was "merely the instrument that God uses because he so wills; for with no more difficulty he might abandon it, and act through himself."[11] Even our food of itself did not nourish us, "but God's secret blessing" thereon.[12] God's special providence controlled not only natural phenomena, but the human world itself: "the plans and intentions of men, are so governed by his providence that they are borne by it straight to their appointed end."[13]

For Calvin, Providence generated all conceivable earthly initiatives and circumstances. Thus, the contemplation of Providence provided a triumph over contingency and afforded "the immeasurable felicity of the godly mind."[14] "Everything seems to us to be confused and mixed up but all the while a constant quiet and serenity ever remain in heaven."[15] Believers gained access to that heavenly quiet and serenity by reordering their perceptions of the chaos and anxiety of their lives within a providential framework:

> Innumerable are the evils that beset human life; innumerable too, the deaths that threaten it. We need not go beyond ourselves: since our body is the receptacle of a thousand diseases . . . Now, wherever you turn, all things around you

not only are hardly to be trusted but almost openly menace, and seem to
threaten immediate death . . .Yet, when that light of divine providence has once
shone upon a godly man, he is then relieved and set free not only from the
extreme anxiety and fear that were pressing him before, but from every care . . .
His solace, I say, is to know that his Heavenly Father so holds all things in his
power, so rules by his authority and will, so governs by his wisdom, that nothing
can befall except he determine it.[16]

Calvin conquered contingency and its anxieties by focusing all initiative
in God. Although Providence itself was an ancient Christian doctrine, Calvin's providentialism stripped away all intermediaries between God and humanity—images, saints, angels, the Virgin Mary—and heralded "a new insistence on God's sovereignty."[17] But if a quest to assuage anxiety drove Calvin
to rest all contingency in the hands of a God with undeflectable purposes, ironically, that same impulse drove Calvin to a doctrine that arguably undercut his
purpose. While Calvin's stress on divine sovereignty had late-medieval roots,
he had only intermittent scattered precedents for his doctrine of double predestination.[18]

Double predestination meant that God had decreed the fate of the
damned from all eternity as certainly as He had chosen his Saints for salvation.
Calvin insisted that to argue otherwise would be to limit the sovereignty of
God's will, and so imperil the Providence that was otherwise such a source of
solace. However, the damned could not plead predestination as an excuse.
They had been "raised up by the just but inscrutable judgment of God to show
forth his glory," but nevertheless their inevitable eternal punishment would
result from "the malice and depravity of their hearts."[19] With its combination
of inexorableness and individual responsibility, double predestination might
not have appeared conducive to reduced anxiety: one had no control over
one's eternal destiny. Calvin himself acknowledged, "The decree is dreadful,
indeed, I confess."[20]

Calvin, however, hoped to lessen its dreadfulness, in fact, to turn it into
a message of hope, with his doctrine of assurance. That doctrine aimed at creating an affirmative experience from his theology of predestination. God had
not hidden his decrees of predestination from mortals: "Let us note that God
has decreed for us what he means to make of us in regard to the eternal salvation of our souls, and then he has decreed it also in respect of this present
life."[21] In this lifetime, the Saints could scrutinize Providence and gain a conviction of their eternal election; they could know with assurance that they
were destined for eternal life. By means of the revelation of the Holy Spirit
dwelling within them, the godly could interpret Providence. They could know

of their election through their faith in Christ's promises, and, to a far lesser extent, through their good works, the external signs of their sanctification.[22]

The doctrine of assurance intensely pleased Calvin; it could assuage the anxiety of believers in no uncertain terms as they discovered that they were inexorably bound for eternal glory. That was the intention anyway. But the Saints only enjoyed intermittent release from anxiety. Like the later Puritans, Calvin warned that the godly were "not only tried by disquiet . . . but they are repeatedly shaken by gravest terrors," so much so that faith's "light is snuffed out." Yet he insisted that throughout their trials, their kernel of knowledge remained.[23] Calvin assured the godly that their painful doubts and afflictions were part of God's work within their psyches: "If there come deepe thoughtes that wey wyth us so farre as even to make us sweat and tremble, or els if we be in such disquietnesse of minde as though we were upon a rock: it is god that worketh in that case: & he summoneth us, because he seeth that we are as it were fugitives."[24]

Similarly, albeit with less emphasis, Calvin insisted that reprobates could experience the first pangs of their eternal torture. The afflictions of the reprobate were "a certain entry of Hell, from whence they do already see a far off their eternal damnation." The doctrine of assurance, intended to dispel anxiety, easily could produce the exact opposite effect. Getting the hermeneutics of Providence correct, distinguishing the anguish of the Saint from the anguish of the damned or the faith of the Saint from the seemingly identical faith of the hypocrite, was to wrack the psyches of generations of scrupulous would-be Saints.[25]

Calvin's providentialism pushed those who accepted it toward divination, and divination of unprecedented urgency, with regard to individual eternal destiny. But some of his statements indicated a skepticism about divining Providence's outward patterns in temporal affairs: "However all things may be ordained by God's plan, according to a sure dispensation, for us they are fortuitous . . . the order, reason, and necessity of those things which happen for the most part lie hidden in God's purpose." The wicked might prosper in this world and God might extend "without any difference temporal punishments to his own children and to the unbelieving, and that in order that it may be made evident that our hope ought not to be fixed in this world."[26]

Such statements sound unequivocal about the illegibility of Providence. If they had been Calvin's last words on the subject, they would suggest a vast gulf of sensibility between him and later Puritans like Dane and Norton, tireless scrutinizers of the intentions of Providence.[27] Yet given Calvin's totalizing ambitions for Providence and the way he conceptualized it working in the human soul, and given that Renaissance culture was itself a culture of divination, such interpretive restraint would have been extraordinary. While there is no evidence that Calvin ever searched for divine messages in the behavior of pigs, as Dane did, he had no doubt that he could, at least to a certain extent, read the intentions of Providence.

God's judgments on sinners, for example, were not always illegible to mortals. Calvin asserted that God occasionally demonstrated by His government of the world that "He is both the avenger of sins and the rewarder of righteousness, and some sparks are seen through the darkness." Calvin reassured the righteous and threatened the wicked that God did not confine judgment totally to the afterlife: "God sheweth that hee will not leave the wicked unpunished: he sheweth it every day, he hath shewed it before we were borne, and if we pursue from age to age since the creation of the worlde, wee shall see that God hath alwayes kept the same rate."[28]

It was the duty of the pious observer to pay attention to "notable punishments, and such as are worthy of special observation," especially since God's judgments on others forecast his impending wrath directed to us: "Whenever we see this or that nation is afflicted by any calamity, we ought to remember this truth, that God seasonably warns us that we may not abuse his patience, but anticipate him before his wrath passes from some side of the earth to us." Indeed, in such spectacles, "If God should set up scaffoldes to execute his chastisements upon: wee could not perceive them more evidently."[29]

Calvin gave examples of contemporary divine judgments. He preached on a theme beloved of later Puritans, the sad fate of Sabbath-breakers ("What more glorious for us than this notable vengeance of God against the despisers of our doctrine?"), and he saw the accidental deaths of Francis II of France and his father as divine judgments on persecutors. The Turks invaded Greece for that country's licentiousness and impiety. But the worst vengeance God inflicted on a people was to leave them alone to sleep in their carnality, as He was doing to the inhabitants of the Swiss city of Constance. The Reformation itself Calvin could explain only in terms of divine intervention. On the private level, Calvin told an elderly correspondent that her present afflictions might have been sent her because of earlier timidity in the cause of God. When Calvin was not sure of God's messages, he attempted interpretation. He assured a correspondent at a time of plague that "we are seeking and searching to find out the misdeeds on account of which God punishes us."[30]

Certain manifestations of Providence appeared as wonders, spectacular and straightforward in their messages. A devil once carried away an impious Genevan (Calvin inspected the route it followed with the eyewitnesses). God showed forth his opinions on current events in the form of the strange freaks of nature known as prodigies. Calvin noted approvingly one of God's editorial comments in the form of the "pope-ass," an utterly improbable creature resembling the Pope, said to have been fished out of the Tiber River.[31]

With Providence inserting itself so lucidly in the sectarian strife of the sixteenth century, it is perhaps not surprising that Calvin's grasp of Providence could even lead him into prophecy. He foresaw divine vengeance on Henry VIII for his arrogance, foresaw that God would punish a church with ungrateful and arrogant members by making it hard for them to find a new pastor, assured his colleagues that "it would not be at all wonderful" for the Lord to avenge slanders directed against them, and predicted a forthcoming great change of affairs during the Council of Trent since "God will not suffer himself to be mocked any longer."[32]

Thus the operations of the world shadowed forth, however irregularly, something of the divine plan. A wrathful God was ever ready to intervene in temporal affairs with tokens of His anger, and He left on individuals the marks of their eternal destinies. In the singular and the unexpected, in the vagaries of contingency, the godly could catch a glimpse of His activities. While Providence was a learned and a difficult doctrine, as Calvin himself acknowledged (and became no easier when he had finished his conception of double predestination), his conception of it as a semiological system linked the doctrine with other contemporaneous attempts to read the "argumentes and sygnes" of the world, ranging from astrology to folk divination.[33]

As with the divination practiced by the Renaissance magus or the learned astrologer, not everyone had access to proper providential interpretation.[34] If the events and phenomena of Providence were a running transcript of the primal text of God's eternal decrees, recovering from them the meaning of that primal text was "the peculiar privilege of the Church," and it came only after God "has adopted us and has shone into our minds by his word."[35] Therefore, providential divination literally offered privileged occult knowledge and power. Calvin, like Reformed orthodoxy after him, was hostile to anything he perceived as smelling of magic, be it from the Catholic Church or be it from learned or popular culture. But that hostility should not obscure the considerable family resemblance between Calvin's providentialism and other forms of divination. In conceiving Providence, Calvin shared some key assumptions with the meanest of village cunning men in England, figures out of the cultural milieu of John Dane.

✳

> Hath hee [God] not as by wonders redeemed us from sondry sad Bondages. God
> did pave a way for our removal, carried us through the sea . . . When these
> things come to be recorded it will be wonderfull.[36]

The web of interpretive possibilities legitimated and focused by the Calvinist deity appeared no less impressive in early Massachusetts than it had in
Geneva. The emigration to Massachusetts, if anything, strengthened the Puritans' sense of a God whose intentions could be discerned. "All gods wayes with
his people are full of wonders," and God's wonder-working Providence was
never more in evidence than when He "by a stretched-out arm brought thee
and thine through seas and dangers, and delivered you wonderfully."[37]

The Puritans' conception of the Church heightened their providentialism once they arrived in Massachusetts. Calvin had proclaimed that God's
Providence was especially concerned with his Church and indeed that "God
will take so peculiar a care of his own Church, as to preserve it even amid the
annihilation of the whole world."[38] The Puritans, like Calvin, made no great
distinction between the Church in Israel and the Church of their times, but
the Puritans' Church had more nationalistic overtones than had Calvin's.
Preachers in England, both Puritan and conformist, drew parallels frequently
between England and ancient Israel. They wavered in their rhetorical flourishes as to whether the parallels were between Israel and the English nation,
Israel and the English Church, Israel and the godly in the English Church, or
Israel and the universal Church, of which the English component was an especially favored part. However, they all agreed that some relationship existed, or
should exist, between national and divine purposes.[39] In Massachusetts the formation of a polity comprised of Saints removed, except for purists like Roger
Williams, the necessity for the ambiguous distinctions between church and
nation made in the homeland.[40] A part of Israel, God's people, had a home.

God worked out His eternal decrees dramatically in the lives and psyches
of His Massachusetts Saints. "There is a mass of miracles met together when a
sinner is converted," Thomas Hooker exclaimed. "Look into [the] first beginnings in all the dealings of the Lord the dispensations of himself in the wayes
of providence ordinances mercies afflictions . . . manie a Saint of God can say
that the Lord hath been wrastling with him from the time of his Childhood,
and all along in the places where he lived."[41] As John Norton put it, "You may
believe it, what God hath done for the Soul of the least Saint of some few years
continuance, were it digested into Order, would make a volume full of temp-

tations, signs, and wonders: a wonderful History, because a History of such experiences, each one whereof is more then a Wonder."[42]

Even life's troubles offered the Saints proof of God's involvement with them. Afflictions were the rods of a chastising father. "There is not any sicke-nesse befalls us or ours, nor any losse in our estates," according to John Cotton, "not any kind of evill that befals the places where we live, so farre as it reaches us: but it is a knocke of Gods hand to turne to him."[43] And the knock of God's hand was not always gentle, as Thomas Shepard warned: "The Lord at first con-version draws his people sweetly, drives them gently . . . But afterwards he suf-fers Satan to tempt, himself deserts them, leads them through a wilderness of Sins and miseries, that they may know what is in their own hearts."[44] Some-times, the ministers warned, as Calvin had done, that God "creates darknesse in the Soule; then it is filled with fear and amazement, and disquietment."[45]

For the reprobate, afflictions were simply a means of setting them "further off from God by discontent with his providence."[46] But the worst that could happen to a person, Hooker warned, was not that God sent misfortunes or tor-ments, but that He simply left him or her alone, as He had done to Calvin's neighboring city of Constance: "We should be persuaded and informed its the heaviest plague that can befal a man, That God should suffer him to sleep in his sins and prosper in a wicked Course: Because it argues (for ought any man knows) that God intends no good to him, nor will work no good for him."[47] New England Saints sometimes had to be assured that worldly prosperity and lack of trouble did not signify that God had abandoned them.[48]

Through His afflictions, mercies, desertions, and judgments, God created a vast, close, and tumultuous drama both within and without the Saints. But how were they to interpret it? Their usual technique of providential divination involved discerning the relationship between God's work—His Providence, which sometimes involved overt supernatural intervention—and His Word, the Bible.[49] Perhaps the simplest way of applying scripture was to study how God responded to the behavior of his Old Testament Saints, and thus how He would respond, and was responding, to the behavior of present-day Christians. In England in the early decades of the 1600s, for example, anxious Puritans mulled over the sins of the Chosen People in the Old Testament, and, as one of them, John Brinsley, put it, "By considering and comparing the same with the times wherein we live, I have ever feared the like plague or a heavier to be hanging over this our sinfull nation." Brinsley's erudite prophesying figured heavily in the thinking of the Saints who fled to Massachusetts, although many were able to draw similar conclusions on their own.[50]

Providential divination usually had some linkage to biblical similitude, and the Puritans were most comfortable when they could tie together God's work and His Word. However, they did not always feel constrained to tie them together strictly. John Cotton, for example, simply assumed that God ordered the affairs of the world to suit his Saints when he foretold the storm that nearly sank the ship bearing the Child petition to England. God also offered forewarnings and editorial comments on His people's activities in the environment around them that cried for unmediated interpretation. His comments ranged from wonders like the monstrous births produced by the religious dissenters Anne Hutchinson and Mary Dyer—witnesses to the monstrosity of their doctrines—to meteorological phenomena, "extraordinary Signes and prodigies from Heaven whereby the Lord gives warning to men of his terrour and Judgment."[51] Those meteorological phenomena varied widely, from the comet that blazed in the heavens shortly before John Cotton's death in 1652, to the companies of armed men who marched in the sky above Long Island one clear morning in 1665. More ominously, a minor earthquake might indicate diabolical commentary, as Thomas Hooker's household speculated when an earth tremor shook their dwelling in the late 1630s as they were discussing the sins of Anne Hutchinson.[52]

For the Puritans, as for Calvin, the Holy Spirit guaranteed correct interpretation of the phenomena of Providence. "The Holy Spirit brings into the soul a self-evidencing light," said John Davenport. According to Cotton, it "tells you what use you are to make of such a Scripture, such a Sermon, such a Providence, such an Affliction." "The Spirit ever shows us things as they are," Shepard exclaimed, "even tho' they be deep things and mysteries . . . Saints do not only see things in Letters and Syllables, and words, but see things as they are in themselves."[53] Illuminated by the Holy Spirit and guided by God's word, the Saints of New England enjoyed an occult communication with their Maker, Cotton proclaimed: "Many secret passages shall their [the Saints'] hearts be made privie to, that others shall never be acquainted with; he wil acquaint us with his secret purpose about a people, sometimes in Prayer, sometimes in Humiliation, sometimes one way, and sometimes another."[54]

Sometimes the Holy Spirit directly delivered an insight through what might be called a revelation, although the term itself was fraught with definitional ambiguity. This insight could come through a Saint's intuition, as in the case of John Wilson's many predictions. Sometimes the insight might come more mysteriously through a dream, like Cotton's dream of his successor coming to Boston, although Puritans could be double-minded about dreams, dismissing them in general even while deciphering the meaning of specific dreams. Scripture verses might flash up in the mind, fraught with contemporary significance; presumably such an impression caused Thomas Hooker to announce to his Chelmsford, England, audience in the late 1620s that "God told me yesternight that he would destroy England and lay it waste." While some Puritans showed more restraint than others about assuming in practice that such psychic phenomena were of divine origin, the only clear theoretical boundary placed around them was that God's primary revelation had been given and finished in the Bible, and the Spirit would not contradict or take precedence over that revelation.[55]

Providential divination might jumble together a mixture of techniques. For example, the minister John Fiske's church at Wenham twice postponed the ordination of three deacons in 1660 because of heavy rains. As Reverend Fiske pondered God's intention in this meteorological intervention, a verse from 1 Timothy 3 was, in his words, "presented to my mind." The verse concerned the necessity of testing the faith of the deacons, and for Fiske it clearly pointed a finger at one of them who had not given a relation of his spiritual experiences. After two agitated church meetings, Fiske had the man removed as a candidate, and God removed His inclement weather.[56]

With God able to manifest His opinions and wishes through so many rhetorically obscure mediums and the Holy Spirit's guidance not accessible for public confirmation, inevitably political controversy surrounded providential interpretation. What did the two false suns shining around the real sun one day in the winter of 1645 mean? Were they a vindication of the doctrines of the Hutchinsonians or a comment on the vaporous quality of those doctrines? Perhaps they spoke of an impending mortality.[57] The Child petition affair of 1646, in which a group of colonists tried to communicate their dissatisfaction with the local government to Parliament, produced a rich array of providences and counter-providences, ranging from the stumbling of horses to the raising of ocean storms, as each side searched for, and found, evidence of divine approval for its course of action and divine judgment on its opponents'.[58]

Revelations, manifesting as they did nowhere but in the mind of their recipient, especially lent themselves to political disruption, as in the famous example of the religious dissenter Anne Hutchinson in the 1630s. Hutchinson lost her defense at her examination before the Massachusetts General Court in 1637 not because she admitted having immediate revelations in themselves (as is routinely claimed),[59] but because those revelations did not sit well with Massachusetts orthodoxy, especially the one about God ruining her examiners and their posterity. John Winthrop, with the full weight of the Massachusetts political establishment behind him, could say confidently at the end of the discussion of Hutchinson's revelations, "I do acknowledge that there are such revelations as do concur with the word [of the Bible] but there hath not been any of this nature."[60] Some sixteen years later, John Wheelwright announced discreetly at the Boston Thursday lecture, "The Lord doth sometyme teach imediately . . . though I do not hereby open a dore to such as slight gods ministry." A half century later, Edward Taylor expressed the political boundaries of revelations more forthrightly: "Extraordinary discoveries of the minde of God, ordinarily, are made to Persons of more than an ordinary, or Common concern . . . Hence it is from Satan that any should assert that Extraordinary discoveries are with ordinary, & common people."[61]

God's activities were not the only ones in the theater of Providence that the Saints needed to discern. As Taylor cautioned, there was also Satan who, with the myriad of demons subsumed under his name, and with God's permission, "laid his Train to blow up all the world by sin" and who "possesseth with craft and power all the souls of the sons of men . . . [unless] the Spirit itself fills and acts that soul." The godly were not immune from his assaults. He would "endeavour to disturbe their peace, and damp their joy . . . He suggests any word that may terrefie them . . . He presents all things unto them in false glasses . . . He useth his instruments to deal with them." New England was not exempt from him. "He will follow Christ into the wilderness, and tempt him there." Satan, his demons, and, of course, his witches followed the colonists across the ocean.[62]

✳

All the wonders of God, some of them quite dark, accompanied the settlers across the Atlantic, and the settlers came well equipped with a rich array of techniques with which to contextualize and interpret those wonders. God's wonder-working, communicative Providence remained intact for the next generation of Massachusetts learned orthodoxy. Witness, for example, some aquatic examples of the "wonderful work of God, that commandeth both the sea and the dry land" from 1666 to 1682, as recorded by the minister William Hubbard in *A General History of New England* (written in the early 1680s):

*On June 6, 1666, a drunken man runs into the sea at lecture time and drowns.

*In June, 1671, a Sabbath-breaker gets excessively drunk and drowns.

*On December 23, 1671, several fishermen on their way to keeping the un-Puritan holiday of Christmas drown.

*Sometime in June 1674, all the fish in the great pond at Watertown swim to the shore and die.

*In the summer of 1676, a "rude fellow," after regretting that some ministers and magistrates had not drowned in a recent boating accident, is himself drowned.[63]

Calvin would have had no problem with Hubbard's conception of Providence—a Providence judgmental, didactic, partisan, and manifesting in the irregular and singular. The conventionality of Hubbard's providentialism is particularly interesting because historians have often singled him out as an example of change coming to New England, a minister with something of an enlightened, less providentially fixated sensibility than his brethren.[64] This historiographical image has arisen for two reasons: first, historians usually contrast Hubbard with his ministerial adversary during King Philip's War, Increase Mather, a dramatically different figure, and second, they usually do not consider his writings as a whole. However, Mather himself in some respects approached the limit of a continuum of acceptable orthodox providentialism, and when Hubbard's work is considered in its entirety, much of what has been seen as a diluted providentialism reemerges as a vivid example of providentialism's cultural politics. Between them, Hubbard and Mather portray the range and uses of Restoration Massachusetts orthodox providential interpretation.

Like his predecessors, Hubbard thoroughly immersed himself in the intense and partisan semiological use of Providence, as his *General History of New England* makes clear. Hubbard's God was not only active, but also not at all reluctant to take sides in sectarian quarrels (Hubbard's sympathy for religious tolerance has been greatly exaggerated by historians).[65] Time and chance happens to all men, Hubbard stated in the *General History*, but he stressed that his caution only applied to Quakers trying to read the hand of God in the sudden deaths of two of their primary New England foes, John Norton and Major Atherton. All the Boston Baptists survived the smallpox epidemic, as their leader, John Russell, observed with providential satisfaction, but then he himself died one year later, "lest he should further translate others from the truth." Hubbard added to the accounts of a storm at sea by earlier historians William Bradford and Nathaniel Morton the detail that the storm that hindered the passage of one of the enemies of Plymouth Plantation was raised by "either the old sins of the owner and undertaker, or the new ones of the last passengers." He even extended John Winthrop's impressive list of the sad ends of the enemies of New England into the 1660s.[66]

Hubbard's *General History* provides vivid glimpses into the providential mentality of seventeenth-century Massachusetts. Hubbard recorded the colonists of New Haven speculating on the intentions of Providence in thwarting their every attempt to move. He noted people's observations of the "solemn remarks of providence" befalling those who were most forward in the popularly inspired execution of Anne Hibbins for witchcraft in the 1650s. He reproduced the speculation that the early church contentions that beset the Wethersfield settlers were due to irregularities in their acquisition of land. While it was true for Hubbard, as for all orthodox Puritans, that Providence usually operated through second causes, it sometimes went above them. Epidemical sickness, for example, were not totally explicable in terms of second causes, but bore the trace of the immediate hand of God.[67]

The only hint of an eighteenth-century "reasonableness" in Hubbard's histories comes from his treatment of prodigies and omens. He made no mention of the comet that preceded John Cotton's death, and he dismissed in his *General History* the sound of guns and drums that were heard south of Boston in 1667 and were subsequently connected with King Philip's War.[68] Furthermore Hubbard showed his awareness of recent English controversies over portents and prodigies, making an unsympathetic, if obscure, allusion in the *History of the Indian Warrs* to blatantly partisan Dissenter accounts of prodigies signaling God's condemnation of the Restoration Church settlement.[69]

Hubbard's skepticism about prodigies had sharp limits, however. Anne Hutchinson's monstrous birth still had a place in the *General History*, as did various other prodigies recorded in Winthrop's journal. Hubbard noted without comment the ominous linkage made between the emergence of a vast quantity of strange humming flies one spring (the colonists' first experience with seventeen-year locusts) and a subsequent mortality, and he added to our knowledge of the ill-fated voyage of the *Angel Gabriel*, the only passenger ship to New England in the 1630s to sink en route, by mentioning that "many things were observed as ominous about which vessel, that threatened some great disaster to like to befal them."[70] It is difficult to generalize about Hubbard's attitude to omens and prodigies beyond saying that he approached them with a highly selective skepticism.

If in his *General History* Hubbard seems a typical Puritan minister, in his publications connected with King Philip's War he seems at times to be arguing in a most un-Puritan fashion against an overly rigorous interpretation of Providence. In the election sermon of 1676, Hubbard announced, "Possibly some upon every Check and frown of providence against us, may be ready with Saul to call for the Lot to be cast, and will be too forward without a perfect Lot, to say the cause is in Saul or in Jonathan, or in the people . . . We must not lye for God, and need be carefull we doe not entile divine Providence to the mistakes of our minds."[71]

In his explanation of the causes of the war in the *History of the Indian*

Warrs, Hubbard explicitly denied that God was singling out New England in punishment for some extraordinary declension: "This is not the first Time that Christian People have been exposed to many Outrages, and barbarous Calamities from their Pagan Neighbours." Hubbard conceded that in a manner generalized to the point of uselessness, the accusation of declension might be accurate: "No doubt but after so long a Time of Peace and Prosperity, as hath been enjoyed, the like Corruptions have began to bud forth as are usual in such a Case." But "the Sovereign Ruler of the World need never . . . to seek of a Ground why to bring a Scourge upon [any sort of men], having also the other holy Ends why he contends with his People, of which he is not bound to render the World an Account."[72] One cannot divine provoking sins from visible afflictions, Hubbard seemed to argue, both in the *History of the Indian Warrs* and in his election sermon.

Puritan disclaimers concerning the ability to interpret Providence always have to be approached warily, however, and Hubbard's are no exception. Hubbard's rejection of a reading of the war as the results of any extraordinary sins of New England, even taken at face value, hardly indicates a rejection of reading the war as a punishment for sin. It was just that the sins came from the outskirts of Massachusetts society, as Hubbard explained in the *History of the Indian Warrs:* "It is the general Observation of all indifferent and unconcerned Persons about the like Troubles: That they have ordinarily either begun, or have fallen heaviest upon those Places and Persons that have had most to do in the Trading with Indians."[73]

Hubbard's blaming of the war on unscrupulous Indian traders was not simply a "natural" causal interpretation, but also a "moral" one: the war was a token of God's wrath on the parts of the colony where the sin of trading was the greatest. Nor did Hubbard display any eighteenth-century reasonableness in defending his reading of God's behavior: "If it be here objected that the same or like Calamities have befallen many of those Places and Persons where no such Evils could justly be complained of, it may be as easily answered . . . that in such publick Calamities, it is not easy to distinguish between the good and the bad."[74]

In fact, a close examination of Hubbard's explanation of the providential roots of King Philip's War as lying on the periphery of Massachusetts society reveals someone who felt only too well the convincing nature of providential reasoning. Immediately after cautioning in his election sermon about reading Providence too hastily, Hubbard explained the reason for his caution: "We know what ammadversions have been made by men of other perswasions, none had need give any occasion to such misconstruction of Gods hand, by an ungrounded suiting of times with events."[75] Such providential speculations had a corrosive effect: "Probably . . . this sudden and unexpected Turn of Providence, may occasion many to think, that either there hath been some notable Declension from former Principles and Wayes, or else the World hath been much abused by former Reports of our prosperous Proceedings here."[76] Indeed, besides hostile Quakers and Baptists, even Massachusetts's providentially minded friends in England drew negative conclusions about the colony's piety from this affliction, just as Hubbard feared.[77]

Hubbard wrote his *History of the Indian Warrs* at least in part as an attempt to defuse the poor providential impression made by King Philip's War, and he did not intend his book merely for a home audience. Anticipation of its English publication killed that market for Mather's history, and Hubbard went to England to supervise the reprinting of his book there.[78] It was Hubbard's very concern with the negative reflection on Massachusetts suggested by the divine judgment of King Philip's War that led to the urgency of his attempt to deny that the evidence justified an interpretation of serious declension: one could not read moral provoking causes from the calamity of the war, and in any event those provoking causes were at the fringes of Massachusetts society. However, convincing such arguments might be, Hubbard saved them for addresses to the world beyond Massachusetts. In sermons intended for home consumption, Hubbard had no reticence in declaring the reality of God's controversy with New England and the Indians' role therein as His scourge.[79] What at first glance might appear to be a designification of Providence on closer study turns out to be an example of the real cultural power of providential interpretation.

If Hubbard's "modernity" fades into near nonexistence when he is considered closely on his own, that modernity seems to reemerge vividly when his account of King Philip's War is compared with Increase Mather's writings on the same topic. Mather had a substantially greater providential vision than Hubbard. For Mather, battles, actors, and strategies were but the shadows of a larger spiritual drama, too unimportant to be written down in detail. Where Hubbard framed the supernatural impetus behind the Indian uprising only in a local sense as a plot instigated by the Devil to destroy the churches of Christ in New England, Mather deemed the war as a sign of the Last Days, a "solemn warning from Heaven, that dismal things are hastening upon . . . the whole World."[80]

The entire war for Mather was an opaque physical veil over a spiritual drama. Guns and drums and horsemen sounding and galloping in the sky all unquestionably foreshadowed the war.[81] The war itself began with an attack on a departing church congregation on a day of humiliation at Swansea, "the Lord thereby declaring from Heaven that he expected something else from his People besides Fasting and Prayer." Thereafter, the struggle went in a downward spiral until the people of New England gave sufficient signs of repentance for their sins. When the General Court began to frame laws for reformation, the English won a victory at Hatfield, and when a sufficiently sincere and general day of humiliation was held in Boston, the tide of victory began to flow with the English.[82]

Victory, according to Mather, was not due to the Lord determining the outcome of battles, as Hubbard portrayed it, but to the Lord determining the outcome of prayer. Prayer frustrated the councils of the heathen, prayer caused them to fight against each other, prayer sent sickness and famine among them, and prayer took away their courage and cut down their leaders. For the English, prayer sent troops and appropriate weather to places in need, prayer protected the captives, and, of course, prayer caused the war to tilt in favor of the English.[83] Hubbard, in his *History of the Indian Warrs*, only once noted the link between the fortunes of war and English prayers, although he elsewhere he connected New England's calamities to the death of John Wilson, whose "faith and prayers" had protected it from "public judgments."[84]

Where Hubbard had been a locally minded conciliator, trying to unite a colony behind its government and trying to counter negative providential interpretations of the war, Mather took up a broader and openly transformative role. He spoke "as God would have me speak," whether to lash the Massachusetts English for their racism, or the government for its lack of moral reform, or the enemies of New England and the Saints everywhere. In one extraordinary passage in which it is unclear whether Mather was addressing hostile Indians, bishops in England, or the foes of the Church throughout the world, he growled, "Notwithstanding the success which you have had you may be the Beast and we may be the Saints of Christ." Given his aggressiveness, it is unsurprising that, unlike Hubbard, Mather was utterly undefensive about the impression his account of a chastised New England might make on outsiders: "If this be done to *Immanuel's Land*, what may other Lands expect ere long."[85] In other publications, Mather rose to heights of sarcasm in displaying his contempt for those who thought that Dissenters made partisan use of prodigies.[86]

But was Mather's version of the war representative of New England providential orthodoxy? His London publisher, Richard Chiswell, complained that he was barely able to sell five hundred copies of the book, since news had gotten out that a better account, presumably Hubbard's, was on the way.[87] The argument made by Michael G. Hall that this decidedly lukewarm reception indicates that Mather's sensibility was out of date requires a demonstration of a period when such ghostly historiography was the norm. Certainly, Mather's supernatural account bears little resemblance to providential histories like Winthrop's and Bradford's. It also bears little resemblance to his account of earlier troubles with the Indians, published a year later, in which Mather acted more the proper historian, as he was at pains to inform his readers in his preface. As Perry Miller noted, A Brief History was a jeremiad writ large, a unique massive conflation of the roles of preacher and historian and a moral drama whose nature Hubbard, for political reasons of his own, did not try to replicate.[88]

Even given that Mather confused the genres of jeremiad and history in his Brief History, his providentialism still seems more extreme than Hubbard's. Some positive evidence suggests that Mather's prophetic providential sensibility did not represent the norm for Puritan orthodoxy, either in England or New England. Mather's intense chiliastic concerns have no counterpart in the published works of his peers, and those peers did not always appreciate his harping on that theme.[89] Just as Mather was more willing than his contemporaries to make exact predictions about the timing of the Second Coming, so was he, also unlike his contemporaries, prepared to commit to print not only general statements of impending divine wrath, but quite specific prophecies of the form this wrath would take.[90] Although Mather's claim in the early 1670s that God's wrath against New England would manifest as a plague of false teachers slipped into oblivion, he hit prophetic pay dirt with his prediction of impending warfare in 1674.[91] Mather also had a stark premonition of the Boston fire of 1676, reminding his audience ten days before its outbreak of the fate of London in 1666. He later claimed to his wife's son that after the sermon, "as I came home I went into my study. I wept there, walking alone before the Lord, & saying O Lord God, I have told the people in Your Name that you art about to cutt off their dwelling, but they will not believe me. Lord spare them &c that I might appear to be a false prophet amongst them when I declare such things as these." Mather, aware that such powerful prophetic communion with the Deity was controversial, added to his correspondent, "The Lord knowest that these things are true. But do you keep them secret."[92]

The evidence from New England places Mather's faith in the scrutability of the intentions of the spiritual world and that world's extreme sensitivity to human activity on the edge of Puritan orthodoxy. The orthodox rarely displayed such fine-honed prophetic powers in any period, and certainly Mather's father, Richard, apart from foreseeing his own death, has left no trace of them.[93] But the evolution of Mather's sensibility within an orthodox context can be reconstructed circumstantially.

Mather studied at Trinity College in Dublin during the Interregnum. At this time, Trinity College's provost was Samuel Winter, a former ministerial student of John Cotton's. Increase recorded in his autobiography that Winter loved him like a son, and that Winter's son, a classmate of Mather's, took a "singular phansy" to him.[94] Such a warm bond indicates at least a mutual sympathy. Winter was memorable partially for his fervent study of, and preaching on, the Book of Revelation, but more so for his dramatic ability at prediction and answering prayers. Like Increase, and later, his son Cotton, Winter experienced his ability vividly and sensually. The borderline nature of Winter's sensibility is indicated by the caution he once received not to predict so confidently, lest he be mistaken for an anabaptist.[95]

Orthodox Puritans generally shunned such extravagant powers, although Winter himself seems to have been respected enough by his peers.[96] Increase's son, Cotton, was later to warn that "many [Inconsiderate Christians] have been, when they have Read the Life of Dr. *Winter*, unaware, led into, an Indiscrete *Affectation* of *Extraordinaries*, and *Singularities*, in the Course of their *Devotions*. This is a Thing which may have Perilous Consequences!"[97]

Mather's history of the war seems to have been acceptable enough to his clerical colleagues, just as Winter's powers of prayer were to his. But there is good reason to think that Hubbard, with his more pedestrian and cautious, but thoroughly conventional, sensibility, was at least as representative of Massachusetts orthodoxy as Mather and not a harbinger of the eighteenth century, or a reflector of advanced trends in the Anglo-American world. Hubbard's confident and partisan reading of Providence, his ability to assert the inscrutability of the Lord's intentions, combined with an irresistible bent toward divining them, and his experience of Providence in the irregular and unexpected put him at one with John Calvin. Hubbard's own preaching appears to have been conventionally evangelical.[98] Hubbard's difference with Mather was simply one of intensity of application, and in this difference of intensity, it was Mather who was the exception, not Hubbard, and both fell within the bounds of a providential orthodoxy that had proven itself remarkably immune to change.

✳

The sharp observer in Massachusetts of the 1680s would have noticed some hairline cracks in this facade of providential orthodoxy among Massachusetts's learned elite. Charles Morton, Dissenting schoolmaster from Newington Green, arrived in Cambridge in 1686 with his own physics textbook in tow, a book distinctly skeptical about most portents and prodigies.[99] While most Massachusetts preachers were still preaching on the mysteries of the interaction of a vast and overwhelming spiritual world with the human being, some ministers in their twenties were striking a new note, telling their auditors that "the Christian sacrifice is a reasonable one" and that it was "most reasonable" that they should repent, and assuring them that their happiness and holiness were identical.[100] What this new vocabulary boded for Massachusetts providentialism can be best seen by examining the source from which it came: the Anglican redefinition of the interaction between the human and spiritual worlds in the second half of the seventeenth century.

CHAPTER TWO

✳

Providence Besieged

The Massachusetts Puritans brought their wonder-working Providence with them from England, where it had existed as one interpretive option within a rich culture of wonders. In the early seventeenth century, the lore of wonders covered a terrain with gloriously vague and disputed interior boundaries, boundaries determined largely by cultural politics. During the disruptions of the mid seventeenth century, the politics of wonders reached such intensity that members of England's learned elite began reformulating the very framework within which a wonder-working Providence could exist.

Boundary disputes about wonders and their interpretation in the early seventeenth century might be between competing religious groups. Miracles had ceased, proclaimed the Reformed churches, in contradistinction to the Catholics, but what did this cessation mean? Certainly it meant that no human possessed the kind of powers the Catholics claimed their saints possessed.[1] But were possession and dispossession of demons intrinsically impossible because intrinsically miraculous, as some Anglicans claimed in order to deny the use of them to Puritans and Catholics?[2]

Disputes might arise between divines and other groups as they attempted to assert interpretive possession and definition of wonders. Did a monstrous birth manifest a miraculous speaking voice of God, as Samuel Willard was still proclaiming at the end of the seventeenth century, or did it result from any of the eleven other circumstances the French physician Ambrose Paré, with his own professional territory to defend, claimed could also induce it?[3] Astrologers and hermetic magicians tended to place a great deal of emphasis on the wonders of secondary causes. Christopher Heydon, when speculating on the cause of the cold winter of 1608, determined that it must have been due to a judgment of God, chance, or natural causes, but he rejected the first two options as "unworthy of a scholar," and chose the last, favoring an astrological line of inquiry.[4] Although the more zealous Protestants wrote and rewrote histories to make the hand of Providence more explicit and omnipresent, Elizabethan playwrights, while officially adhering to the omnipotence of Providence, referred often enough to fortune and chance.[5] Were lots and games of chance inevitably under God's special providence, or did they escape such direct supernatural surveillance?[6]

Boundary definition could also fall along lines of learning, to a certain extent. Educated English people were more likely to be critical of wonder stories than the masses. Divines rejected traditional omens, as when "an Hare starteth out before a man in the way, or a Fowle flyeth beside him," while explaining to their listeners how to recognize messages from God in events.[7] William Fulke recounted contemptuously the great stir made by a story that the Devil had flown over the Thames, landed at Stratford, and been captured and put in the stocks, yet he had no hesitation in speaking of aerial phenomena like "sightes of armies fighting in the ayre, of Castles, Cities, Towns . . . burialles, processions . . . arms of certayne noble men . . . the very similitude of persons known to the beholders."[8] The "wyser sort" might "utterly scorn" vulgar prophecies, yet those prophecies "leave an impression in the myndes that seem most to scorn them."[9] For all factions, whatever their religious, professional, or social concerns, sympathies and resonances, spirits and wonders filled the world and provided a rich treasure house of interpretive possibilities, whether or not that mass of possibilities was fitted into a providential framework.

Just as wonders functioned within a broad consensus in English culture, God's wonder-working Providence existed within a broad theological consensus in the English Church. The doctrine of the Church of England had been, unofficially, up until the middle of the 1620s, Calvinist.[10] Therefore, there was not any radical difference in the doctrine and use of Providence between Puritans and hierarchical churchmen. A Puritan, almost by way of definition, was likely to be more religiously scrupulous and concerned with signs of his or her election than others, and so given more to scrutinizing Providence and framing current events in a biblical context, but hard and fast lines between Puritans and other groups cannot be drawn. Thomas Beard, for example, author of the treatise usually taken as the epitome of Puritan providentialism, *A Theatre of God's Judgments*, has been recently characterized as not a Puritan firebrand but a "complacent Jacobean Calvinist conformist." A future bishop, Joseph Hall, vividly described the ministry's providential divinatory role: "The *Seers* of God have ever from their watch-towers descryed the judgments of God afarre off."[11] The Puritans' providentialism functioned along a continuum within the Church.

Even the anti-Calvinists, leaning toward an Arminianism that questioned the helplessness of the human will and emerging in as a formidable presence in the church hierarchy in the 1620s and 1630s, had a strong supernaturalist background. "Liberal" Protestants still spoke affectively about the union of Christ and the soul.[12] Archbishop Laud shivered at the bad omen of his portrait dropping from his study wall and considered that his sins had drawn down the judgment of his execution upon him.[13] Thomas Jackson, perhaps the most theologically acute (or at least involuted) of the Arminians, wrote, but never published, a treatise on "ominous presagements, or abodings good or bad, whether given, taken, or affected; and of Prodigies."[14]

A sharp observer might have noticed signs of a disentanglement of the close linkage between the natural, supernatural, and human realms within learned culture in the years of Puritan migration to Massachusetts. Astrology did not have quite the amount of elite respect in the 1630s as it had at the turn of the century.[15] In that decade, the Great Tew circle was in the process of developing a piety independent of a precise delineation of the supernatural.[16] Earlier, the great scientist and statesman Francis Bacon had called for a rigorous separation of concern for secondary and final causes and was skeptical of most claims that events in nature were related to events in the human world. His rejection of authority and his demand for the rigorous and communal documentation of phenomena offered a potential hazard to the comfortable edifice of tradition, hearsay, and private judgment on which the lore of wonders rested, and when his standards became widely accepted in the second half of the seventeenth century they had that corrosive effect. From such signs, a Whig historian could trace an ascending line of modern rationality into the early Enlightenment from the hermetic and neoplatonic magi/scientists of the Elizabethan period like John Dee and Giordano Bruni to Francis Bacon's purified nonilluminist natural magic to the mechanized worldview of the later seventeenth century.[17]

However, that line would obscure the relative status of ideas in the earlier period, the existence of dialogues, conversations, tolerated inconsistencies, and even abusive controversies across a range that would not be accepted within learned culture by the end of the century. Bacon, for example, for all his scientific skepticism, was one of the "wyser sort" who could not quite dismiss prophecies.[18] He also favored the project of compiling a history of "the remarkable events and examples of God's judgments, though late and unexpected, sudden and unhoped for deliverances and blessings, divine counsels dark and doubtful at length opening and explaining themselves."[19] The observer would have had to have been very alert and somewhat prophetic to read very much of a historical direction from scattered protomodern conceptualizations.

Decisive impetus for change came not from the internal dynamics of ideas, but from the turmoil of the Civil Wars and Interregnum of the 1640s and 1650s. A close and legible supernatural realm manifesting both in Reformed theology and the world of wonders threatened the stability of the state and the social order. As a consequence, conservative English thinkers began three overlapping projects aimed at rearranging the hierarchy of acceptable forms and contents of knowledge in an effort to eliminate the destabilizing potential of the supernatural. The first project involved recasting basic assumptions in Reformed theology and their experiential results, the second involved sharply limiting the scope of providential divination, and the third reformulating the practices and assumptions of science. The projects attempted to marginalize in learned culture those who still resisted them, and prominent among their targets were the Puritans and the Puritans' providentialism.

✳

Theology bore dangerous fruits in the 1640s. The Calvinist concept of free grace and the authority of the Holy Spirit proved powerful forms of legitimation for dissidents in those times of social unrest. Anabaptists and antinomians flourished in the New Model Army, and the radical democratic implications of their understanding of baptism, election, and free grace threatened existing social hierarchies. Radicals proclaimed that "poor, plain countrymen" inspired by the Spirit could interpret scripture better than unregenerate doctors, they founded alarmingly democratic congregations, and they traced their spiritual ancestry to such orthodox Puritans as John Preston and Richard Sibbes.[20] Worst of all, the government tolerated them, and they seemed to be spreading in profusion. While the outbreak of "independency" appalled orthodox Calvinist Presbyterians as much as it did the Anglicans, the latter held the former responsible for the mess. As a vivid variation on a common Anglican genealogical analysis put it, "this *Independent* is but a bastard *Presbyterian*, or an *illegitimate* child, begotten of the *luxurious* seed of the Presbyterians, and the frothy sperme of the fanatick people."[21]

Accordingly, even before the Restoration, Anglicans intensified their campaign to overturn Calvinism and remove its tenets from within the circles of respectability. The doctrine of predestination, the linchpin of Calvin's Providence, came under severe attack. Anglican leaders like Henry Hammond put pressure on their brethren to reformulate their Calvinist beliefs in a manner more suitable to social stability. Rejection of predestination came to be a badge of those speaking for the Restoration Church.[22] By 1660, "moderate" Anglicans could claim that "*none* of all the Doctrines of the *Romish Church* is so scandalous, and so derogatory from the *justice, truth, goodness,* and *mercy* of God," as that of the "*absolute* irrespective *Decree* of God, touching *Election* and *Reprobation.*" Indeed, such a doctrine could "reside nowhere but in the Breasts of Fiends and Devils."[23]

The doctrine of absolute predestination did not only reside somewhat abstractly in the breasts of fiends and devils, but, more to the immediate social and political point, also among "our *Antinomians* and *Enthusiasts,* and other *Sects* among us (whom no conceit without this could have seduced to their several *frenzies*)." Therefore, the denial of free, predetermined grace effectively delegitimated the "humoursome doating on a party, which self-admirers are pleas'd to call the Elect, that is those of their own fashion and likeness. They . . . fancie themselves the favourite and special darlings of Heaven."[24]

Also in need of debunking was the experimental edge of Reformed piety, specifically the idea that the Deity communicated directly with the faithful, that holiness involved privileged information about the ways of Providence. William Clagett spoke for many Anglicans when he said, "We can remember what infinite dishonours have been done to God in the late times, by men . . . pretending to the *special Guidance* of the Spirit."[25] The individual must not have the opportunity to claim a source of authority independent of the consensus of the Restoration community. After the Restoration, Anglican clerics went to some length to disabuse the laity of the notion that they could in some way sense the Spirit working inside them. A person's psychological states were his or hers alone, and in no way reflected communication with the divine. The Anglicans spoke disparagingly of "Stories of God's *Withdrawings* and *Desertings;* and again, of his *Shinings in* and *Stealings,*" derived from "a fanciful application of some Scripture or other," and doctrinally based on naught but the "abuse or misapplication of . . . Old Testament phrases."[26] They sneered at the Dissenters that the Dissenters themselves could not deal with the social effects of encountering the Spirit; even in "the *other,* and as you think, the *Purer, England,*" the civil authorities had to be called in to repress Anne Hutchinson.[27]

Individuals claiming contact with the Holy Spirit laid themselves open to the damning charge of enthusiasm: "a pretence to inspiration, without any proof of it."[28] Delineating the boundaries of enthusiasm in a Protestant culture where anyone's correct understanding of the scriptures came only with the aid of the Holy Spirit was invariably political.[29] Unsurprisingly, during the politically charged 1640s and 1650s the term began to be used with increasing frequency. It became paired with another term emerging at the end of the 1650s, "fanaticism," and both became associated with the "vulgar."[30] Attacks on enthusiasm were not new, but what was new, besides their growing frequency, was the way Anglicans covered once relatively respectable groups like the Puritans with their once relatively respectable practices and beliefs with the label.[31] The orthodox Dissenters, although they were perhaps "ashamed to talk like the lowest form of Enthusiasts," laid themselves open to the charge with their extempore prayer and preaching and discoursing on the influence of the Spirit. Talk of such dealings was no longer fashionable, the Anglicans claimed: "The better sort of Hearers are now out of love with these things." The Dissenters' theology itself put them beyond the pale of respectability and common sense: only "the *Enthusiast* . . . will teach you strange and desparate *Doctrines*; such as, Absolute *Reprobation* . . . of Gods being the Author of mens sins . . . that Gods *Grace* is irresistible to some, and equally *Impossible* to others." Said Gilbert Burnet at John Tillotson's funeral, when referring to Tillotson's Puritan youth, "even before his mind was opened to clearer thought, he felt somewhat within him that disposed him to larger notions and a better temper."[32]

The rejection of God's absolute decrees and of intimate communication with the Holy Spirit did not necessarily require a rejection of the central Reformed theological doctrine of justification, the concept that the sinner's salvation was due entirely to the imputation of Christ's righteousness. But this doctrine still implied an uncomfortably close connection with the divine, with all the attendant problems as it was processed into experience. Some influential divines, in a wish to distance themselves emphatically from the scourge of antinomianism, began to develop a concept of justification different from any previous ones, Catholic or Protestant. In the new concept, it was not Christ who was the cause of our justification, by His imputing His righteousness to us through His substitutionary atonement on the cross, but our own faith, supernaturally assisted to be sure, but still our own. We were saved by our own faith; we were most emphatically not saved by a mysterious fusion with a divinity.[33]

The new theology of justification represented the vanguard of Anglican thought, however.[34] Although perhaps not widely accepted in its details, it did express a pervasive mood in Restoration Anglicanism. C. John Sommerville, in his survey of popular Restoration religious literature, notes that Anglican devotional manuals and popular literature of this period in general suggested that the new nature of the convert was to grow out of the old, and if this literature mentioned justification at all it did so in a manner that emphasized human responsibility far more than divine action.[35]

An alternative to redefining theological propositions was to pay little attention to them. Even though many Anglicans resisted a drastic technical redefinition of how the supernatural interacted with the believer, and indeed, a few overt Calvinists remained among the Restoration bishops, the issue of justification did not inspire the same heat as it had done before the Civil Wars, when a veiled remark in a liberalizing direction by a cleric could bring down the wrath of the House of Commons upon him, as Richard Montague discovered.[36] Unless doctrines perceived as bedrock, like the Trinity, came under attack, Anglicans mostly were content to let sleeping dogs lie. Said one in response to some intricate questions on free will and innate depravity, "These *Controversies*, which so miserably *distracted* the *Church* in the last Age, are now happily laid *asleep*, and he must not be very *wise*, who wou'd endeavour again to *wake* 'em."[37] Even those clergy who had retained the doctrine of Christ's imputation of His righteousness preferred to concentrate on such mundane and relatively easily regulated details as morality and the practical benefits of religion for the believer, than on the nature of grace, Christ's interaction with His faithful, and the more knotty questions of theology in general. The doctrine of moral, as opposed to dogmatic, certainty in theology grew popular in this period: one could not have absolute conviction regarding the mind of God; only Quakers, papists, Puritans, and other undesirable sorts made that kind of claim. The best one could hope for, indeed, all one needed, was a prob-ablistic moral conviction.[38]

That probablistic moral conviction was not to be reached by investigating the deep points of the supernatural realm or by a leap of divinely guided faith, but by the use of "reason."[39] While what "reason" consisted of was never made precisely clear, it did not depend upon a mysterious illumination of the Spirit, nor did it rely upon the intricate verbal and theological dissections that characterized both conformist and nonconformist preaching before the Civil Wars.[40] Whatever it was, Anglicans were agreed, it was not to be found in Dissenter preaching.[41] Reason, as the Anglicans tried to appropriate it, was more or less empirical and nonspeculative, not infallible but competent enough for human needs, socially located as roughly comprising the common sense of a sober and pious conformist man of breeding. Reason would show that the scriptures were unquestionably the word of God, from the reasonable argument of the internal evidence of the Bible, and that the truths absolutely necessary for salvation contained therein were simple, unenthusiastic, and eminently reasonable. A reasonable faith that Jesus was the Messiah, a hearty repentance, and a resolution to mend one's ways formed the pillars of the edifice of salvation.

Reason was hardly intended to be politically neutral. If reason prevailed, and fine points of theology were not worth debating, because not capable of

being resolved, theology could not legitimately be used to justify opposition to
the state church:

> The *speculative* Christian . . . passeth over those things which are plain and easy
> to be understood, and applies himself chiefly to . . . matter of controversy and
> subtle dispute, as the doctrine of the *Trinity*, *Predestination*, *Free-will*, and the
> like . . . of [this] rank usually are the heads and leaders of parties and factions in
> religion, who . . . hinder themselves and others from minding the practices of
> the great and substantial duties of a good life.[42]

Reason dictated the avoidance of hair-splitting theological debates as a socially divisive waste of time. As Samuel Parker concluded bluntly, "The way
then to prevent Controversies, and to avoid Schisms, is not to define, but
silence groundless and dividing Opinions."[43]

Parker's point of view is a reminder that the Anglican reformulation of
Reformed theology and religiosity did not just take relatively gentle persuasive
forms like argument, redefinition, ridicule, and contempt. If Dissenters per-
sisted in retaining a supernatural economy that placed them beyond the pale
of reason, then it was reasonable enough to deal with them by force, rather
than futile reasoning.[44] In the Restoration Church settlement, the Anglican
hierarchy effectively set its own terms for the return of Dissenting ministers to
the Church of England, guaranteeing the decline of Calvinism within the
Church, and the Clarendon Code ensured an intense, if sporadic, legal ha-
rassment of those who remained outside. The Licensing Act of 1662 put up a
large, albeit not impenetrable, barrier to the printed dissemination of Dissenter
viewpoints.[45] Through redefinition of theology and spiritual experience, and
through ridicule, contempt, and legal pressure, Providence was to be restrained
from playing upon the soul in the way it had before the "Troubles," when it had
been capable of constructing the religious subject as a seer of God.

✳

Not only the religious individuality licensed and formed by the older conception of Providence needed to be reconstructed. Many Anglicans felt that
the range of phenomena themselves accessible for providential interpretation
had proven out of control and socially disruptive in recent years: "This wild
amuzing mens minds, with *Prodigies*, and conceits of *Providences*, has been one
of the most considerable causes of those spiritual distractions, of which our
Country has long bin the *Theater*."[46] Puritans, Anglicans complained, confidently interpreted events to legitimate all sorts of unfortunate actions: "How

often have we been told (in some solemn Sermons of Thanksgiving before the late long Parliament) . . . that now God had plainly decided the controversie, and all might see (but the obstinately blind) who had the juster part of the quarrel?"[47] While Royalists could scarcely see the precipitous restoration of Charles II as anything but providential, they inexorably connected the tendency to "read" Providence with the Puritans: "They have cried out *Judgments! Judgments!* so long, that they are even become judgments themselves: indeed the greatest and sorest that a nation can groan under."[48]

Anglicans did not have the slightest reservation about the reality of Providence per se. That God governed the world in its minutest details, that He was capable of intervening in its ordinary course, and that He took a special care of His Church and His faithful were not points that Anglicans would dispute. Indeed, to dispute these points would be leading one down the slippery path to atheism. It was the confident reading of special providences, God's commentaries and pronouncements upon human activities, that contributed to social unrest. People had to be disabused of the notion that a wide variety of phenomena lent themselves to providential interpretation. Accordingly, Anglicans began to reconstruct what might be termed practical applied providentialism.

This task was given added urgency by the fact that after the Restoration and the beginning of the removal of nonconforming ministers, unreconciled Puritans produced compilations of prodigies seen on land, water, and in the air, and of dreadful judgments befalling those clergy who chose to conform, or even those onlookers who made too merry at the executions of the regicides.[49] Providence clearly encouraged resistance to the new order, as the editor of one of the compilations stated: "Though he [God] hath suffered this year so many *hundreds* if not *thousands* of our able godly *preaching Ministers* to be *removed into corners*, yet the defect of their Ministry hath been emminently supplied by the *Lords* immediate preaching to us from *Heaven*, in the great and wonderful works of his Providence."[50]

In New England in 1665, John Davenport, reviewing the wonders in the home country of the last five years, exclaimed "Did ever God speake so loud, & shew soe cleerely, by multiplied signes, in heaven, earth, & sea . . . as he hath done to England since the late change of government?"[51] While a moderate Dissenter like Richard Baxter might think that such compilations of prodigies like the *Mirabilis Annus* series did the Dissenters' cause more harm than good, he himself took note "about the time of the silencing of Ministers, how many Churches in *England* were torn at once with terrible lightning, and almost no place else."[52]

Faced with such destabilizing interpretations of God's current interventions in the natural order, Anglican clergy aggressively began to discourage the tendency to read special providences—"this *melancholy*, this *frightful*, this *Astrological* humor," as future bishop Thomas Sprat put it, in his *History of the Royal Society* (1665).[53] Sprat, heralding a theme that was to become more common as the century progressed, proclaimed that to focus on the extraordinary interventions of God insulted Him: "It is enough for the honor of his *Government*, that he guides the whole Creation, in its wonted cours of *Causes*, and *Effects*: as it makes as much for the reputation of a Prince's wisdom, that he can rule his subjects peaceably, by his known, and standing Laws, as that he is often forc'd to make use of extraordinary justice to punish, or reward."[54]

Sprat emphasized that the regularities of God's Providence, His general Providence, in other words, were more accessible to human analysis than His special Providence. Sprat did not deny the reality of God's extraordinary interventions, only the possibility of interpreting them in any but the most general way: "Whenever therefore a hevy calamity falls from *Heven* on our *Nation*, a *universal Repentance* is requir'd; but all particular applications of privat men, except to their own hearts, is to be forborn."[55] Other Anglicans attacked Sprat for his *History*, but their criticisms centered upon his perceived overemphasis on the ability of reason to encompass religion and his optimistic belief that natural philosophy could serve as a substitute for theology and traditional education. His assessment of special Providence met, if silence can be so interpreted, with assent.[56]

John Spencer, a clergyman and later the country's most distinguished Hebraic scholar, in an influential response first published in 1663 to the Dissenter compilation of wonders, did not deny the existence of strange signs and prodigies. Instead, he sought to define them in such a way as to make them inaccessible to political use. The time when God used miracles had ended, Spencer claimed. He interpreted current unusual phenomena not as signs from the Lord, but in Baconian terms as anomalies of nature with no signification. Apparitions and meteorological signs, when real, were either due to unknown natural phenomena, or, rarely, to demons attempting to mislead people. Even when phenomena were clearly prodigious, like Anne Hutchinson's and Mary Dyer's babies ("monstrous beyond the possibilities of Nature"), their interpretation was beyond the skill of mortals.[57]

Although Spencer wrote his book expressly to defuse the impact of Dissenter publications, he avoided attacking Calvinism directly. Yet he clearly implied a link between Calvinism and a wonder-working Providence. Besides criticizing the logic of interpreting prodigies, Spencer, like Sprat, disliked that activity's emotional tone. Prodigies had always been considered portents of misfortune, and Spencer, pointing out that the "common reverence of Prodigies . . . detains men under . . . servile fears," linked them with the conception of "an envy in God and a delight to do evil . . . too much countenanced by some Christians." The Calvinist conception of a God of wrath, a deity of "an envious and troublesom disposition," led to the "easy conclusion, that all Prodigies are a kind of Van-guard to give notice of the many troops of furies and miseries marching after."[58] The unhealthy frame of mind, melancholy, as Sprat had called it, that made prodigies plausible did the same for Reformed orthodoxy.[59]

Just as Anglican divines had openly expressed the social and political utility of their redefinition of the way that Providence worked in the soul, so too were Spencer and Sprat quite open about the utilitarian advantages of their project of redefinition of the outer workings of Providence. The designification of prodigies, Spencer claimed, would "make men more manageable to the commands of Authority," and it "ministers to the quiet and tranquility of the State."[60] Similarly, Thomas Sprat deplored the tendency to "discover in every Turn of human Actions many supernatural *Providences,* and miraculous *Events,*" for there was "nothing more injurious than this, to mens public, or privat peace."[61] Both Sprat and Spencer did well by ministering to the tranquility of the state; Spencer was appointed head of Corpus Christi College in Cambridge in 1667, the only master of that period who cannot be identified with royalist activity during the Interregnum.[62] Sprat was to become Bishop of Rochester.

Spencer and Sprat did not go so far as to deny that God could intervene in human affairs or even that His actions were always beyond interpretation, nor did Anglicans in general. Anglican preachers retained a lively interest in the doings of Providence in the Restoration period. Their emphasis, though, fell on God's dealings with the nation rather than with the individual. Preachers concerned themselves more with explaining how Providence had a special concern for the king and how Providence demanded obedience from the subjects than they did with encouraging individuals to scrutinize Providence for themselves.[63] "Divine Providence looks after the minutest things . . . but it is more especially and particularly engag'd in ordering and managing publick affairs," the popular preacher Benjamin Calamy explained in 1682.[64]

Accordingly, Anglican preachers still divined the meaning of providences. They still spoke of national judgments and of God's dealings with their nation. Fire, plague, and bad harvests brought forth from them pleas for repentance and warnings that God's patience with England was not limitless. But their sermons had changed since the first part of the century in two important ways. First, Anglican divines grew reluctant, as they had not been before the Civil Wars, to draw too close a parallel between England and Israel, now that they had seen the kinds of behavior authorized by such readings. They stressed the more general rule that national sins received national judgments, without denominational discrimination.[65] Second, even though Anglican preachers still preached on public judgments, they avoided attempting to read the causes of those judgments too specifically. That restraint came partially from the Restoration emphasis on moderation, but also directly from the bad example of the Puritans. While Anglicans remained committed to an extraordinarily intervening God, they were also committed to keeping Him from creating any political disruption.

The Anglicans produced one treatise on judgments during the Restoration period, and the treatise prominently displayed these two commitments. A Staffordshire man, John Duncalf, in 1677 rashly swore that his hands should rot off if he had stolen a Bible he was accused of taking. Lo and behold, not only his hands but also his legs rotted off, an episode dramatic enough to be remembered three-quarters of a century later.[66] Simon Ford, a local Anglican minister, preached several sermons thereafter on the subject of judgments that he subsequently revised and published. In his treatise Ford had no intention of denying that the hand of God could be read in interventions as clear as the one the people of Staffordshire experienced, and indeed he stressed the duty of all pious people to mark God's hand in such occurrences. Aware that he was playing with dynamite given England's recent history, Ford hedged his encouragement to note the hand of God with a number of significant strictures. "*Publick signal Judgments* . . . are a sort of Divine Providences which God more *rarely* than is ordinarily believed, exhibits to the world." Furthermore, when they did happen, their "*certain interpretation*" was more difficult than it had been in biblical times. To rush to a conclusion in those instances was "not more *easie and frequent*, than . . . *sinful* and dangerous."[67]

If Ford wanted to discourage the assumption that judgments occurred frequently and could be easily interpreted, he also wanted to make clear to Dissenters that judgments had no partisan nature. Ford deplored the tendency of "dissenters of all sides to impute the sufferings befalling their *opposites*, to Divine displeasure." God was entirely above party and could not be expected to intervene in the domestic religious quarrels of England, Ford insisted. "*Gods great and signal Judgments*" were only inflicted "for such Crimes as are generally condemned in the *judgment of all Mankind*, or at least, *the generality of Chris-*

tians." He warned that it was a "foul and hainous crime" for anyone "out of a *misguided zeal* for God . . . to become a *forger* of Divine Judgments."[68]

Caution in the interpretation of judgments served as a marker by which Anglicans located Puritans outside the bounds of respectability after the Restoration. Anglicans did not refrain entirely from stooping to partisan use of judgments, but even then, they took care to distinguish themselves from the Puritans. For example, Henry Hesketh, when preaching on the anniversary of Charles I's execution, a standard Anglican occasion for rhetorical bashing of Dissenters and reflecting on the mysteries of Providence, wished "those men that have used to be such bold interpreters of Providences, might do well to consider" that their failure to mourn for their sin of killing the king was bringing down the judgments of God upon England. But Hesketh quickly added that he "did not desire to be counted a bold pryer into God's secrets . . . and shall never (I hope) fall into that presumption, which hath added to the guilt of those mens sins." He then allowed that his interpretation might not be certain. Similarly, John Standish in a sermon recounted a tale of one of Cromwell's officers. The officer on the eve of the Battle of Worcester boasted of how he was going off to hunt deer and hoped to bag the large buck (Charles II). Some years later one of his servants accidently killed him while they hunted deer. At the tale's conclusion, Standish intoned, "whether all this was but an ordinary blind Mischance, I determine not, but leave to God and the World to judge." Anglicans still practicing overpresumptuous providential discourse felt obliged to wash their hands of that practice, even while engaging in it. Simon Patrick's Conformist told the Dissenter in their "friendly debate," "I my self could tell you strange but true Misfortunes that have befaln some of your way; which I will not interpret to the justifying of our cause or the condemning of yours."[69]

✳

The attack on the Puritans' providentialism was part of a broader campaign that did not only concern itself with religious topics, narrowly defined. Radicalism in the Puritan Revolution not only took the form of antinomianism and anabaptism, it also included the unbridled pursuit of topics like astrology, alchemy, and hermetic magic. Such topics, like Puritan theology and providentialism, gave too much scope for individual illumination and, unlike Puritanism, too much scope for a self-sufficient universe, to satisfy more orthodox and socially conservative Englishmen.[70] Foes of Puritanism had long characterized the Puritans' exploration of God's eternal decrees as a kind of presumptuous occult probing of divine matters either inherently secret or best left so. Now they conflated the Puritans' providentialism with those very occult disciplines that the Puritans looked upon with horror. Sprat compared zealous providentialists to astrologers, Spencer more sweepingly linked them with "the *Rosy-Crucians* . . . some kinde of *Chemists* . . . *Figure-casters* in Astrology." In 1659, a new edition of an account by the Elizabethan magus John Dee concerning his communications with spirits had a preface equating Dee's impious activities with the religiosity of the Puritans, and rumor had it that leading Puritan divines tried to get the edition suppressed.[71] English learned culture increasingly considered private illumination, be it via occult forces or via the Holy Spirit, as unacceptable.

The Anglicans' conflation of Puritans with astrologers and chemists demonstrates how the struggle over the nature of Providence did not limit itself to religious issues, narrowly defined, but inevitably was played out in natural philosophy. Conservative natural philosophers in the 1640s and 1650s began reaching a consensus on a methodology in the approach to nature that, like the reformulations in theology, would leave little scope for "enthusiasm." They emphasized thorough and collective inquiry, the patient accumulation of facts, and an extreme restraint both in rhetoric and in the formulating of dogmatic hypotheses. They stressed experience, but only such experience as could be communicable to, and repeatable by, the learned community to be valid. The Royal Society, founded in 1660, unofficially codified the new consensus.[72] This stress on moderation and a consensual, provisional attitude to reason, with its exclusion of private, illuminatory insight, bore a striking resemblance to the Anglican reformulation of theology; it is no accident that Thomas Sprat proudly proclaimed that the Royal Society was free from "*the Artifice, and Humors, and Passions of Sects.*"[73]

The new modes of discourse in natural philosophy would satisfactorily marginalize the "enthusiastic" investigator claiming private or occult sources of knowledge. The mechanical philosophy, of which Descartes's was the most widely known variety, would resolve the corresponding problem of a pantheistic, magically charged universe. The world, matter, of itself was inert and lifeless: it could do nothing, create nothing, without the intervention of higher powers. English thinkers interested in natural philosophy adopted it partially for this reason, just as French thinkers had somewhat earlier in the century.[74]

The mechanical philosophy, however, if uncongenial to enthusiasts, could be appropriated by the atheists, who were also assumed, on slender evidence, to be running amok as a result of the disorder of the times.[75] It left an opening for interpreting the world as a clockwork that ran of itself and had no need of a spirit or an intervening God, with Thomas Hobbes's *Leviathan*, uncharitably read, being the most notorious example of that interpretation.[76] While appreciating the mechanical philosophy's intellectual clarity and the limited scope it offered for "enthusiasm," pious English thinkers had to protect it from appropriations they abhorred.[77]

Attempts at integrating the mechanical philosophy and the doctrine of Providence varied. The Platonic clerics Henry More and Ralph Cudworth posited that if matter were entirely inert there must be an intelligent "plastic spirit of the world," "the grand *Quarter-master General* of divine Providence," as More termed it, serving as a creative and formative link between spirit and matter.[78] The great scientist Robert Boyle, whose version of the mechanical philosophy was influenced by the same medieval theological roots that inspired Calvin,[79] rejected More's conception but claimed nevertheless that the study of nature, "a machine so immense, so beautiful, so well contrived," would lead rationally to an acceptance of Providence. Only a continually active Providence could explain so well made and continually well functioning a device. Boyle could hope that "the consideration of God's providence, in the conduct of things corporeal, may prove, to a well-disposed contemplator, a bridge, whereon he may pass from natural to a revealed religion."[80] With such observations, pious natural philosophers found ways to reconcile the mechanical philosophy and religion, in a synthesis that remained satisfactory to the religiously inclined until the advent of Darwinism.

The political configurations through which the mechanical philosophy was introduced into England ensured that it stressed the ways God worked through the universe's ordinary operations, not His extraordinary interventions. Toward the end of the seventeenth century, controversial clergymen like Thomas Burnet, in his *Sacred Theory of the Earth* (1684), and William Whiston, in *A New Theory of the Earth* (1696), extended that stress by seeking ways to explain the miracles of the Bible in mechanical terms. They suggested that Moses had adapted his account of the early days of the Earth to suit the primitive mentality of his listeners and was perhaps himself no natural philosopher. Burnet and Whiston generated a flood of publications. Conservative clergymen felt uncomfortable with the attempt to bind God thoroughly to the ordinary laws of nature, while emboldened deists seized upon the new hypotheses to support their contention that God had set up a clockwork universe and the Bible was a fable.[81] The point of these disputes is not that the learned community reached a consensus about the nature and extent of biblical miracles, for it certainly did not. Nor is the point to suggest that pious English thinkers felt, or should have felt, any contradiction between believing in the mechanical philosophy and believing in a still active God.[82] These controversies' significance is that they mark how the parameters of debate in learned culture were changing in a way unfavorable to an extravagant conception of extraordinary providences.

For many learned English people, Newton's hypothesis of universal gravitation satisfied any potential conflict between God's extraordinary and ordinary providential interventions.[83] His theory of gravity allowed itself to be interpreted as a proof of the continual intervention of God in the operation of the world, while leaving the contemporary universe largely unsubjected to the idiosyncrasies of a personalistic and politically unreliable supernatural order. The very regularity of the universe became as great a miracle as any of the supernatural interruptions recorded in the Bible.

Calvin discovered and interpreted God's power in the world's contingencies; the new Restoration piety found it in the world's regularities. The appearances may have been saved for religion, but those committed to an older sense of Providence noted that the Newtonian definition of miracles obscured the wonder and unpredictability with which the Reformed tradition had previously firmly associated them: "The Supreme and All-mighty Being doth not confine himself to *Mechanism* and the Common Principles of Natural Motion," thundered John Edwards, the last prominent Calvinist in the Church of England and friend of Cotton Mather. Although gravity was certainly not explicable in natural terms, Edwards agreed, "*Rarity* and *Wonder*" distinguished a miracle, whereas the effects of gravity were "common and usual," and excited no "amazement."[84] But such a fine-tuned sensibility for God's wonder-working Providence was uncommon in educated circles by the end of the seventeenth century, and popularizers like William Whiston, Richard Bentley, and Samuel Clarke loudly proclaimed the miraculous nature of the commonplace phenomenon of gravity.[85] By the 1690s, natural philosophy and Providence had reached a satisfactory accommodation quite remote from the formulations of the early seventeenth century, but suitable enough for the Anglican mood of the Restoration.

✳

The three overlapping projects, theological, practical, and scientific, formed the basis for the Anglican attack on the divinatory providentialism of Puritanism and the sects. The theological project denied the theoretical and experiential supernatural framework that gave confidence to close providential readings, while the practical and scientific projects discouraged the very readings themselves. Not all learned Anglicans agreed with, or participated uniformly in, each of the projects (nor I am suggesting that the origins, meanings, and attractions of these projects were exclusively political, or that their politics were directed solely against Puritans), but those projects increasingly defined the parameters of acceptable learned knowledge as England moved into the early Enlightenment.[86]

The success of the projects hardly indicates the triumph of a universalistic reason. Stricter standards of evidence might render many specific wonders unlikely, but beyond that point the projects did not draw their strength from their superior rationality. Much of the knowledge generated in the discourse of wonders was partisan and self-serving, but the knowledge that replaced it was hardly free of that taint. Why should God's honor be more served by His ordinary government than by His extraordinary interventions; why should He interfere only in large-scale events or in those around which Christians had created an interpretive consensus; why should the activity of the Holy Spirit in our minds not be discernable; why should people not be able to know that they were among the saved? These were not questions to be resolved by the application of a self-evidencing reason, and certainly not by appeals to the Bible, which has ample deconstructive mechanisms against totalizing readings, but by the learned community's own mechanisms of inclusion and exclusion.

One of those mechanisms was the attractive force of prominent individuals who could serve as cultural models and indicate the boundaries of acceptable discourse, and one of the most famous of such models was John Tillotson (1630–90). Tillotson, who ended his career as Archbishop of Canterbury, was at the cutting edge of the first two of these three projects, and he was perhaps the most influential preacher of his time. His widow received 2,500 guineas for the rights to his sermons, and these sermons were held up as a template for rhetoric and piety throughout the eighteenth century.[87] Tillotson is particularly important for this study because, for reasons to be discussed below, he did not represent a role model only for Anglicans, but he had a powerful impact on the Dissenters, including those in Massachusetts. William Brattle and John Leverett introduced his writings to Harvard by the 1680s, and Tillotson became perhaps the most widely read author in the colonies. In 1722, Benjamin Franklin satirically claimed that theological study at Harvard consisted solely of copying long passages out of his works.[88] Since Tillotson had such a widespread following in Massachusetts, he is the natural choice through whom to trace the newly molded contours of Anglican providential thought as it came to be assimilated into Massachusetts.

Unsurprisingly, Tillotson regarded the concept of Providence as crucial. Belief in Providence was one of the tenets of natural religion; God had written the doctrine in our hearts: "the belief of this is the great foundation of religion."[89] People could be assured that God regarded prayers, constantly observed them, and would eventually deal out appropriate rewards and punishments.[90] However, for all his faith in Providence, Tillotson, like many other contemporaneous Anglicans, conceived of it very differently than had English theologians in the earlier period of Calvinist consensus. The foundation of Calvin's providentialism, predestination, in particular, worried Tillotson, for it created an unacceptable god: "We [must] be sure we ascribe nothing to him [God] that is *evil*, or in any ways unworthy of him; That we do not make him the sole author of our salvation, in such a way, as will unavoidably charge upon him the final impenitency and ruin of a great part of mankind." If predestination created the wrong emotional tone for the Deity, it also had an unfortunate experiential edge that boded badly for social stability: it stirred up people unnecessarily. In "good men," predestination engendered "groundless fears" and "great perplexity and discomfort." In bad men, the idea that humans were saved absolutely, and through no strivings of their own, had the "natural consequences" of "tending to licentiousness and a neglect of the precepts of the gospel." Tillotson preferred to think that while God may have predestined a few "extraordinary examples" like Saint Paul for salvation, most people were given "sufficient grace," which they were free to accept or reject.[91]

Tillotson carried on his experientially edged reconstitution of Providence into its work in the human soul. While discussing the process of salvation, Tillotson took pains to tear apart the close and detailed intertwining of the human and supernatural realms that had recently authorized so much disturbance in England. He made no distinction between preparatory work to regeneration and regeneration itself, and he denied any difference between regeneration and sanctification. Justification itself was not the mysterious encounter and union between the believer and God, but "signifies no more, but the pardon and remission of sins." Further, "So soon as we believe in him [Christ], and heartily embrace his doctrine, we are united to him." Furthermore, justification created no discernable permanent mark of favor: "our continuance in this state of grace and favour with God, depends upon our perseverance in holiness."[92]

Tillotson never denied the necessity of supernatural grace for salvation, but he denied the possibility of massive extra-social supernatural empowerment in the process. A person could not achieve repentance without grace, but grace was "never wanting to the sincere endeavours of Men." "If we do but heartily, and in good earnest resolve upon a better Course, and implore the Help of God's Grace to this purpose, no degree of it that is necessary shall be wanting to us." He was skeptical of any sudden infusion of grace at any stage in the process of salvation, even in the case of dramatic conversions. Against the Calvinists he denied that there was any irresistible act of God involved in conversion, except in rare cases like Saint Paul's, and even that divine action he preferred to call "very *forcible* and violent," rather than irresistible.[93]

Just as Tillotson denied massive empowerment by supernatural agencies, so too did he deny that those agencies' activities were directly legible in the Christian's inner life, although he certainly did not deny their transformative importance. Tillotson doubted those who believed that they received from the Holy Spirit an "extraordinary impression upon their minds." Although the Holy Spirit could cast thoughts into our minds, in practice, divine thoughts were indistinguishable from our own. Tillotson reassured people who thought that their lack of religious ardor meant that God was abandoning them that such occasional abatement in zeal "naturally proceeds from the inconstancy of mens tempers."[94] In keeping with his rejection of the harsher aspects of the Reformed supernatural economy, Tillotson believed that the Devil had no control over our imaginations, and he thought it an "uncomfortable consideration" to believe that the Devil could cast "blasphemous and despairing thoughts into the minds of men."[95] Tillotson wanted no one to regard his or her mental states as having any kind of supernatural authority.

Nor did Tillotson wish to encourage the conception of an angry God, a conception that had driven providential divination. His desire to reshape that conception guided his treatment of afflictions. For Tillotson, afflictions were hardly the products of an actively wrathful God. Instead, they were the almost unnatural results of human "obstinacy and intractableness." These human qualities "constraineth, and almost forceth him [God] against his inclination, to take the Rod into his hand, and to chastise us with it . . . If he afflict us, it is not because it is pleasant to him to deal harshly with us, but because it is profitable and necessary for us to be so dealt with."[96] God afflicted us out of sorrow, not out of wrath.

When He did afflict us, according to Tillotson, we should not respond by anxiously scrutinizing those afflictions for their messages. Rather than divination, afflictions were to encourage pragmatic philosophizing. Tillotson pointed out that when "good men" met with abuse in this world, it served both to humble their pride and at the same time to secure their reputations. For by humbling their pride, good men "secure the reputation which they have, and which would otherwise be in danger of being lost."[97] Afflictions also encouraged us to consider that if they were so grievous, so much worse would be the torments of Hell.[98]

Afflictions had benign intentions and advantageous practical results, and Tillotson took that optimistic perspective on religiosity in general. Religiosity improved our health, our reputations, and our worldly estates, both through the inoculation of good habits and because "God's more especial providence" accompanied good men.[99] This stress on the worldly advantages of religion had important political implications. The devout were not to look to supernatural signs for indications that God approved of them, but instead to the extent of their successful integration in the existing social order.

While the terrifying Providence of Calvin encouraged a lively effort at divination, the more benign Providence of Tillotson discouraged it. That discouragement did not limit itself to the work of Providence in the life of the individual; it extended to Providence's work abroad in the world. Tillotson did not deny that God issued extraordinary judgments of the type that filled folio volumes in the earlier part of the century, but he did deny that they could be, or should be, read:

> When we see the judgments of God abroad in the world, and to fall heavily upon particular places and persons, we should argue thus with ourselves: for what reason the holy and wise providence of God hath dealt so severely with others, I know not . . . it is not for me to pry curiously into the counsels of God, and to wade into the depths of his judgments: but there is one use which I am sure it concerns me necessarily to make of it, to look into myself . . . lest while I am gazing upon others, I fall into the like or greater calamities.[100]

He did acknowledge that occasionally a judgment appeared so striking that its interpretation was obvious, but in general, Tillotson rejected trying to scrutinize judgments for their meaning: "It is rash to conclude from little circumstances of judgments, or some fanciful parallel betwixt the sin and the punishment, what sinners and what persons in particular God designed to punish." In any event, "no man can with certainty conclude, from the greatness of the judgment that falls upon any one, that such a man was a more grievous sinner than others, who have escaped the same or the like judgments."[101] Tillotson did not especially interest himself in special providences, except as they brought a person to repent, something he or she should have been doing in the first place. He did not find scrutinizing Providence a particularly effective evangelical device: "Does not our own experience tell us how little effect the extraordinary providences of God have had upon those who were not reclaimed by his word?"[102]

The one area in which Tillotson did preach on God's judgments with some frequency was the area of "national judgments." God could deal with individuals in the afterlife, explained Tillotson in the standard fashion, but nations had to receive their rewards and punishments in the present.[103] The variety of disasters that God inflicted on England after the Restoration—plague, fire, declining commerce, war, poor harvests—resulted from England's sins. But when cataloging these sins, Tillotson preferred to remain unspecific and uncontroversial for the most part ("It will not, I think, become us to be very particular and positive in such Determinations"), referring broadly to infidelity, immorality, and church divisions.[104] Tillotson's faith in providential national guidance was dramatically confirmed by the Glorious Revolution of 1688.[105]

Although Tillotson occasionally acknowledged extraordinary judgments, his providential devotionalism did not focus on God's extraordinary interventions, but rather on the general and governing aspects of Providence. When discoursing on this theme, Tillotson could rise to an Emersonian pitch of feeling:

> God does not commonly prove his providence to men by extraordinary instances of his power . . . but . . . by the constant course of nature, in the returns of day and night, in the revolutions of the seasons of the years, *in that he gives us rain from heaven, and fruitful seasons, filling our hearts with food and gladness* . . . They are daily miracles, . . . and we should be strangely amazed at them, but that they are so very frequent and familiar.[106]

Given his emphasis on a strange amazement at the common and natural (and politically reliable) course of Providence, rather than on the extraordinary instances of God's power, it is not surprising that Tillotson himself became a Fellow of the Royal Society in 1671.[107] In doing so, he neatly sewed together the strands of the three overlapping projects that together transformed the Anglican conception of Providence.

For Dissenters, Tillotson played an especially important role, because he represented the acceptable face of this transformation. Tillotson himself had been a Presbyterian in the 1650s, and he shared many of the concerns of the moderate Dissenters. He never showed great attachment to the specific forms of the Church of England, and he labored intermittently, although unsuccessfully, to make the Church more comprehensive. Rigorously anti-Catholic and personally friendly with many Dissenters, Tillotson retained the strict personal piety of his Puritan youth and admired much Dissenter piety. He read with approval Cotton Mather's biography of John Eliot and achieved immortality in the annals of early New England by assuring Increase Mather of his "resentments of the injury which had been done to the first planters of New-England."[108] Thus, Archbishop Tillotson, obviously a figure of great cultural importance, swathed in a widely admired personal piety, unattached to the Church forms that Dissenters loathed, and above the overt day-to-day clash of Dissenter-Anglican politics, offered the Dissenters a powerful new model to follow on the road back to respectability. They might not accept all his theology, yet still strive to imitate his tone of moderation and stability and his experiential desiderata. Tillotson's example ensured that young ministers in Massachusetts could come to grips with the Anglican reconfiguration of Providence without having to confront the fact that they were going over into territory formulated in opposition to Puritanism.

✳

Cultural politics were only part of the elements reshaping discursive assumptions in Restoration England. That period was a time of accelerated economic change in England, and historians have linked changes in providentialism to underlying economic shifts. Margaret C. Jacob has explained the style of providentialism promoted by divines like Tillotson, with its stress on "sober self-interest," and its orderly, mechanical universe with a restrained but ever-present Providence, as an attempt to Christianize an emergent liberal capitalist market system wherein possessive self-interest was running rampant.[109] Keith Thomas speculated that contingency itself, the control of which was Calvin's chief boast for his providentialism, did not seem as threatening in the second half of the century to the English elite as it had previously. Thanks to improved agricultural techniques, England no longer saw the famines of the first half of the century. New schemes of insurance provided some protection against the vagaries of Providence. Newly emergent economic and social sciences traced the fortunes of society in secular terms, and the development of probability theory brought order into contingency itself.[110]

Jürgen Habermas, in a effort to understand broad European institutional and discursive change, has argued that England's commercial expansion and movement toward free commercial exchange in the second half of the seventeenth century stimulated the beginning of the consolidation of a "bourgeois public sphere." This public sphere manifested itself within new social sites of discourse, coffeehouses, journals, periodicals, clubs. Those sites, among which should be included the Royal Society, encouraged ostensibly unforced critical judgement and reasonable exchange, a free exchange in the commodity of ideas: the discursive pattern of the early Enlightenment.[111]

The new cultural sites of the public sphere and the mode of discourse they promoted represented a shift from an authoritarian world in which power embodied in special persons, be they magi, ministers, or kings, displayed itself before the people to a world in which power was constituted by a discourse in which the people participated and criticized.[112] With their stress on the free exchange of information, they were not sympathetic sites for privileged appeals to supernatural sources: a 1665 pamphlet on coffeehouses portrayed a "virtuoso" (scientist) at a coffeehouse dismissing claims of prodigies by a "sly Phanatick."[113] While Habermas linked the emergence of a public sphere to England's economic development, cultural politics demonstrably helped to shape its discursive contours.[114] Tillotson, for example, was the divine of choice, both for rhetoric and content, for immensely influential new-style cultural arbitrators like Joseph Addison of the *Spectator*.[115]

However powerful the political, economic, and cultural encouragements of discursive change, educated Anglicans hardly abandoned the world of wonders instantaneously. Isaac Newton, besides being a devout, if heretical, theologian and student of eschatology, studied alchemy into the 1690s, and in that decade, John Aubrey, Fellow of the Royal Society, busied himself collecting stories of ghosts, astrology, and magic.[116] Throughout the eighteenth century, many Anglican ministers did not hesitate to predict the descent of God's wrath on a sinful nation. Nevertheless, in the late seventeenth century, the discourse of wonders clearly underwent a process of constriction in educated Anglican circles. The new and increasingly influential providentialism glorified God by utilizing the gifts of a beneficent providential order, rather than by anxiously scrutinizing the world for His messages.[117]

The older Providence, the Providence of signs and wonders, remained inextricably tied up with the older theology that the Dissenters preserved. Calvinism, strong doctrines of grace, an intrusive Providence, and religious practices and experiences frowned upon by much of England's elite went hand in hand into the eighteenth century. The arrival in London of the Calvinist French Prophets in the first years of the century precipitated the largest eighteenth-century outburst of enthusiasm, as well as criticisms of enthusiasm, before the midcentury revivals.[118] John Mason, an Anglican clergyman who created a stir when he gathered his flock to await the millennium in Northamptonshire in 1693, was also a Calvinist with a fondness for extempore prayer. An observer of his activities neatly summed up the Restoration Anglican perception of the link between Calvinism and enthusiasm: "There may be I grant, some valuable Persons who are lightly touch'd with the apprehension of Absolute Reprobation, &c. and may (as they think) make it serve to some serious purposes: but he that ruminates upon it . . . must either Despond or Prophecy."[119]

The observer of Mason's activities noted disapprovingly that his followers cited the great Congregational divine John Owen to claim that those who have the Spirit "know they have it and cannot be deceived."[120] That sort of privileged, illuminatory knowledge, the knowledge of the Puritans, was being pushed to the fringes of Restoration learned culture.

✳

And what of Massachusetts? Did it simply sit out this process of cultural marginalization? Was it content with its armies in the sky, with the workings of the Spirit in the soul, with the intricacies of closing with Christ, and with the endurance of an endless controversy with an angry God? Although the orthodox Dissenters—officially almost the only group in Massachusetts— have been largely mute in this chapter, they were participants in the providential debate. They did not intend to give up their wonder-working Providence without some struggle, and Massachusetts, if mainly in the writing and organizational capacities of Increase Mather, was to play a significant role in that struggle.

CHAPTER THREE

※

Israel Strikes Back

Massachusetts was hardly isolated. The Anglicans engaged in a vehement campaign for the redefinition of Providence precisely because they struggled with an opposition. As the Dissenting divine John Collinges put it, "Who sees not that there is a New Mess of *Divinity* bringing into the world, which is not like to be well digested, or received indeed while the N.C. [Nonconformists] are in any reputation?"[1] The orthodox Nonconformists' response to the Anglican campaign to redefine Providence took two approaches. The first vigorously reasserted old doctrine and practice, and the second explored how much the forms of discourse being developed by the Anglicans could be accommodated to old assumptions. Massachusetts ministers participated in both types of response, and the intellectual development of Massachusetts cannot be properly understood without examining their role in the Dissenter response.

✳

In the spring and early summer of 1683, Increase Mather preached a number of sermons on the subject of Providence at the Thursday lectures at his Boston church. Some of the sermons later appeared as a book *The Doctrine of Divine Providence Opened and Applyed*.[2] Mather had Providence on his mind at this time; he was also working on an elaborate project for the recording of special providences.

Mather was not alone among Massachusetts ministers in pondering the mysteries of Providence in this period. Far from being inward looking, the ministers were linked to Europe in an active two-way flow of communication, and they knew that Israel's troubles were not limited to their own colony.[3] The Church in Massachusetts suffered the disaster of King Philip's War, bitter internecine feuding among the godly, and hostile royal attacks on the colony's charter, but the Church abroad suffered under the blows of oppression and a newly resurgent Catholicism. Waves of persecution swept over the ministers'

brethren in France and central Europe, while Dissenters in England, just recovering from the terrifying, if imaginary, perils of the Popish Plot, were being
hit by the very real perils of a severe Anglican persecution, with a Catholic
heir to the throne waiting in the wings.

With Israel so besieged, who could not be concerned? "God hath a controversy with the world," Mather said in 1683, in his usual dramatic fashion,
and other ministers echoed him. Samuel Willard lamented in 1684, "At this
day in many places of Christendom the ways to Zion mourn, the Harps are
hanged up; the mournful Ditty is that in ps. 123." "The Design of Christ now
in the world is to see who will be faithfull to Him," John Allin claimed in
1683. The ministers organized fasts and encouraged prayers on account of the
"calamitys on the Church abroad." They warned their congregations that the
churches in Massachusetts should not expect to remain isolated from the
troubles of the churches elsewhere. "We know not how soon our Turn may
come," Timothy Woodbridge said at a day of prayer organized for the French
Protestants at the South Church in 1681. John Danforth at a fast in Dor-
chester warned his listeners in 1681 to pray for the foreign churches for the
pragmatic reason that Massachusetts would need their prayers "when the cup
of Divine Wrath comes about to us as certainly it will." The ways of Providence abroad in the world were of immediate concern to the godly of Massachusetts; seventeen-year-old Cotton Mather nervously queried himself at the
end of 1680, "What shall wee do to stand by the Truth in a Time of danger?"[4]

If Increase Mather shared a concern about the doings of Providence with
his fellow Massachusetts ministers, he also knew well that in doing so, neither
he nor they followed an isolated, colonial line of thought. As he noted in the
preface to The Doctrine of Divine Providence Opened and Applyed, "This subject
of Divine Providence has been largely and Elaborately handled . . . by several of
our own Nation in their Discourses lately published: In special by Mr. Flavel,
Dr. Collins, Mr. Charnock, and Mr. Crane."[5] What is significant about the list
of authors with whom Mather associated his own efforts is not that they were
just of his "nation," but that they were all Dissenters. In a period when the
Anglicans produced not a single extended treatise on Providence, the Dissenters produced five, Mather's being the last.[6] Mather's only justification for
adding his particular treatise to this series of exceedingly lengthy books was, he
claimed, its brevity. He deliberately omitted some of his more theoretical sermons on the nature of Providence from his publication "lest the discourse
should become too Voluminous for such Readers whose Edification is particularly
aimed at."[7]

The Dissenter treatises have not yet been examined in depth by scholars, nor has Mather's effort been examined in light of the others. Together those treatises are important for they comprise a transatlantic learned response to the Anglican redefinition of Providence, and they show that Massachusetts, far from being isolated in the Restoration period, shared fully in the Puritan culture of the time.

All five of the treatise writers were battle-scarred veterans of the religious struggles in England. Crane, Flavel, and Collinges had been ejected from their ministries in 1662 by the triumphant Anglicans. Mather returned to Massachusetts rather than conform. Collinges was known for his "ill affections to the Crown," and Charnock was suspected of plotting against the government in the confused period after Charles II took the throne. All but Crane were well-known figures and prolific writers. Charnock was studied into the nineteenth century, and the latest new edition of a work by Flavel came out in 1963.[8] The writers of these treatises were not marginal "phanaticks," for all that the Anglicans wished to construct them as such, but products of, and participants in, England's learned culture.

The treatises do not form a perfect unity. Crane and Flavel took evangelical approaches, focusing mostly on the role of Providence in the life of the individual Saint. Charnock and Mather focused more on Providence as it interacted with the Church as a corporate body. Collinges, in the longest of these books, included a lengthy defense of Calvinist orthodoxy in explicating the "hard places" in Providence. Nevertheless, they sufficiently resemble each other to be treated as a group, and my discussion will focus on their common themes.

The writers understood that their elaborate defenses of Providence were something novel. Collinges, the second after Crane to produce a treatise, remarked in 1679 that he knew of nothing comparable to his work except his predecessor's.[9] They also knew that they were engaging in an argument, defending a wonder-working divinatory Providence that was falling into disrepute in Anglican-dominated learned culture. Crane defended his point of view immediately in his preface: "Far be it from me to affect lying-Legends; and as far be it from me (because of lying-Legends in the World) to bury the Works of God in the grave of a contemptuous Oblivion."[10]

Collinges noted that some who granted to Providence a "universal influence," "love not to hear of any *Specialties* of it," and "few or none make any *observations upon* the motions of Divine Providence."[11] Flavel, disclaiming any attempt to convert atheists, explicitly and correctly linked the decay of interest in special Providence with the decay of interest in experiential religion. Flavel said, "My Business here, is not so much to deal with professed *Atheists*

. . . But rather to convince those that . . . never having tasted Religion by Experience, suspect at least, that all these things which we call *special Providences* to the Saints, are but *natural Events,* or meer *contingencies.*"[12]

Like the Anglicans, and like Calvin before them, the Dissenters all agreed that the ways of God were inscrutable in their full scope, and that, as Solomon was said to have put it, no man could know either love or hatred by all that was before him in this life. In fact, they gloried in the mystery of Providence.[13] But whatever their theoretical claims about God's inscrutability, in practice the Dissenters, like their predecessors, seemed to acknowledge only a limited sphere in which they could not comprehend Him. As if to live up to the Anglicans' worst expectations of them, they proceeded to register in great detail, with examples from biblical, Church, and contemporary sources, just how Providence worked and could be interpreted.

The Dissenters based their interpretive confidence on the temporal and ongoing presence of God's Word, as it had been delineated in its authorized text, the Bible. God's Word was emphatically not discrete, not confined to its text, wherein it could cause no contemporary disturbance, but still active and formative in the contemporary world. "The Two Volumes of the Sacred Scriptures, and Divine Providence . . . are Comments on, or Expositions of each other," Crane said.[14] As Charnock put it, "What God doth now is but a copy of what he pourtrayed in his word as done in former ages . . . The Births of Providences are all of a like temper and disposition. We cannot miss of the understanding of them if we compare them with the antient Copies."[15] Flavel expressed the same idea in a more evangelical manner: "Bring those Providences you have past through, or are now under, to the Word; and you will find your selves surrounded with a marvellous light; and see the verification of the Scriptures in them."[16]

These Dissenters' sense of an active and engaged supernatural power whose patterns of behavior had been revealed in the Bible gave them the confidence to read providences. "Every single providence hath a language wherein Gods mind is signified," Charnock declared, in a sentiment that all the others would second. Collinges, confident enough in his ability to discern the significations of God's mind, claimed, against all Anglican denials, that one could infer the nature of someone's sin from the judgments passed upon him or her, although he charitably added that all we could make in such cases was a judgment of probability.[17]

The Dissenters did not base their comprehension of God's intentions purely on rational analysis. Flavel claimed that the Saints could inwardly sense impending troubles, and he himself was later said to have foreseen his own death.[18] Although they would have seemed to have come out on the short end of the Restoration settlement, the Dissenters remained convinced that the universe still bent to the power of their prayers. Mather exclaimed, "A praying People (tho' but few in number) can do marveilous things." The Deity worked through the prayers of his Saints. "When God would do any mighty work in the World," claimed Charnock, "he first stirs up his people to pray for it, and their prayers by his own appointment have a mighty influence upon the Government of the World." Furthermore, a close scrutiny of Providence would validate the power of prayer. "Christians . . . are well assured," said Collinges, "that many of the Providences that befall them are, and can be no other than the return of their Prayers." Prayer was validated, according to Crane, "from the signal appearance of *Providence* at or nigh the very time that prayer is made."[19] The Dissenters' Providence remained a wonder-working Providence, still breathing the inspiration of the Spirit.

Thus for the Dissenters, the study of Providence led to more than simply an accepting resignation before the will of God. It had an illuminatory quality, opening up the most fundamental activity of the world. As Collinges said, "nothing more conduceth to true Spiritual wisdom." All the other authors seconded him, and Flavel assured his readers that by the study of Providence, "you may maintain sweet and sensible communion with God from day to day." But sweet and sensible communion with the Deity was just what the Anglicans were trying to discourage. An Anglican concerned about the Dissenters' activist Providence would not have been reassured by Charnock's claim that each providence offered "something to be practiced," nor by Collinges's statement that "from the observation of the motions of *Divine Providence* . . . considerate Christians may . . . give a very probable conjecture, if not form a certain judgment, both what God is about to do, and what *Israel ought to do*."[20] Memories were still fresh about what Israel had done under providential inspiration in recent English history.[21]

Furthermore, these Dissenters had no doubt just who represented Israel in Restoration England. Whether in England or across the ocean in Emmanuel's Land, the Saints wrapped themselves in a cloak of cosmological significance, a cloak visible enough even in a time of censorship. Not for them the Anglican Simon Ford's assertion that God's Providence was above parties. Collinges confidently asserted that a study of special providence would enable a person "to go a great way in making up a Judgment, who they are that make up the true Church of God." For example, such a study showed that "Sometimes the Providence of God raiseth up his people to such a considerateness, as to the commerce and trade of a Nation; that they cannot be rooted out without cutting the sinews of a nation, and breaking the strength of it" (he discreetly gave a biblical example).[22]

God continued to look after His people in Restoration England. According to Collinges, God's elect in general enjoyed more protection from sickness and accidents than did others.[23] Flavel exclaimed, in the middle of a section on how God could work "above the Power, and against the course of natural causes," "Do we not behold a weak, defenceless handful of men, wonderfully, and (except this way) unaccountably preserved in the midst of potent, enraged and turbulent enemies?" Crane, asserting what became an axiom among the Nonconformists during spells of persecution, reassured his listeners that "What men do to ruin God's people ends often in the ruin of them and theirs." Dissenters would learn, according to Charnock, from a study of Providence, of the extent to which the nation depended on them. "Gods people (whatever their Enemies suggest to the contrary) are a blessing in the midst of a Land; their interest is greater than the interest of all the world besides . . . The Providence of God, being chiefly for the good of his People, cannot well fall upon them but some drops will fall upon those involved with them in a common interest." Mather, predictably, claimed that "the setting up of Christ's Kingdom in this Part of the world, is one of the Wonders of divine providence, which this last age has seen."[24] The English state might have jettisoned God's elect, but the study of Providence reassured Dissenters on both sides of the Atlantic that God Himself had not.

John Spencer had claimed that the Dissenters' providential interpretation sustained its intensity through their sense of a wrathful God, and certainly the treatise writers used that sense to come to terms with their persecution. They were more wont than the Anglicans to stress that their God did everything for His own self-interest, not humanity's. As Collinges said, "God in all his great workings, both of Judgment and Mercy . . . is pursuing one and the same great end, *viz.* the glory of his great and holy Name . . . The deliverance and good of his people is subordinate to this, so is the ruin and destruction of their Enemies."[25]

Since they did not expect their carnal self-interest and God's to coincide, difficult circumstances in the Restoration period caused them no interpretive difficulties. "The Providence of God as to its works," Collinges explained, "relating to his Church and people, rarely as to circumstances, answereth the expectations and confidences of the best of Gods people." Charnock stated, "'Tis indeed Gods usual method to leave the Church to extremity before he doth command help." In any event, the persecutions themselves, Flavel claimed, stemmed from "our own turnings aside from the Lord," and "Times of extremity make us more humble, and humility like the Plow, fits us for the seed of mercy."[26] If the Lord afflicted His people on both sides of the Atlantic, that only confirmed their connection with Him.

There are only two major differences between Mather's work and that of the other Dissenters, one idiosyncratic, the other the effect of geography. Mather made brief but emphatic references to the impending Last Days: "I am perswaded, that er'e this Generation be passed away, the Lord Jesus will do more marvellous works in the world than ever was done in one Generation since the world began." Flavel, Charnock, and Crane remained silent on the theme, one that had figured so prominently and disappointingly in the decades of Puritan rule, while Collinges cautioned that concern with dating the arrival of those days "commonly produceth *error in our imaginations, vain thoughts, bold determinations of the Councels of God, groundless prophecies, erroneous apprehensions both of God and of his ways.*"[27]

Conceptually, the other difference between Mather's treatise and his English models was that Mather had a far more national orientation. The interests of God's Church were far more clearly the interests of New England than they were of old England. Correspondingly, the sins of New England were more evidently the sins of Church members than they were in old England, and Mather ended his treatise with one of his usual lashings out at the sins of Massachusetts. The English Dissenters had little incentive to identify Israel with England.[28]

The Dissenters' treatises demonstrate that the logic of their providentialism had not greatly changed since the early years of the century. God remained partisan, close, and communicative, and touchy about His prerogatives. The Dissenters' relationship to Providence remained actively divinatory; the world was intelligible to those with the gift of deciphering its biblical analogies and similitudes. But that particular logic, the logic of similitude, was passing out of fashion in English learned circles. The theologians and natural philosophers who rejected close readings of special providences and an extraordinarily intervening God were also developing new forms of discourse that avoided reasoning by similitude and authority, divine or otherwise, and that answered the question of how to determine the meaning of a phenomenon by exact and "objective" observation, and by the comparison of quantifiable elements, not by analogical reasoning and a presumed correspondence between the moral and natural worlds.

Orthodox Dissent understandably hesitated to pick up modes of thought intended to eliminate it. The dominant groups in English society, however, favored those modes of thought, and even the Dissenters' treatises bear some witness to them. All the treatises except Mather's brief one include attempts to codify the working of Providence, to generalize covering laws to explain its operations. Codification represented the only new element in these treatises, an attempt to rationalize a previously unselfconscious set of practices.[29] However, a skeptical reader wading through these attempts at discerning Providence's covering laws would probably not be convinced by the effort. Mather, alone of the five authors considered above, would try to adapt the providential sensibility of the Puritans more rigorously to the new disciplining of perception being promulgated by Restoration natural philosophers.

✳

Mather remained largely alone in this attempt at adaptation, but he did not originate it. As already noted, the instability of the Interregnum years led a great many Anglicans to grow wary of the perceived abuse of Providence as a device for legitimization of undesirable behavior. Their wariness caused them to limit drastically the use of Providence as an interpretive category, as part of an overall redefinition of the supernatural. Puritans too worried about the abuse of Providence by enthusiasts (from which category they excluded themselves, of course), but their response to the identical concern differed from that of the Anglicans. The Puritans had no intention of jettisoning their conceptions of Providence or the extraordinary interventions of God because of the way those ideas could be used by sectaries any more than they had jettisoned their concept of grace because of the way it could be used by antinomians.

Loath though they were to part with their concept of Providence because of the way some groups had used it, the Puritans had to acknowledge that it presented challenges. The problem with Providence in this time of social disorder seemed to be that it was a purely plastic interpretive term, subject to no outside controls. Providence lacked proper surveillance. A socially approved group needed to retain interpretive possession of it, through means that the larger elite community would acknowledge. Providence had to be wrested back from the enthusiasts while leaving it intact in the process. The Anglicans were accomplishing the former, but at the expense of the latter.

The Puritans made two attempts to recover learned control of Providence, the first by the erudite Presbyterian Matthew Poole in the late 1650s and the second by Increase Mather in the early 1680s. These attempts are interesting for two reasons. The first is that in their effort to meet with new learned standards, they tried deliberately to modernize an area of discourse that previously had been unselfconscious and unproblematic, at least to its practitioners. The second is that they failed in this attempt. Their total published results consisted of two volumes, one by Mather and one by a sympathetic Anglican, neither reprinted.[30] Their project was out of step with the times.

The first attempt, conceived of by Poole in or shortly before 1656, left its traces primarily in a manuscript preserved at Cambridge University.[31] The manuscript contains Poole's proposal for the "registring of Providences" and a commentary upon that proposal. In this project, Poole consciously tried to deal with the dilemma facing believers in a traditional wonder-working Providence. On the one hand, sectaries were giving the concept a very bad name—"the credulous world [has] not been so deluded with such foule impostures as it is now."[32] On the other hand, the discursive forms that had been used traditionally to "prove" the existence of that Providence were sadly lacking by evolving learned standards. The old form of demonstrating illustrious providences, which relied on authority and the didactically satisfying way in which stories fit into a predetermined framework, was no longer self-evidently convincing. That form, as Poole accurately summarized it, was based "mostly upon the single Testimony of some one Man, & hee many times not the first Author. there being alsoe a great mixture of false and foolish & unwitnessed fictions not only in Legends, but also in other Authors, to the infinite disparagement & discredit of all true relations."[33]

Poole had given careful thought to the methodology by which he would reestablish the credibility of special providences. Reports were to be "followed to their Originalls, & collected from their several fountains & evidenced by such proofes as may convince gainsayers." To further these ends, Poole suggested setting up a network of correspondents throughout the British Isles. When these correspondents heard of a likely case, they were to "draw a short, yet full narrative of the Case, & get it subscribed by the Witnesses (naming the place of their abode & (where it is convenient:) the Quality of the Person witnessing it:) & that they will be ready to sweare it, whenever legally required to doe it, & those that can be persuaded, that they make affidavit before some Justice." Poole would print these materials for "publick benefit," and preserve the originals in Sion College, London, unofficial headquarters of English Presbyterianism.[34]

Poole, as Keith Thomas has pointed out, laid out a Baconian line of inquiry.[35] He emphasized the factuality of events and the quality of witnesses, an approach that the Royal Society would codify. The line of inquiry favored by the Royal Society was not neutral, however; God and the human soul were excluded from purview, and the Royal Society's historian, Thomas Sprat, proudly proclaimed that the Royal Society from the beginning was intended to be free from "*the Artifice, and Humors, and Passions of Sects.*"[36] Thus, Poole, representative of a passionate partisan worldview, was attempting to use a mode designed to exclude just that. Given that orthodox, educated Dissenters feared sectarian excess almost as much as Anglicans, it is perhaps not surprising that some of them felt little reluctance to use a tool that ultimately was to be used against them.

The forms of inquiry that the Royal Society used, besides being intended to eliminate "enthusiasm," were intended to work out areas of consensus in a fractured society. The problem of consensus also haunted Poole's project. A correspondent, otherwise enthusiastic ("I dare not confine it [the project] to any humane Invention but must confesse the great appearance of God"), feared that the project would be "reported to bee a stratagem only to advance a Presbyteriall Faction."[37] To avoid innuendos of partisanship, he suggested that Poole not mention in his proposal the plan to preserve the materials of the inquiry at Sion College, because of its inevitable associations with factionalism.[38]

In the interest of consensus, the correspondent also stressed the necessity of bringing sympathetic Anglicans into the project, but that raised another problem. Poole was especially interested in two sorts of reports of providences: "Apparitions of Spirits, witches . . . [and] Judgments upon all Sinners, so especially against such, as have falne away from God's truth and Ordinances."[39] Although the inclusion of apparitions and witches would have met with the approval of many pious Anglicans, those Anglicans were not likely to agree with the Presbyterians about what constituted "God's truth and ordinances" and thus what constituted divine judgments for breaches thereof. Poole's correspondent favored changing the phrase in question to "such as have fallen away from the love of truth & from the wayes of God."[40] The correspondent's favored phrase created a broader, but vaguer interpretive category, such as Restoration Anglicans like Ford argued for, and it affords a good example of the effects of the necessity of social consensus in interpreting illustrious providences. Correspondingly, it illustrates the difficulty of setting "objective" standards for evaluating them in a pluralistic setting. Tolerance among mortals dictated tolerance from supernatural beings.

Poole pursued his project to the end of the 1650s. While it attracted some attention, he never managed to set up the network of correspondents on which it was to rely.[41] Thus the project itself did not get far enough for the difficulties implicit in its approach to emerge. However, those difficulties came fully into evidence in Increase Mather's subsequent attempt to move the project along.

Mather came across Poole's project indirectly. Someone sent a copy of Poole's proposal to the New Haven divine John Davenport. Increase Mather assumed that the sender was Samuel Hartlib, scientific and social reformer and indefatigable correspondent across party lines. The assumption seems reasonable enough, given that Hartlib regularly sent Davenport books and manuscripts on social, scientific, and religious developments in Europe and was himself an avid collector of "histories of illustrious providences."[42] Davenport, however, had either little time for or interest in the project, and the topic does not seem to have been pursued further in England, since the Anglicans were not interested and the Dissenters had more pressing concerns.

The matter might have ended there had not Davenport's friend, Increase Mather, come across it in his deceased friend's papers and decided to revive the project in 1681. Mather's revival of this project coincided with his increasingly active interest in natural philosophy at the beginning of the 1680s.[43] That interest, overlapping with his more immediate concerns about the intentions of Providence, bore fruit in a short-lived philosophical society he formed in Boston, a book on comets, and *An Essay for the Recording of Illustrious Providences*.[44]

Mather had mulled over the idea for a collection of special providences for some time. Previously the idea had been connected with the history of New England "for the benefit of Posterity, that they might see how God had been with their fathers, in keeping the Foundation of the Churches, and of the Commonwealth."[45] Such a history would have been overtly structured within a predetermined general argument—the divine plan for New England—and there had been recurring calls for that history since the earliest days of the colonies. *Illustrious Providences* was to be something quite different.[46]

On 12 May 1681, a general meeting of Massachusetts ministers led by Mather approved some proposals to get the project on providences under way. They first defined the boundaries of their inquiry. Like countless generations of the pious before them, they were to seek the hand of God both when nature veered off its accustomed course and in subjective human experience:

> Such Divine judgments, tempests, floods, earthquakes, thunders as are unusual, strange apparitions, or whatever else shall happen that is prodigious, witchcrafts, diabolical possessions, remarkable judgements upon noted sinners, eminent deliverances, and answers of prayers, are to be reckoned among illustrious providences.

The project was to be based upon reports collected by ministers inquiring in the "places whereunto they belong," with care taken that "the witnesses of such notable occurents be likewise set down in writing."[47] The only significant departure from Poole's scheme lay in the expanded scope of the inquiry.

An Essay for the Recording of Illustrious Providences (hereafter referred to as *Illustrious Providences*) has been discussed often enough to make a thorough account of its contents redundant.[48] I will thus forgo retelling accounts of witches and stone-throwing poltergeists and focus instead on the way in which the essay represented an effort to cast an old subject in a new discursive manner. Mather knew that he had to talk about providences in a untraditional way. In the preface to *Illustrious Providences* Mather singled out for praise Robert Boyle's rules and methods for creating a natural history. That praise gives an indication of Mather's understanding of the direction he had to take.

Boyle was more than just a prominent scientist. He was a deeply pious man, as well as a tolerant one. Although an Anglican, he served as governor of the Corporation for Propagating the Gospel in New England, the bulk of whose members were Dissenters.[49] While perhaps the foremost scientist in Restoration England, unlike some of his compatriots, he was enough of a transitional figure to have a suitably pious dread of supernatural phenomena and to be devoutly providentialist.[50] He was also a nobleman and possessor of a sizable fortune. Like Tillotson, Boyle served as a powerful emblematic figure linking piety, experimental philosophy, and social respectability. Mather visited him on a number of occasions while in London at the end of the 1680s, and Boyle presented him with copies of his works.[51]

Boyle had been appalled by the religious creativity of the Civil Wars and Interregnum. He took a prominent role in developing the acceptable style of discourse in the Royal Society, dispassionate and factual, and not wandering far from the details of observation, a style, in fact, deliberately distanced from his own early writings.[52] Boyle at one point codified guidelines for proper reporting of phenomena, and those guidelines make Mather's discursive goals in *An Essay* intelligible. Boyle stressed observation, not interpretation. Focus on specific cases, he stated, and do not attempt premature system-building and generalization; write in a clear and unrhetorical manner. Be modest and undogmatic in presenting your opinion; qualify your assertions with phrases like "perhaps," "it seems," and "it is not improbable"; do not spend time refuting others' opinions unless necessary if you do not have experimental objections derived from experiments, and then do so "with moderation and civility." Appeal to other writers not as judges and authorities but as witnesses. Use the essay form as a means of avoiding the temptation to make sweeping statements.[53]

Boyle's guidelines shared the Anglican emphasis on moderation and probabism, and they were contrary to the old way of demonstrating illustrious providences. In the old manner, writers would first set out their categories of God's behavior and then rummage around in any source that came to mind to illustrate their predetermined conclusions. A source found in another author was as good, if not better, than an eyewitness account—one pre-seventeenth-century connotation of "probable" was "approval by textual authority."[54] Events were commentaries on a predetermined text, and it was the text, not the commentaries, wherein the interest lay.

How well did Mather follow his model? The structure of *Illustrious Providences* can seem confusing. "Some digressions have I made in distinct chapters," Mather warned in the preface, and in fact four of the eleven chapters—one on natural philosophy, another on the reality of demons, a chapter on apparitions (which noted at the onset that there were few of these in New England), and a chapter of cases of conscience—have little to do with the recording of providences. These chapters are peripheral to the goals of the project as set forth in the preface. Accordingly, they should be considered separately from the creation of an essay for the recording of providences.

In the essay proper, Mather stayed very close to the guidelines Boyle set out. He diligently badgered his correspondents for details and more details of providences. He eventually omitted stories of which he could not get sufficiently thorough accounts.[55] Mather gave sources for most of his stories and dated them whenever possible. He offered as many circumstantial details as he could. The effect is one of the re-creation of specific events for the reader to evaluate with as little authorial interpretation as possible. Mather did cite other writers, as Boyle allowed, but he clearly appealed to them as witnesses, not as authorities, just as Boyle recommended. Thus an account of a miraculously preserved New England skipper was followed by a similar story from Flanders. The story of the haunted house of William Morse was followed by an account taken from Joseph Glanvill of "a disturbance not much unlike to this," the drummer of Tedworth. A story of dreadful judgments upon New England Quakers was followed by a "true and faithful" account from England, and so forth.[56] Contextualizing New England providences in this manner demonstrated their normative nature.

Mather's prose in the essay itself stayed restrained and "objective," and he kept moralizing to a minimum. Significantly, only in the digressive chapters did a "prescientific" mode of discourse emerged. Here Mather included long chains of inadequately detailed, and occasionally wildly improbable, stories, seemingly allowed only on the basis of the personal authority of the authors in which Mather found them and clearly subordinated to the general thrust of Mather's argument. Mather freely engaged in generalizing and moralizing in these chapters.

In short, *Illustrious Providences*, exclusive of the digressions, seems an admirable brief model of late-seventeenth-century amateur "scientific" writing. Mather presented his stories with a maximum of corroborating detail and concern for accuracy, and he kept argumentativeness to a minimum and restrained generalizations. Ironically, the net effect of Mather's virtuous attempt was to demonstrate why the concept of special providences was becoming marginalized during this period. The earlier collections of providences—Beard, Batman, Clark, or even Mather himself in collections like *Wo to Drunkards* and *A Brief History of the Warr with the Indians in New England*—left no doubt about the judgmental nature of Providence. God rewarded the good and punished the wicked, and the Church prospered.

Mather's collection of providences in his essay, by contrast, was notable for its random nature, as scholars have noticed.[57] Lightning killed the godly as easily as the ungodly. Storms and tempests occurred, but to no apparent end. Mather did make an effort to discern moral rules: poltergeists often afflicted those hiding some secret crime, the godly might die terrible deaths to warn the ungodly what *they* could expect, and God often sent judgments to Quakers to awaken them to their evil ways. But such interpretation was in short supply in the book; the new mode of discourse that focused upon individual events rather than the analogical moral linkage between events allowed little room to go beyond those events, and Mather rarely did so. The moral order of the universe remained hidden, except perhaps in the extreme cases of drunkards and Quakers, and Mather's restrained prose did not force any conclusions to which the evidence itself did not lead. He used a discursive mode that dissolved the very phenomenon it examined.

Mather's own effort demonstrates why no one else was pursuing his line of investigation. The new mode of discourse Mather used in *Illustrious Providences* conflicted with the doctrine he wished to document; in effect, Mather dealt with the problem of reconciling the old providentialism and the new science by segregating them. Mather's handling of an event reported in both *Illustrious Providences* and *The Doctrine of Divine Providence* clearly illustrates the different possibilities of his different discursive manners. Connecticut suffered two substantial floods in the summer of 1683. In *Illustrious Providences* Mather did note that they had a sacred dimension:

There is an awful intimation of Divine displeasure remarkable in this matter, inasmuch as August 8, a day of public humiliation, with fasting and prayer, was attended in that colony, partly on the account of Gods hand against them in the former flood, the next week after which the hand of God was stretched out over them again in the same way, after a more terrible manner than at first.[58]

After his brief and speculatively restrained remarks on God's purposes, Mather expounded at far greater length on the possible natural causes for the floods, which included the previous appearance of a comet, together with a conjunction of Jupiter and Saturn, a south wind impeding the flow of the river, and the fact that the floods followed a great deal of rain. Mather, in effect, spatially marginalized the issue of God's purposes in causing the floods and thereby drew the attention of the reader to the secondary natural causes.

Mather also dealt with these floods in *Divine Providence*, but here, where he felt no obligation to experiment with new Restoration discursive modes, his approach was considerably different. He made no mention of possible natural causes, and what in *Illustrious Providences* was merely a sentence intimating divine wrath became six pages devoted to outlining the provoking sins of New England.[59] The reader was left in no doubt as to where the stress of Mather's discourse belonged. The floods existed as a mere illustration of a given eternal verity, with Mather the privileged interpreter of the Deity's intentions.

Likewise, in *Illustrious Providences*, Mather described in minute detail a whirlwind in Cambridge and a tempest in Connecticut as extraordinary phenomena of nature, but without editorial comment. He used the same phenomena in a sermon delivered while he was working on his essay, and to a quite different effect:

> Hath not the Sword been raging in the midst of thee, O *New-England?* Hath not the Lord been marching through the Land in Indignation? . . . Was it not so two years ago, in a Place not far off, when one that stood in the way of that Whirlwind of the Lord was dashed to death in a moment? . . . And I am informed that there was this Summer, in a neighboring Colony, a Tempest no less prodigious; which in the Woods, for eight miles together, carried all clear before it. Certainly these are Signal, and Speaking Providences.

Here Mather's storms overtly carried a message at which they scarcely hinted in *Illustrious Providences*. He took them, along with other natural disasters in New England and Europe, to presage a general descent of God's wrath.[60]

The Puritans' providentialism could only be sustained in such a heavily didactic and exhortatory framework, an authoritarian supernaturalism, where messages were assumed in advance. Their providentialism was embedded in a particular discursive patterning of the world, one that was passing out of fashion in England. It is not surprising that when Mather came to London at the

end of the 1680s, and preached at Dissenters' meetings, some found his sermons "more *Affected and Quaint* than those of the Nonconformist Teachers,
who are most famous in that Way."[61]

If Mather's project stumbled over the discursive horn of the dilemma that
Poole did not have to confront, it also stumbled over the other horn, the conflict between judgments and pluralism. Even New England offered an example
of the social hazards of proclaiming judgments. That example took the form
of a judgment upon Quakers that did not make it to the pages of *Illustrious
Providences*. Stories of a fatal horse race that some Quakers attempted to conduct on Long Island on a Sunday in 1681 had traveled widely enough for Edward Taylor of Westfield, Massachusetts, to refer to it in a letter to Mather. In
the locality where it was reputed to have happened, however, some people
claimed that one of the men involved had been already sick and that the other
did not die but was only ill for a long time. The local minister reported that
attempts to read the event as a divine judgment were producing a great deal of
local contention, since "there are few in that place that make any conscience
at all of the Sabbath, & therefore no wonder if they be unwilling to take notice
of such a judgment." He requested that Mather neither report the incident nor
use his name until fuller information was acquired, which apparently never
happened.[62]

The incompatibility of Mather's project with the temper of English
learned culture is demonstrated by the fact that although Mather considered
his essay modestly "no more than a specimen" and hoped that others would
"go on with the undertaking," there would be only one more such project
brought to print. In 1697 William Turner published a large folio volume *A
Compleat History of the Most Remarkable Providences Both of Judgement and of
Mercy which have happened in this Present Age*, replete with accounts of revelations of future things, remarkable judgments, strange conversions, astrology,
remarkable friendships, witches, apparitions, remarkable promises kept, remarkable charity, remarkable protection of the good in times of danger, and
the memorable speeches of the late Queen Mary, among many other providential topics.

Turner was an Anglican, but he had striking sympathy for Dissenters and
Dissenter religiosity, as contemporary observers noticed.[63] Not only did he glorify Dissenter spirituality, he clearly conceived of his project in an illuminist
way that smacked of "enthusiasm." He proclaimed that with his project, he
had "scaled the Mountains and *scrabbled above the Clouds*, and open'd a little
the Curtains that hid and separated the Secrets of Heaven from Common
View; and at a distance looked into the Divine Councels."[64] Turner had an

equally archaic natural philosophy: he still insisted on the reality of the Ptolemaic universe.

Turner viewed himself as carrying on the project set forth by Poole, which he seems to have known only from the account of it in *Illustrious Providences*. Like Mather, he included eyewitness accounts and specifically invited submissions from divines, but the similarity ended there.[65] He practiced far more archaic discursive practices than either Poole recommended or Mather practiced, jumbling eyewitness and secondhand, contemporary and ancient accounts together, with little discrimination between them. Far from maintaining a control on the "quality" of his witnesses, he solicited accounts by newspaper advertisements.[66]

Clearly the project of recording illustrious providences was not attracting minds on the cutting edge of English intellectual life. Turner simply ignored the issues over which Mather stumbled. Poole's and Mather's hope of fusing the discourse of special providences into the discursive practices being developed in the new natural philosophy would not be realized. The task was an impossible one. Those practices were developed in part to exclude the assumptions upon which illustrious providences were based, to create situations in which it was not possible to talk about such things; and the schizophrenic structure of Mather's book itself demonstrates their effectiveness. Furthermore, as the alterations suggested to Poole's project indicated, the concept of determining the hand of God was bound to be controversial in any sort of pluralistic society.

Turner's compilation represented the end of a genre more than one hundred years old. The next publication in this vein originating out of learned culture was Alexander Pope's satire *God's Revenge against Punning* (1716), in which an outraged deity struck England, for its various heresies, with that dreaded scourge.[67] The Newtonian William Whiston in 1749 could still reflect on the need for a history of judgments, in order to demonstrate "the interposition of a particular divine Providence sometimes for the Punishment of notorious wicked Men." But he attempted no such project, and he had himself been the target of ridicule both for his Arian heresy and his earnest chronologies of the Last Days for some forty years.[68]

※

Mather's essay stands alone as the only example of the Dissenter providential genre to engage seriously, for better or worse, the new discursive standards of the age. Despite the elaborate "empirical" observations about the workings of Providence that filled the Restoration treatises, and that Mather systematically worked out, interpreting Providence ultimately fell outside the framework of the new disciplining of perception. It remained occult, eluded the new communal surveillance, and depended on the spiritual state of the individual observer. Flavel, in a sober moment, noted, "We cannot know from the Matter of the things before us, whether they be sanctified or unsanctified to us . . . .the *manner* in which they befal us, and the effects and fruits they produce in us . . . distinguish . . . whether they be sanctified Providences, and fruits of the love of God, or no."[69]

The interpretation of Providence depended on its inward effect. As Collinges said, in reading providences, if you would "gain a *spiritual wisdom, let your eye affect your heart.*"[70] Charnock bluntly asserted the necessity of assuming the end of Providence in interpreting its effects: "Let this aim of God at the good of his Church be the rule of your interpretation. Without this Compass to steer our judgments by, we may both lose and rack our selves in the Wilderness of Providence, and fortify our natural Atheism and Ignorance instead of our Faith."[71] Once faith in Providence failed, its interpretation became impossible; God's plan turned into a wilderness. The Dissenters' divinatory providentialism was not sustained by the authority of reason, facts, and dispassionate observation, but by the authority of faith and the correspondence between biblical patterns and contemporary events.

The providentialists based their interpretations upon a sense of qualitative correspondence and the insight of private experience, neither of which the new natural philosophizing admitted as legitimate sources of objective knowledge. Ironically, in the Restoration period the Puritans found themselves in much the same position in regard to the norms of learned culture as practitioners of occult arts that Puritans generally shunned. For example, John Crane had waxed eloquent in his treatise on Providence over Providence's harmony and sweet accords, and he contrasted this harmony with "bastard-Harmonies cry'd up and doted on" like judicial astrology.[72] Astrologers were also attempting unsuccessfully to rewrite their harmony in terms acceptable to the Royal Society, and they failed for much the same reasons that the "providentialists" did. The mechanical universe serious challenged astrology's theoretical underpinnings, such as they were, and that art proved extremely resistant to being reduced to a set of generally agreed-upon rules based upon accumulated, if necessarily theory-laden, observances of natural phenomena.[73] Thus two forms of divination that had taken the roles of mortal antagonists now found themselves lumped together as enthusiastic by protagonists of a new and increasingly influential sensibility. The Puritan was sinking in elite esteem along with the practitioners of the occult arts that the Puritans had generally despised. Their common fate is an indication of how close a formal relationship can be in spite of intensely felt distance, opposition being true friendship, as William Blake said. Mather's attempt was doomed to failure.

The efforts to save the older conception of Providence were not helped by the fact that Dissenters themselves did not put up a united front in the matter, for reasons both structural and chronological. Barriers to mutual influence between Anglicans and Dissenters were not as high as the labels themselves might imply.[74] Many Presbyterians looked earnestly to a reunification with the Church of England, a dream some of them did not give up until the second decade of the eighteenth century.[75] With that dream, they moderated their strict Calvinism in accordance with Anglican trends. Furthermore, with no institutionalized political power behind them, debates about religious toleration in the Restoration period encouraged from the Dissenters an emphasis not on authority and dogmatism, the emphasis of the God of judgments, but on reasonableness and tolerance. Meanwhile, the Republican wing of the political alliance that fought the Civil Wars against the king drifted off to a deism increasingly hostile to authoritarian appeals to the supernatural.[76] The political shelter for Dissent, Whiggery, did not encourage authoritarian supernaturalist discourse, since it fitted under its umbrella widely diverse religious groups and was constructed against High Church Anglicans and divine-right monarchists, who relied heavily on such language themselves.

Time worked against the Puritans' wonder-working Providence, as well. Presbyterian or Independent, those Dissenters who aspired to be members of a greater learned culture could not isolate themselves forever from its trends. In the sphere of piety, younger Dissenters, like Edmund Calamy in England or John Leverett in Massachusetts, did not share in the apocalyptic, sharply bifurcated religious mood of the midcentury; "that Heat and Rancour and vindictive Disposition . . . have had time to subside, abate, and wear off," as Calamy put it. They became more receptive to Anglican virtues of moderation and "reasonableness" than many of their elders, and they began to imitate the "reasonable" preaching of Anglicans like Tillotson.[77] The Glorious Revolution of 1688, with the resulting Toleration Act of 1689, led to the end of many of the institutional barriers between the Dissenters and the Anglican mainstream in England, just as it did in Massachusetts, with the new charter that ended colonial self-government. Some observers dated the taming of orthodox Dissent in England from the following decade, while at the same time in Massachusetts, liberals began planning the Brattle Street Church.[78] Aggressive learned cultural resistance from Dissenters of the kind represented by the treatises on Providence had largely come to an end by the beginning of the eighteenth century. While Anglicans continued to criticize traditional Puritan piety and providentialism into the eighteenth century using Restoration arguments, they did so without the undercurrent of political anxiety that flowed through the earlier critiques.[79] An Anglican in 1707 could confidently claim that "the awkward style and blunders of the old Nonconformists are now to be found only among Quakers and Anabaptists."[80] The writers of the providential treatises had no successors.

$$*$$

If Increase Mather ever perceived the insecurity of his position in learned culture, he never confessed to it. Although the early 1680s marked the end of his published involvement with science, his private interest remained. He visited Robert Boyle while in London at the end of the 1680s. He continued to purchase the *Philosophical Transactions* of the Royal Society into the eighteenth century, as well as *The History of the Works of the Learned* (a journal containing synopses of recently published learned books). Mather clearly kept abreast of intellectual trends ever more indifferent to his assumptions about Providence.[81]

In spite of his continued interest in new intellectual currents, however, Increase appears not to have been deeply touched by them. He never wandered too far out of the dark enchanted providentialism of his earlier years.[82] In the eighteenth century he told stories of damned souls (or were they devils?) in the shapes of birds singing of the terrors of Hell to surprised listeners who subsequently died and of demonic voices heard at sea speaking of the souls they were going to shore to fetch. In 1712 he mulled over the "strange Blast" that had settled on the apple trees of towns whose inhabitants inclined too much to the abuse of cider. In 1715 he considered writing another book of remarkable providences, this time focused, finally, upon the history of New England. In 1719, twenty-six years after the Salem witch trials, he commended King Saul for his execution of witches, and he warned his listeners that devils lay in wait to snatch their souls when they died. It does not seem to have occurred to him that science could be a serious threat to religion, and attempts to reconcile natural philosophy and the Bible left him completely uninterested. "There is in the Holy Scriptures admirable *Philosophy* . . . But the design of the Blessed Scriptures is not to make men *Philosophers*, but to make them *Pious*."[83]

Increase Mather, as will be shown in the final chapter, typified older Massachusetts ministers, whose intellectual development was set before they had to confront the full implications of changing cultural norms. The disjunction between the modes of providential discourse Mather employed in *Illustrious Providences* and elsewhere did not disturb him; he was old enough and politically battle-scarred enough to be able to explore new Restoration patterns of organizing knowledge without regarding them as normative. For the investigation of the uneasy interaction of old and new providentialism in Massachusetts, Increase's son Cotton is a far more rewarding subject.

CHAPTER FOUR

✳

Cotton Mather
and the
Hand of God

I n July 1693, Cotton Mather (1663–1728) decided to write a history of
the New England Puritans. It was a daunting task he had set for himself
since "the dispensations of his wondrous Providence towards this People
. . . cannot but afford matters of *admiration* and *admonition*, above what
any other story can pretend unto."[1] Mather worked on his project for
five years, with divine assistance, he claimed, and sent it to London to be published in 1700. Finally, on 29 October 1702, Mather held a thick folio copy of
Magnalia Christi Americana in his own hands. He promptly set apart the next
day for "solemn THANKSGIVING unto God," little suspecting that he had just
published the last great document in the orthodox providential tradition.[2]

Needless to say, Mather saw the hand of Providence everywhere in his
lofty history. God sent the Puritans into Massachusetts and supervised their
affairs in general. He occasionally intervened dramatically, sending rain in answer to prayer, raising a storm at sea to force a document damaging to New
England to be thrown overboard, strangely conspiring the bad luck of the English in King Philip's War until they took reformation to heart, and even sending an apparition of a lost ship into New Haven harbor to quiet the minds of
those who still grieved for the passengers.[3] Providence also sent mercies and
judgments, gave the Saints some protection against epidemics, and, on occasion, commented on the actions of mortals in the form of prodigies.[4]

Mather's Saints inhabited a wonder-filled universe, but God did not work
only externally. Mather illustrated God's wondrous activities in the soul with
many spiritual biographies. Some of God's most exalted servants even acquired
the gift of prophecy.[5] Of course, Providence also included the Devil's operations, which, besides ordinary tempting, ranged from creating thunderstorms

74

and throwing lightning at churches, to enticing mortals into witchcraft, possessing Quakers, and besieging Cape Anne.[6] In short, Providence in the 1690s functioned the way one would expect a Puritan's Providence to function.

Mather's Providence was the Providence of the Great Migration as well as the Providence of John Calvin. That the heavy weight of a long tradition sat on Mather's shoulders hardly surprises. His own name came from ancestors John Cotton and Richard Mather, two of the most important first-generation preachers in Massachusetts.[7] Indeed, in Cotton Mather many of the currents of seventeenth-century Puritanism ran in full force: not only theological currents, although Mather was a defender of the *Westminster Confession* until his dying day; not only political currents, although Mather admired Oliver Cromwell and his reign; but also murkier, more unpredictable streams: demonology, witchcraft, judgments, and special providences.[8] He was a student of the treatises discussed in the last chapter: Charnock's and Flavel's works he recommended as essential parts of any minister's basic library; he praised Collinges's treatise on Providence; he quoted, unattributed, from Crane's treatise; and he used both Crane's and Flavel's terminology and rhetorical devices in his own sermons on Providence.[9] Mather quite consciously wrapped his discourse in the authority of orthodox Dissenter providentialism.

But that authority no longer carried the weight it once had, even among Dissenters. Already in the 1690s, as Mather penned the *Magnalia*, the cultural and institutional structures of Massachusetts itself were slipping out of Puritan control. If Mather wished to keep his privileged cultural position in Massachusetts, he would have to adapt his providentialism to the religious and intellectual reconfigurations of the recent past. His search for new "cultural capital" drove Mather's adjustment to those reconfigurations, and in the end it drove him across the line that separated the Puritanism of the seventeenth century from the Dissent of the eighteenth.

✳

In the 1690s Mather still envisioned Massachusetts within the framework of Stephen Foster's definition of Puritanism: "The magistracy guaranteed the social conditions under which the laity, part volunteers and part conscripts, pursued their individual destinies in a collective context interpreted and mediated by the clergy."[10] Confident that the institutional and social structures of his society supported his providentialism, Mather anchored it in traditional New England piety. Like the *Magnalia* itself, his sermons throughout the 1690s grew out of the New England orthodoxy of the seventeenth century. They consisted mostly of jeremiads, calls to the unconverted, and detailed analyses of the stages of regeneration. Those sermons scarcely reflected the influence of the new divines of the Church of England, whose theology Mather was capable of acidly dismissing on intertwined political and theological grounds.[11]

Mather's construction and use of divine judgments demonstrates just how fully he regarded his providentialism as embedded in the institutional structures of his society. In his election sermon of 1696, for example, *Things for a Distress'd People to Think upon,* a typical New England jeremiad, Mather gave a long list of the blows of God's rod against New England. He then asked his audience to try to determine what the provoking sins of New England might be. He stressed caution in determining those sins, since the judgments of God were inscrutable and the designs of Providence intricate. He also warned against rash conclusions about others' guilt, without self-examination. Nevertheless, with those cautions, Mather remained confident that, despite the turmoil of Massachusetts in the 1690s, the community could reach a resolution on what God meant by His messages: "Let us have our *Debates.*"[12] He called on churches to engage in covenant renewal and on heads of households, jurymen, town officers, magistrates, and ministers to work together and radiate reformation throughout the entire community.

Mather's sermon presented the classic clerical Puritan vision of a communal social order dedicated to piety and reformation. He still had faith in the organic nature of his society and in its ability to come to a consensus about what message God spoke to that society. He had no less faith in his place as an oracle for the community, reading for it the signs of the times and encouraging it to understand the message of those signs.[13]

Mather displayed that same confidence in two sermons he preached in 1697 on divine judgments, published in Boston as *Terribilia Dei.* Mather felt no scruples about illustrating the doctrine of judgments with local examples, examples that must have been familiar to his congregation and readers. He mentioned a woman in "a church not far off" who was struck down by God for slighting the Lord's Supper; "wretched young men" known personally to Mather on whom God showered deadly judgments for their debauched lives; a young man stricken with a fatal cancer of the lip after cursing Governor Prince of Plymouth; a town that voted one year to allow its two "very eminent ministers" only thirty pounds each as salary, subsequently losing three hundred pounds worth of cattle in one disaster.[14]

One can almost hear the stories of *Terribilia Dei* being circulated among ministers and pious lay people. Mather did not hesitate to circulate them further, both orally and in print, sure enough about his position to manifest no great concern about the controversy those stories might engender. The community of the godly was the Massachusetts community, as far as Mather was concerned. The judgments themselves strikingly and supernaturally vindicated the social and religious hierarchy of church, state, and family. Respect the magistrates, respect the ordinances of the Church, respect the ministers, respect family values, or risk divine retribution—Mather could interpret these judgments because the social structure of Massachusetts was so finely tuned to God's purposes.

Mather's confidence in the supernatural support of Massachusetts institutions and in the support those institutions gave him suggests that the new charter of 1691, placing Massachusetts under a royal governor, committing it to official religious tolerance, and granting the vote to non-Church members, made but a minor impact on his perception of the nature of New England. Mather still viewed himself as functioning within a shared local dominant Puritan culture, broadly united in its assumptions, even if heavily contested within those assumptions. Larzer Ziff—while pointing out that in preparing the *Magnalia*, Mather relied extensively upon anecdote, folklore, and hearsay—has claimed that the *Magnalia* served to document the "perception of reality common to members of all classes within it."[15] Although Ziff may exaggerate, it is fair to say that Mather believed he was doing just that, speaking for the Massachusetts community.

The colony Mather constructed in his sermons, however, would soon have to be readjusted to shifting cultural and institutional realities. By the 1690s, Boston had a substantial group of ministers and laity who had accommodated their Calvinist past to the new cultural imperatives dominating England. They advocated a religion of balance and order, admired Anglican divines like Tillotson, and avoided heavy use of providential divination. This "catholick" party, represented by young clergymen like Benjamin Colman and their lay supporters like Thomas Brattle and John Leverett, was evidently as up to date as any Congregationalists or Presbyterians in England.[16] If some of Increase Mather's English auditors at the end of the 1680s found his sermons "*affected and Quaint*," some of Colman's in 1695 found his "polite" mode of preaching too avant-garde, before he went on to become a great success in the fashionable spa town of Bath.[17]

The origins of the "catholick" movement are usually dated to the mid-1680s, when the young Harvard tutor John Leverett introduced the writings of Tillotson to his students, beginning what has been called "the First American Enlightenment." Unfortunately, exactly what induced Leverett to make this decision must remain a mystery. The factors usually connected with it include the vulnerability to outside influences of a colony reeling from King Philip's War and the loss of its charter, combined with the influence of specific immigrants like Dissenting schoolmaster Charles Morton, who arrived in 1685.[18] Yet specifically local situations need to be placed within a broadly shifting English context; the fact that the decision chronologically parallels similar decisions being made by young English Dissenters suggests that cosmopolitan Boston was not dramatically different in terms of the cultural pressures at work in it from any other provincial English Dissenting community.

Massachusetts's relationship to the Anglican Church had always been more ambiguous than that of the Independents in England. New England orthodoxy had long been split between its positions of congregational independence and nonseparation from the Church of England. Some members of New England's clerical elite replaced their separatist zeal of the 1630s with a renewed appreciation of clerical control in the 1640s and professions of solidarity with English Presbyterianism, just as some of their brethren in England were doing.[19] By 1660, some of the ministers and leading figures in New England shared the hopes of the Presbyterians in England for a properly reformed national church upon the return of Charles II.[20] Historians have spoken of a party in Restoration Massachusetts that worked for closer ties with the homeland. Members of this group domestically favored an expanded national church (created through the Halfway Covenant) and intolerance to anyone outside the bounds of that church. Their ecclesiological goals bore a structural resemblance to those of English Presbyterians like Richard Baxter, who admired the New England church reforms immensely, as well as Anglicans like Tillotson.[21] Harvard had a teaching fellow in the late 1660s widely suspected of leaning to Anglicanism, and during the Restoration Boston even attracted some Anglican immigrants, presumably thick-skinned ones, hostile to Puritanism and the very idea of a biblical commonwealth.[22] Thus, while resisting political pressure from the English government, New Englanders remained in touch, intellectually, culturally, and religiously, with diverse groups in England. As Dissent in England slid into accommodation with Anglicanism, Dissent in New England slid along with it. There would be cause for surprise only if there had not been young, culturally ambitious Dissenters in Boston in the 1680s exploring Tillotson.

By the late 1690s, that slide in New England had achieved a critical cultural velocity, of which the most serious manifestation was the founding of the Brattle Street Church in Boston in 1698. The wealthy founders of Brattle Street, "catholick" in their sympathies, wanted their church organized with slightly more emphasis on ritual and less on the centrality of spiritual experience than had been customary in New England, while they denied the scriptural basis for the individual covenanted church that had been at the heart of New England church polity. Cotton and his father's early attempts at harmony with the Brattle Street Church degenerated into a nasty little pamphlet war by 1700, out of which that church emerged unscathed.[23] With the settling in of the Brattle Street Church, new English cultural standards institutionally situated themselves in the heart of Puritan Boston, their presence announced visibly by way of the church's most un-Puritan spire piercing the Boston skyline.

Not coincidentally, the year 1700 marked the beginning of Mather's engagement with the Restoration Anglican reconfiguration of English religiosity. Mather signaled the engagement that year with a tract titled *Reasonable Religion*. He said at its beginning, "Instead of saying *Shew your selves Regenerate Christians*, we will only say, *Show yourselves Rational Creatures*." In the first half of the treatise, Mather attempted to show that it was reasonable to assume that there was a God, that Jesus existed and did what He was claimed to have done, and that sin was foolish and unreasonable. For his proof of the truth of Christianity Mather relied heavily on the credibility of the witnesses of Jesus's career and miracles and the way in which He fulfilled prophecies.

By vindicating Christianity in that manner, Mather limited himself to the standard "reasonable" arguments stressed by Restoration Anglican apologists. The Anglicans emphasized these indubitably public and evidential proofs at the expense of the earlier Reformed emphasis on the scriptures' self-evidencing authority, via the Holy Spirit.[24] In following the Anglicans, Mather shifted the weight of persuasion from dogmatic certainty and private illumination to a moral, probablistic certainty arrived at from weighing matters of public documentation. For the first time in his career, Mather used a substantial body of arguments and rhetoric that would have been unexceptional in up-to-date theological circles in England. In the process, he evoked, if only implicitly, a very un-Puritan kind of religious subjectivity.

What brought about Mather's choice of such a novel approach? That Mather stayed alert to new trends is not in itself surprising. As historians often point out, he aspired to be a universal example of Christian piety, and of learned Christian piety at that, and his voluminous, extraordinarily wide-ranging publications amply testify to his aspirations as a disseminator of a universalistic evangelical discourse.[25] In those publications, he defended Dissenting orthodoxy and located himself in the shared culture of wonders of its godly community, but he also remained intensely alert to new religious and intellectual trends emerging from England and beginning to affect Boston—"the *first* in the whole *Province* and *Provinces* of *New England*, for universal Literature," as Benjamin Colman characterized his range in his funeral sermon.[26] To turn his back on his godly tradition, as the "catholicks" appeared to be doing, would be to abandon his evangelical roots; to ignore new expectations within the transatlantic "Republic of Letters," expectations brazenly being trumpeted by the Brattle Street Church, would threaten the universality of his discourse.

But to acknowledge new expectations is not the same as accepting them. Scholars have sometimes assumed that *Reasonable Religion* represented a major change of direction for Mather—a new attraction to reason—and that Mather in *Reasonable Religion* reacted purely to English intellectual trends, "the result of his understanding of the implications of natural philosophy for religion."[27] The new terminology Mather used, however, rose to cultural prominence as a result of politics; given Mather's heavy investment in the Puritan tradition, he would not take up that terminology without political considerations of his own. *Reasonable Religion* appeared at the height of Mather's controversy with the Brattle Street Church, and while scholars have focused on Increase and Cotton's vitriolic feud with Brattle Street, Mather did not respond to the Brattle Street Church simply by attacking it.

Reasonable Religion, rather than a change of mind, is a strategic attempt to demonstrate the universality of Mather's own position, meeting the local enemy on their own ground by employing the religious language of more fashionable circles. Mather deliberately tried to wrap his preaching in a mantle attractive to elements of the local population who might have found his usual approach old-fashioned. He noted in his diary "how useful it [*Reasonable Religion*] might be, especially to some sorts of People," and he planned to distribute at least two copies in each of his neighborhood visits.[28] The growing sensitivity to English mainstream culture in Boston required a similar sensitivity in Mather's evangelical tactics.

That sensitivity had sharp limits, however. Having authorized *Reasonable Religion* with a Tillotson-like framework, Mather then discarded it. He denounced "rational preaching," gloried in the "Great Mystery" of redemption, and punctuated his discourse with rhetoric that would make English exponents of reasonable religion cringe and confirm their worst impressions of Dissenting preaching.[29] Mather in fact was not able to hold on for long to "an Enlightenment-like regard for reason," with its implicit naturalizing emancipation of the human subject (or such subjects as were deemed capable of reason).[30] *Reasonable Religion*, in its stress on human depravity, the limits of human understanding, and dependence upon grace, was no different from contemporaneous publications in which he referred scornfully to the "*Reason* of silly, shallow, sinful *Mortals*" and claimed that "Our *Understandings* are Enfeebled by *Sin*."[31] Mather's concessions to reasonable religion may have been more tactical than fundamental, at least for the time being; still, *Reasonable Religion* is important in that it marks his acknowledgement of shifting domestic cultural power: even in New England he had to allow new and distinctly un-Puritan theological trends discursive space.

Mather arrived by similarly circuitous means, with similarly limited results, at another theme prominent in Anglican religious circles around the time he published *Reasonable Religion*. Not by coincidence did he give two Thursday lecture sermons on the imitation of Christ at the height of his controversy with Brattle Street in 1700.[32] This theme was not alien to Puritanism, nor to Mather's earlier works, but emphasis on the imitation of Christ was more ordinarily associated with Anglican preachers who stressed morality above the experience of grace and of Christ's sacrifice.[33] Mather knew this and broadcast his knowledge to his audience. Early in his first sermon he warned, "It has been a *Satanic Stratagem*, to press the *Imitation* of Christ, with an intent thereby, to draw off the minds of men from Faith in the *Satisfaction* and *Propitiation* of Christ." Mather persevered, regardless of Satan's stratagems, covering himself by a statement at the beginning that the imitation of Christ was impossible without a prior regeneration.[34]

But why risk Satan's stratagems in the first place? In persevering, he presented himself as someone above party and stressed his disapproval of those of "a *Sectarian Spirit*, that will be *Zealous* for the particular and speculative *Opinion* of their own *Parties* in *Christianity*."[35] Presumably, Mather's introduction of ecumenical material both in these sermons and in *Reasonable Religion* demonstrated his transcendence of the partisan spirit he was displaying so amply in his contemporaneous attacks on Brattle Street. It is unlikely though that people drawn to rational religion would be any more attracted to his version of the imitation of Christ than they would have been to his version of reasonable religion, since both of Mather's versions emphasized far more altered consciousness and overwrought emotionality than they did rational and moral behavior.[36]

The timing of Mather's forays into "reasonable religion" in 1700 indicates that the impetus for his engagement with new trends in religiosity did not come out of any soul-searching on his part or dissatisfaction with his inherited Puritan tradition. Rather, it was the shock of seeing members of Boston's elite gravitating to Colman and the Brattle Street Church that drove Mather to expand his rhetorical repertoire. Mather acted because he perceived that evangelism in Boston required new tactics and new language if he wished to retain influence with groups that were indifferent to traditional Puritan rhetoric.

Other events at the turn of the century forced Mather to face a wider and irrevocably non-Puritan world impinging on Massachusetts. In May 1699, Massachusetts received a new royal governor, the Earl of Bellomont. Bellomont was nobility, albeit down-on-the-heels nobility, and, excluding Edmund Andros and his short and hated reign, the first non–New Englander to rule Massachusetts. He was also a Whig and a Calvinist, although a member of the Church of England, and as governor of New York he had shown himself to be a godly magistrate. His arrival in Boston in May 1699 occasioned one of the most ostentatious displays of ceremony the town had ever seen, and the next year Mather preached the election sermon before him.[37] That sermon distinguished itself from New England tradition in its remarkable freedom from readings of God's wrath and predictions of doom, and in Mather's insistence that while Massachusetts might not be all that important a part of the English empire, materially considered, spiritually it was its crown jewel. Mather spoke to the governor as the polished representative of a province perhaps not very important measured in material terms, but in terms of piety, rather impressive.[38] In that rhetorical context, the God of judgments had to take a back seat.

✳

Mather's exploration of new forms of evangelical and providential preaching in 1700 can be treated as a symbolic measure of his awareness of shifting institutional bases of power in Boston. The city had new forms of church organization, the province had a governor outside the communal Puritan framework of the past, and Mather experimented with new non-Puritan emphases in his preaching. Thereafter the institutional basis of Mather's support in Massachusetts quickly eroded further. Bellomont died in 1701. A Massachusetts man, Joseph Dudley, replaced Bellomont, but Dudley, an adept imperial politician if indifferent at best as a godly magistrate, proved sympathetic to the Church of England and hostile to Mather. In 1701, Mather's father lost the presidency of Harvard, and both Mathers stopped attending its corporate board meetings. Cotton Mather hoped to be given the presidency in 1707, upon Samuel Willard's death, but instead it passed to John Leverett, whose seemingly unruffled accommodation with preachers like Tillotson alarmed Mather exceedingly.[39] Boston also had in the eighteenth century a thriving, expanded Anglican church and aggressive Anglican missionary efforts by the Society for the Propagation of the Gospel, as well as several distinctly un-Puritan houses of prostitution.[40]

The institutions, official and otherwise, of Massachusetts were slipping away from Puritanism, and with them were going the province's communication networks. In the early years of the eighteenth century, Boston began to develop its own "public sphere," wherein information could circulate outside, and in opposition to, the old authoritarian channels within which Puritanism had developed. Boston's first ongoing newspaper appeared in 1704, rich with information about the rest of the world and filled with local advertisements and notices, and it was joined by two more by 1721, including Mather's particular nemesis, the overtly hostile *New England Courant*. In the 1710s, with an outbreak of disputes about the local currency, the press served as a medium in which debate, not consensus, was normative.[41] Boston had four coffeehouses by 1720, and Mather throughout his career recognized coffeehouses as discursive sites threatening to his authority. By the 1710s, Boston also had a group of people at home in the norms of the new science.[42]

The institutional structures and networks in Massachusetts no longer firmly anchored Mather's religious discourse, nor the traditional discourse of the clerical "standing order," in general, and Mather knew it.[43] One result of that shifting cultural power for Mather was a very different handling of divine judgments. He first retreated from his traditional providential divinatory formulas in his election sermon of 1700 when he faced an English nobleman, and shifting political, cultural, and social conditions in Massachusetts offered him no incentive to return to them. In the seventeenth century, Mather had mediated a collective interpretive context; his readings of divine judgments had institutional authority behind them and in turn reinforced that institutional authority. But after the turn of the century Mather had largely lost political influence, and he clearly represented only one faction in the ministry.

Therefore, Mather could no longer draw lines of consensus across society by interpreting divine judgments. If Mather were to present himself rigorously as a seer in the new situation, he would not be mediating a collective context, he would only be isolating himself. Like Anne Hutchinson many years earlier, he now lacked the power of the state or of a godly society to vindicate his providential divination; unlike Hutchinson, Mather, as a male, a prominent Bostonian, and a member of the learned elite of Massachusetts, knew enough, and cared enough, about how power worked in society to know when to lay off prophesying. He could not maintain a role of oracle to a community skeptical of him and other clergy trying to retain their sweeping interpretive authority over judgments. Mather complained in 1714, "We must not be discouraged, by the Derision of a few Foolish, and Flashy, and Prophane Creatures . . . who Scoff at all *Sermons* of an *Historical Importance*."[44]

It is not that Mather ever lost his belief in the reality of divine judgments. Fires, storms, earthquakes—Mather responded to them all by explaining how

God had sent them in response to sins.[45] But Mather did get discouraged by the derision of flashy and prophane creatures, as that derision implied the breakdown of a traditional collective Puritan context. He abandoned the structure of the traditional jeremiad with the turn of the century.[46] Although he occasionally preached on judgments in a threatening manner reminiscent of his earlier style, even in such sermons he toned down his rhetoric considerably.[47] Most significantly, that preaching underwent a process of decommunalization, a process that motored the decline in prophetic preciseness; the Massachusetts community Mather invoked in his sermons, the framework within which God handed down His judgments, had changed dramatically since the 1690s.

For example, in 1711, Mather decided to repeat his performance of 1697, *Terribilia Dei*. He again gave a sermon on divine judgments in order to make profitable "the strange Punishments inflicted by God on many Sinners in the World."[48] Mather remained just as emphatic as in 1697, if not more so, about God's moral interventions in the world, "Can't you *See*; Oh, fearful Blindness if you cannot *See!*—most sensible *Judgments* of GOD arresting many Sinners before your *Eyes*." Drunkards meeting terrible ends, whoremongers falling into unaccountable impoverishments, rakes humiliated, disobedient children dying young, railers at religion destroyed, possessors of ill-gotten gains blasted—the list was a long one and, in principle, terrifying.[49]

Yet in 1711, Mather hesitated to move from the statement of principle to specifics. He still had stories, but he drew back from sharing them:

> There is a Report of some things Extraordinary in some Late Judgments of God. It is likely, there may be various Misrepresentations of many Circumstances attending that matter. I will not therefore depend upon everything that may be Reported. But I suppose, no body doubts, There has been a very High Degree of Profaneness discovered by some Unhappy Men; and that God presently singled out some of them, in a manner that much Awakened the Neighbourhood. But whether that matter have so much in it, as has been said, or no . . .[50]

Mather then changed the topic midsentence and retreated to a tale about a marginal member of the community, a poor and discontented woman who took to drinking, became convinced that Satan was speaking to her, and eventually committed suicide by jumping out a window.[51]

The passage with its retreat from a controversial judgment suggests that Mather had become distrustful of the authority of the godly oral network that transmitted the remarkable judgments of God, and he knew that he did not have a united community behind him in recounting this story. Anglicans like Simon Ford had cautioned about the divisiveness of judgments in a divided society; Increase Mather had come across the same problem in assembling *Illustrious Providences*; now Mather encountered it at the heart of Puritan New England. In an appendix, Mather did reprint a few detailed judgments, but these were European in origin and not likely to raise much controversy in Boston. Certainly, Mather's one specific local example of the sad end of a depressed alcoholic did not suggest the sweeping divine legitimation of Massachusetts social institutions offered by the judgments in *Terribilia Dei*.

Mather's last publication on judgments, *Boanerges*, eloquently demonstrates the process of their decommunalization and of the corresponding evacuation of their meaning. Mather preached this sermon at the Thursday lecture of 14 December 1727 as an attempt to keep up the religious fervor engendered by an earthquake that had been felt across New England on 29 October. Mather addressed the questions of how the community should interpret and respond to what God had meant by sending the earthquake, and in dealing with these questions, he made it clear that the old interpretive community of the seventeenth century had broken down.

In this sermon Mather emphasized the individual, not the polity. The only institutions he mentioned were the churches; now they alone held responsibility for the salvation of New England. Mather even exulted that the churches had been praying for a revival for months and "wondring what was become of our *Prayers*," when God sent his earthquake to terrify guilty sinners.[52]

If Mather no longer conceived of Massachusetts as a godly polity, it still remained a society where people still took God's judgments seriously, as shown by the great concern the earthquake engendered. Mather spent some time in the sermon on the topic of how to search out the provoking sins and reform them. Just as he had done in 1696, Mather cautioned against overhasty judging of others' faults and an overemphasis on trivial matters.[53] Yet, unlike in 1696, Mather also cautioned against an intensive collective scrutiny of hidden sins. He called for no debate on what the provoking sins might be, and he did not even suggest striving for the type of consensus he envisioned in 1696. Mather certainly had his own opinions on what provoked the earthquake, but he did not insist on them. When he suggested to his auditors that God might be angry with New England for the sorry state of ministerial salaries, he prefaced that suggestion by saying, "if Things not yet by all Good Men *Agreed on*, may be spoken of."[54]

Instead of calling on his listeners to develop a consensus about their sins, he called upon them privately, with a discretion Tillotson would have approved, to scrutinize their own hearts for whatever unspecified faults they might find there: "Whatever *Miscarriages* in your *Lives*, you felt your *Hearts*, when the *Earthquakes* rowsed them, *smite* you for, Oh! Forsake them."[55] In fact, the only thing that all "Wise Men" in Massachusetts were agreed on in 1727, according to Mather, was the need for a very ecumenical, "catholick," piety: "And let our *Main care* be for, a SOUL so full of *submission* to GOD, a SOUL so full of *Benignity* to *Man*, as the Gospel calls for. This is what all Wise Men are *agreed in*."[56] Although Mather directed his audience for their salvation to the Covenant of Grace between God and the individual believer, he made no mention of covenant renewal, as he had in 1696. Renewal was to take place within each individual, not even within the churches as a collectivity, and certainly not within Massachusetts as a political unit.[57]

Only once did he address New England as a collectivity, over the neglect of the Sabbath. Here a flash of the old Mather reappeared:

> Where, where are the True *New-English Sabbatizers?* Must we repair unto the *Sepulchres* of our *Fathers* to look for them? Where are the *Housholders* that *Remember the Sabbath* . . . Where are the *Nehemiahs* [i.e., rulers], who will do all they can to lay Restraints upon those, who would *bring Wrath upon* us by *profaning the Sabbath?* Can the *Ministers* of the Gospel do no more, that the Remote Inhabitants of their Parishes . . . may be put into the Best Method of spending the *Holy Time* in the Best manner . . . If we won't *Rest* with and in GOD on His Day, GOD will not suffer His *Earth* to Rest under us . . . [The prophet Amos], having foretold, That in that *Earthquake*, the Lord would *Rore out of Zion*, he mentions the *Transgressions* that would call for such a thing. One of them is This; *Ye say, when will the Sabbath be over?*[58]

Householders, rulers, ministers, the founders, and the works of the Lord compared with His Word, within an unabashedly threatening context—a classic example of seventeenth-century communal, authoritarian, supernaturalist jeremiad rhetoric in the middle of an eighteenth-century sermon. Mather perhaps knew that the passage had an archaic tone out of keeping with the rest of his sermon, for he bracketed it by adding at its end, "I will not have this called, A *Digression*. However, I will go no further in *This*."[59] While telling his audience that God would send them worse punishments if they did not reform, Mather added, "I do not speak these things as a *Melancholy Visionary*."[60] He was dead within six months of preaching *Boanerges*.

✳

A changing distribution of cultural and political power dictated changes in perceiving and interpreting divine judgments; that same changing distribution of power also dictated an intensified exploration of the increasingly useful and relevant religious language of the early Enlightenment for evangelical purposes. Although Mather had only rarely engaged in intricate theological discourse in the past, shortly after 1700, his sermons consciously began to bypass theological complexities.[61] By the end of his life he had deliberately jettisoned the out-of-fashion scholastic conception of reason on which the extraordinary theological castles in the air of the past had been built.[62] By the end of the first decade of the eighteenth century, he began to speak of the process of conversion in a manner that stressed human initiative and displayed an impatience with the intricacies of the process.[63] As the complexities of the intricate spiritual world that had authorized Puritan seers faded in his sermons, Mather increasingly punctured his discourse with appeals to reason, while emphasizing good works and the glory of the eminently reasonable Golden Rule, just as the Anglicans had done. At times Mather even seemed to lose sight of the basic Reformed doctrine that true good works without saving grace were impossible.[64]

Again, the spur behind that exploration was politics. Preaching morality was a defensive response to the Anglican critique of Puritanism: "[Moral preaching] will help to Vindicate us abroad in the World. It shall be known that Morality and Moral Honesty is as much inculcated by the Preachers of CHRIST as it is by any of those who aspire after no higher Flights of Christianity."[65] More important, Anglicans had simplified doctrine and stressed morality for the sake of ensuring political unity. Mather used the same tools for the sake of creating a new alliance of the godly to replace the old, manifestly collapsed one, and his eye was not only on local audiences as he adjusted his evangelical rhetoric to new standards.

In fact, Mather had never taken his cues simply from his local environment. Although he never traveled far from Boston, he always saw himself as a transatlantic figure, a person out to make his mark on a European intellectual and religious world, which he did with a respectable degree of success. He corresponded with many prominent figures in Great Britain and on the continent, received an honorary degree from the University of Glasgow in 1710, and was elected a fellow of the Royal Society in 1713. Most of his most important treatises were printed or reprinted in London, his opinion was solicited in English religious disputes, with positive effect, and some of the most prominent English Dissenting ministers of two generations wrote prefaces to his works.[66] Nearly a hundred years after his death, he remained in England "well known to the world by his many valuable writings," and his works continued to be reprinted in London into the nineteenth century.[67] "Take him altogether, I do not know his equal left," wrote the Scottish church historian Robert Wodrow, upon hearing of his death.[68] Mather's ability to position himself among the more important Dissenting ministers of his day speaks well for his competence at analyzing and adjusting to transatlantic cultural trends, and that competence did not encourage maintaining seventeenth-century Puritan stances.

In the 1710s, as unity in Massachusetts crumbled, Mather grew preoccupied with the necessity of unity among Christians throughout all of Christendom and started addressing his publications more frequently to an international and interdenominational audience. While Mather had a long-standing interest in church unity going back to the early 1690s, up to the second decade of the next century he thought of unity in terms of compromises in details of church polity.[69] Now he conceived of it as entailing drastic compromises in theology, especially since the most active movement in Protestant devotion was coming from Lutheran pietists, not from the Reformed tradition. For Mather the basis of unity would have to be what he called "vital piety," a Christian fervor that transcended differences of doctrine.

Accordingly, in 1713, Mather began to mull over the need to reformulate the essentials of Christianity in a way that could help to bring together the people that were to be the "stone cut out of the mountain" at the coming Last Days, a considerably more diffuse communal religious impulse than his earlier one.[70] The result was the "maxims of piety," the basic propositions necessary for a true Christian to believe in. Mather eventually honed these maxims down to three, which he announced to the world in 1716: "The Glorious GOD is infinitely worthy of all our *Love*"; "our *Life* must lye in the *Faith of the Son of* GOD"; "a Man ought heartily to *Love* and *Help* his Neighbour, and never *offer* to him any thing, which he would judge it as *Hardship* to receive of him." The ability to say these maxims of piety formed a "*short* and *sure*" test of regeneration.[71]

With the maxims of piety Mather could claim, considerably more accurately than in 1700, that he had produced a "*Reasonable Religion*"; it is hard to imagine John Tillotson having any scruples about assenting to his maxims.[72] Indeed, from the perspective of vital piety, Mather could loftily proclaim, at least for an English audience, that no important difference existed between an Arminian and a Calvinist.[73] The only value of religious doctrines came from the opportunity provided by their variety for Christians to "exercise that *Goodness* towards one another in a *Mutual Forbearance* for which there is occasion in such *Varieties*." Otherwise, doctrinal controversies were punishments of God. By the 1720s, Mather even had kind words to say about Quakers, a sect he had previously classified as tools of Satan and objects of God's exemplary judgments.[74]

But Mather's theological ecumenicism did not come without a price. Earlier Puritan ministers were certainly no less pious than he, yet they experienced piety and theology as inseparable. Erroneous theology and erroneous piety went hand in hand. Thomas Shepard, for example, dismissed Arminians as "not understanding it [Grace], because they never felt it in themselves . . . and hence maintain apostacy from Grace."[75] From the earlier perspective, Mather, in his desire to hold together a coalition of the godly, was losing his hold on the intensely defined, politicized supernatural economy of the seventeenth century. But from Mather's point of view, an overly nice concern with theology and the nuances and politics of spiritual experience was a luxury he could no longer afford.

※

Mather did not adjust his practical divinity simply as the result of a positive attempt to extend his evangelical outreach or of a reluctance to serve as an oracle for an increasingly complicated society; he also adjusted in order to preserve his own standing within elite culture. If the universal quality of Mather's evangelical discourse was threatened by cultural and political change, no less was his privileged position as its disseminator. As Boston assimilated the values of Restoration Anglicanism, those values produced the sting they had originally been intended to produce: they made Mather and his beliefs and practices vulnerable to attack and ridicule. Some Bostonians mocked him as an enthusiast, and Colman made unflattering comments about his *"Extacies."*[76] Others discovered that praising Anglican rational preaching was an especially effective way of getting his goat.[77] Mather felt the sting of these attacks: "Real and Vital PIETY . . . is almost banished out of the *Earth*, and where it should be most look'd for, tis by the men who *mind Earthly things*, decried & exploded as, nothing but *Enthusiasm*."[78]

It is not surprising that Mather, who prided himself on his urbanity, occasionally betrayed a nervous awareness of, and vulnerability to, the shifting cultural standards those attacks implied; religion was to be evaluated by the new standards of learning and politeness, not vice versa, and his inherited religion, tainted by "enthusiasm," might not reach those standards. In a publication that laid uncharacteristic stress on good works and the maxims of piety, Mather expressed the hope that he offered a religion, "which the more accomplished any Men of Letters are in Literature, the more they reckon *This* the most valuable of all Accomplishments."[79] In another publication Mather attempted to re-create the major tenets of Reformed orthodoxy by relying almost entirely on reason alone. The purpose of this singular work was to produce a "*Philosophical Religion*, yet . . . *Evangelical* too . . . and the more it is examined by the more *Pensive* and *Polite* part of Mankind, the more it will be justified."[80]

Mather seems not always to have been entirely certain that his religiosity, if presented in the traditional way to the pensive and polite, measured up to their new cultural standards. He was not the only Dissenting minister in the transatlantic world committed to both respectability and a religiosity based on "vital piety" to display that uneasiness.[81] Politeness, which began its ascendancy as a normative social value in the upper and middle ranks of English society in the late seventeenth century, grew to be understood as stressing ease, naturalness, affability, and humor while disparaging dogmatism and solemnity, traits prominently associated with Puritanism. With its emphasis on relaxed sociability rather than inwardness, politeness represented a significant departure from the earlier English ideal of the virtuous gentleman, an ideal that, as Lawrence E. Klein has pointed out, "rejected utterly being beheld (except perhaps by God) as an occasion for the constitution of personality."[82]

Writers like Joseph Addison and Richard Steele took on the task of promoting politeness while Christianizing it, but they assimilated it to the Christianity of divines like Tillotson, not an ambience for the cultivation of an intense providentialism. Addison's *Spectator* had an influence, it has been claimed, second only to the Bible in the eighteenth century, and Mather, along with many others in New England, responded to that influence's discipline. In the early 1710s, he acknowledged the *Spectator*'s power as a cultural arbitrator by musing about sending it "some agreeable Things," while he concerned himself with the politeness of his children's education and his epistolary style. Perhaps not coincidentally Mather shortly thereafter began to fine-hone his latitudinarian-styled maxims of piety.[83]

Given that politeness and Puritanism made for uneasy yokemates, it is unsurprising that Mather's accommodation to the cultural norms of the early Enlightenment was deeply ambiguous. He might need approval from the pensive and polite, he might desire to preach to them effectively, and he certainly wanted to be counted among their number, but he also lamented "the *Depraved Gust* [taste], into which we are of later years degenerated," a "gust" that "renders everything unpalatable but what shall have qualities which I will never be reconciled to," and he lashed out at the regulative power of the new cultural arbitrators.[84] Perhaps it is not coincidental that Mather's visions of end-of-time apocalyptic destruction grew increasingly violent as the eighteenth century wore on.[85] His search for new sources of authority involved not so much a change of mind, but a split in sensibility. In order to retain his position and effectiveness among the pensive and polite in a changing Boston and a changing transatlantic world, Mather explored a providentialism that did not rely on the encounter with, and interpretation of, an overwhelming and sharply politicized supernatural world.

At the same time, however, Mather continued to assert much of the traditional conception of Providence. He certainly never abandoned his Calvinist orthodoxy, nor did he abandon his sense of an active and legible supernatural order. Mather might have grown restrained in his perception and exegeses of Massachusetts judgments. His, however, was a de facto discursive recognition of shifts of cultural and political power in Massachusetts only; he did not hesitate to predict descents of divine wrath on distant countries, or more generally, on the world, and in private, he read judgments with as much partisan verve as he ever had.[86] Nor did he entirely write Massachusetts out of the sacred history of the world.[87]

Similarly, for all that Mather invoked reason often enough and experimented with the language of rational religion and its implicit construction of self-regulated and naturalistic human activity, he never sustained that language for any length of time. To the end of his ministerial career, he insisted to his audiences that God was constantly and legibly at work in the human soul, enlivening and awakening His elect or else withdrawing His grace mysteriously and deserting the believer, either for instruction or simply for the display of His sovereignty. Mather dismissed Anglicans who medicalized the experience of the divine as misreadings of bodily humors; surely "the many Volumns written on this CASE, by Men of Reason in the Congregation of God, have not been all Foolishly thrown away on a meer *Mechanical* and *Chymerical* Business."[88] Mather remained all his life a preparationist, convinced that the ordinary process of conversion included preliminary terrors and convictions of human inadequacy and of the necessity of Christ.[89] He never abandoned his belief in divinely inspired "particular faiths," supernaturally bestowed temporal insights, a form of knowledge the Anglicans had been particularly desirous to delegitimate, nor his rapturous angelology.[90] Mather juggled two languages, one of human agency, reasonableness, and morality, the other of a complex and vital supernatural realm and a depraved, if occasionally supernaturally privileged, humanity.

The unresolved juxtaposition of two languages suggests why historians have come to no agreement about the nature of Mather's religious development. Some have seen him as a proto-Arminian, glorifying the abilities of humans, while others have claimed that he returned to a Calvinism purer than that of his immediate predecessors. The most careful interpreter of his theology and preaching has seen him as adapting an unchanging message to a changing world.[91] Mather never became an Arminian, or even, except in scattered passages and publications, a proto-Arminian. Unlike others in Boston he approached Anglican theologians like Tillotson with suspicion; the only Anglicans he recommended were stout Calvinists like James Ussher or John Edwards.[92] Yet to even conceive of a piety that trivialized differences between Calvinists and Arminians, let alone Quakers, that experimented with rational religion, and that shied away from seeking divine commentaries on the human social and religious order was to invoke a providential order very different from that of his predecessors. Mather never thought out the implications of the concessions he made to reasonable religion, and he always eventually returned to themes of grace and intrusive divine power, so perhaps it is most judicious to say that Mather's preaching in the eighteenth century constructed very different providential economies, economies with different recent ancestries and with different implications, without trying to determine which ones he "really meant." He meant different things in different contexts, and he found himself evangelizing in contexts that his Puritan forebears could not have imagined, contexts that did not so readily make room for Puritan seers.

CHAPTER FIVE

✳

Cotton Mather and the Perils of Natural Philosophy

I t was no ordinary cabbage root that Cotton Mather examined in Boston in the summer of 1688. One of its branches looked like a cutlass, another like a rapier, and a third like an Indian club. Such prodigies boded no good: disruptions of the human sphere soon followed disruptions of the natural sphere. This was not the first ominous cabbage to be seen in New England, and Mather later grasped its meaning, he explained to a Boston audience in 1689, along with the meaning of other prodigies occurring around the same time—a fall of red snow, earthquakes, and, in the sky, flaming swords and the sound of guns—when war subsequently broke out with the Indians.[1]

Like earlier Puritans, Mather keenly studied prodigies. As someone anxious to keep up-to-date in English learned culture, he also avidly followed developments in science, eventually becoming a correspondent to, and Fellow of, the Royal Society.[2] Given that science was being reconstituted after the Restoration to eliminate contexts in which interpretive activities like divining prodigies made sense, those were perhaps not the most compatible of interests. Indeed, historians have noticed that Mather had a sometimes uneasy relationship to the new science. However, they have projected on him fears there is little evidence he felt, such as Pascalian alarm over the infinity of space or dread over the atheistic implications of a self-sufficient mechanism. In general, historians portray Mather's anxieties about science as being stilled by Newtonianism, with its God-directed regular laws of nature.[3]

Mather did grow to have concerns about science, but those concerns were neither primarily philosophical nor were they in fact ever resolved. Left to his own devices, he would have been able to reconcile Newtonian physics and a wonder-working Providence without strain, if only because he never method-

93

ically submitted himself to science's new forms of perceptual and conceptual discipline. But he was not left to his own devices. Rather, he grew aware that the transatlantic learned culture in which he avidly located himself scoffed at wonders and dismissed believers in them as vulgar enthusiasts. Mather's attachment to a wonder-working Providence ran him the risk of ostracization from that culture, a risk he took seriously; did not the *Spectator* itself make fluency in natural philosophy a mark of gentlemanly piety? Science positioned Mather where he could maintain his aura of polite universality "above the contempt of envious Men," as he noted when hearing of his being made a Fellow of the Royal Society in 1713.[4] Mather never perceived his position as threatened by science itself; the new limitations on legitimate discourse within the circles promulgating the new science caused his anxiety.

Mather became aware of the restraints of the new science only slowly. His first published praise of science, *The Wonderful Works of God Commemorated*, preached in 1690, exulted in the harmony between the glories of natural philosophy and Mather's traditional providentialism. Mather's exclamations in that sermon on the wonders to be seen through microscopes and telescopes are frequently quoted. Less quoted from the same sermon are his equally joyous remarks on the wonders of God's active control of Providence, or his exhortations for his listeners to remember each night all that the Lord did for them that day and to keep a journal of their experiences for their progeny, or his lament that so few histories of "*Remarkable Providences*" had been written. The revelations of the telescope and the microscope formed just a small part of the revelations of God's wondrous Providence.[5]

Mather's hymn to science also included as an appendix the sermon he gave in 1689 discussing New England prodigies. In that sermon Mather revealed that although he felt secure in his wonder-working Providence, he knew that elements of its "natural philosophy" were contested. As he told his Boston audience when informing it of the prodigious cabbage root, "I have seen the *Nonconformists* reproached for the minding of *Prodigies*." Mather dismissed such rebukes; they came from "the loose Pens of certain Writers, whom, weighing well their Accomplishments by their own Rule, *we ought not to mind.*" He regarded these partisan writers as no more deserving of heed than other skeptics, like "Those who deny *Original Sin*," emerging from those sectors of the English intellectual nation that had strayed from Calvinist orthodoxy. Mather admitted that reports of prodigies had to be taken warily. It was easy to be deceived, and "those things ought not always to be accounted *Prodigies* which are *Extraordinaries*." Nevertheless, so contrary to reason was it to doubt prodigies that he was not sure if skeptics should "be called *Gentlemen*."[6]

Mather's talk of controversies surrounding prodigies illuminates the intricacy of issues of natural philosophy in the late seventeenth century. As he was aware, prodigies needed to be subjected to exact observation and discrimination; they were therefore a scientific issue. As his allusions to theology and Nonconformists indicate, they were also a religious and political issue. Questions of prodigies, natural philosophy, religion, and politics were thoroughly intertwined. Mather suggested that what one thought of prodigies had a great deal to do with one's religious orientation; as he knew, differences of opinion about prodigies followed religious fault lines formed in the period of the English Civil Wars and Interregnum.

Mather was saying that debates about prodigies were as much conflicts about power as conflicts about scientific truth. Who determined who possessed the coveted status of "gentleman," those who believed in prodigies and related wonders or those who did not? Therefore, whose opinions were on the fringe of learned culture, the believers' or the skeptics'? Mather could keep separate at this time the new science and the ideological impulses hostile to Puritanism that had helped to generate it without feeling his own status as a gentleman threatened in the process. But as the new natural philosophy institutionally and culturally rooted itself around the turn of the eighteenth century and as it increasingly erased the traces of its own controversial origins from its discourse, maintaining that separation would become increasingly difficult for him.[7]

Mather's efforts to maneuver his way between the discursive restraints of the natural philosophers and the wonder-working Providence he had inherited involved a complex set of cultural negotiations, here traced in three sections. The first section explores Mather's various commentaries on Genesis 1 in his "Biblia Americana." Those commentaries display the farthest extent of his conscious unease with science itself. The next section chronicles the history of Mather's shifting attitudes to prodigies. That history makes clear the kind of pressures he felt the new science subjected him to. With those pressures clarified, the last section considers his best-known piece of scientific writing, *The Christian Philosopher*, in which Mather struggled to reconcile his inherited religious universe with the world being constructed by the natural philosophers.

✳

When conflict with science arose for Mather, it occurred obliquely, for the most part, rather than head-on. The exception appeared in Mather's discussion of the Creation, Genesis 1, in "Biblia Americana," a massive, never finished biblical commentary he began in 1693 and worked on for the rest of his life. While discussing Genesis 1, biblical commentators traditionally demonstrated the harmony between the Bible and natural philosophy. In the past theirs had been a straightforward task, and Mather leisurely started writing his commentary on Genesis 1 without any evident sense of urgency or direction, discussing miscellaneous questions about the writing of Genesis, the Mosaic distribution of plants, and evidences of the Trinity in the Creation story.[8]

Sometime in the late 1690s, however, Mather came across William Whiston's heavily revisionist account of the Creation, A New Theory of the Earth, published in 1696. From it he learned that, measured by the scientific expectations of the late seventeenth century, "the common glosses" of the Mosaic account of the Creation were "full of difficulties." Mather made an eight-page summary of Whiston's version (Moses did not describe the creation of the universe but only of the earth, and, not being a natural philosopher, he did not necessarily understand that which he was reporting accurately). Whiston's account may have been superior to the common glosses of Genesis, but it troubled Mather deeply, for two reasons. It localized and therefore trivialized the Creation story, but not only that, it trivialized Moses himself, whom Mather fondly considered the first and greatest exponent of the mechanical natural philosophy.[9] Unsurprisingly, Mather cautioned the reader at the beginning of his summary of Whiston that "You must not expect, that I declare myself, how far I concurr, with every point, that shall be offered," and at the end he reiterated "As for a Judgment upon this Description of the Creation, I will presume to make None at all." He was clearly not happy with Whiston's account; however, that was the way learned culture seemed to be going, and he had to move with it. Mather could console himself with the thought that Whiston's version did not change the fact that our globe was "pitch'd upon" by God as the spot of the Messiah's incarnation.

Mather followed his account of Whiston's hypothesis with an abstract of a more congenial blend of science and religion: Richard Bentley's famous 1693 London Boyle lectures, in which Newtonian physics demonstrated "the Order and Beauty of the Systematical parts of the World," while the Newtonian concept of gravity afforded an "Invincible Argument for the Being of a God."[10] Mather found the glimpse into the mind of God offered by gravity exhilarating: he followed his account of Bentley with a long quotation from the English jurist Matthew Hale that proclaimed how much more sublime and intricate the construction of the world really was than any scheme a natural philosopher could devise.

Although science clearly and magnificently affirmed the presence of the creator, Whiston's challenge to a literal and sufficiently reverent reading of

Genesis 1 remained to rankle Mather. He was obviously relieved in 1702 to come across *Physica vetus et vera*, the newly published book of Edmund Dickinson (1624–1707).[11] Mather summarized the elderly Dickinson's far more conservative account of Creation on eleven pages and inserted them in his manuscript immediately after Whiston's version, proclaiming that "The *Theories* of the *Creation* (Particularly what I last offered you) by the modern philosophers do certainly make too bold with the *Mosaic* and *Inspired* History." Moses, according to Dickinson, indeed gave the story of the whole Creation, and in fact he was the first "corpuscular" (mechanical) philosopher. Moses's corpuscularism, as Dickinson elaborated it, was a peculiarly seventeenth-century hybrid of Cartesian, scholastic, and alchemical assumptions, but Mather never raised any questions about it, in the "Biblia" or elsewhere.

Perhaps Mather sensed a certain disorder in these varied accounts of the natural history of Genesis 1; at some point in 1717 or later, he inserted, without editorial comment, at the start of that commentary another more recent account of the Creation story, "agreeable to the Modern Discoveries." The account was a paraphrase by an Anglican minister, Thomas Pyle, a Newtonian who drew heavily on a contemporary author Mather appreciated, William Derham. Perhaps Mather was attracted by Pyle's own aspiration to universality; he claimed he had "endeavoured so to express every Circumstance, as not (directly and explicitly) to clash with any one particular *Hypothesis* or Opinion."[12] But Pyle's account hardly resolved the conflicts between the texts Mather had previously cited; it simply sidestepped them in its brevity. If that sidestepping troubled Mather, he did not show it.

Mather was not a synthetic thinker, and he left his commentary on Genesis 1 with the jumble of Newtonianism, historicism, corpuscularism, and alchemy unresolved. His faith in the accuracy of Genesis remained intact, nor did he ever doubt that the natural philosophers were restoring the science known to Moses. The only scientific explanation of Genesis 1 with which he expressed any overt dissatisfaction was Whiston's, and if Whiston's account of Genesis marked the high-water mark of the conceptual attack of science on Mather's faith, he seems to have driven it back quite successfully. In any event, his concern with Whiston did not have to do with philosophical issues, it had to do with questions of excessive liberty with the biblical text and lack of sufficient reverence for Moses. Mather's proclivity to jumble together wildly different scientific hypotheses demonstrates just how unoriginal and unsynthetic a thinker he was.[13] As long as scientific fashions could be adopted to his own devotional and polemical purposes, Mather eagerly adopted them. When they could not, as with Whiston's speculations, Mather clearly became unhappy, but he seems to have carried out his retreat to safe territory with little mental strain. He was recommending Dickinson to ministerial candidates in 1726.[14]

Yet all was not easy in Mather's relationship with science. Even in the absence of positive evidence, one is tempted to assume that he must have been troubled on some level by the rapid adjustments he had to make in his account of Genesis. Be that as it may, there is more concrete evidence to show that he knew that the assumptions of the natural philosophers, if not the actual contents of natural philosophy, and the assumptions of his cultural inheritance were growing apart.

*

In 1689 Mather had been certain about both the reality and the respectability of prodigies. Yet, despite the forthrightness of his 1689 pronouncement about the validity of prodigies, he never again interpreted them in print. In fact, three years later, as witchcraft was breaking out at Salem, he announced in a sermon, "I freely confess my particular indisposition to be moved by many things that are often accounted *Prodigies*." After listing New England's moral failings, he concluded that "A thousand *Comets* Blazing over our Heads, or views of *Armies* Fighting in the *Air* would be less Cloudy Premonitions of Impending Evils, than these *Prodigious Inequalities* [i.e., New England's sins]."[15]

Thereafter prodigies silently disappeared from Mather's publications. In the *Magnalia*, finished in 1698, Mather erased many of the prodigies of New England's past. The famous comet that blazed before John Cotton's death vanished, and no cabbages sent forth prophetic roots. The monstrous births of the antinomian leaders, too prominent in New England's history to be ignored, were handled discreetly. Mather noted that Anne Hutchinson's miscarriage was generally considered to have been prodigious, but he added that those present at the birth found nothing exceptional, only a "false conception." With Mary Dyer's monster, Mather, in an eerie passage, chose to emphasize the sorcery of the midwife, Jane Hawkins, rather than Dyer's deformed fetus. Only one instance of armies heard in the sky before King Philip's War retained its full prodigious glory.[16] Thereafter, Mather occasionally affirmed the reality of prodigies, in a general sense, but he did not interpret specific instances. Like witchcraft in educated circles in the eighteenth century, prodigies became for him a matter of belief rather than interpretive practice.[17]

What caused the retreat of prodigies? Mather never gave a forthright explanation, but he left behind hints that can be pieced together to form a plausible account. In the same publication of 1692 in which he indicated skepticism about interpreting prodigies, he mentioned that "a Learned Man Writing against the Regard of *Omens*" acknowledged that demons could appear as foreshadowings of futurities. Sometimes, Mather quoted the unnamed author as saying, demons could "be seen as it were upon the Stage before Execution; that men may considered into whose hands, in likelihood, their Iniquities have Betray'd them." The learned man Mather quoted was none other than John Spencer, discussed in chapter 2, one of the first Restoration Anglicans to attack prodigies and Dissenter use of prodigies.[18]

Spencer's book had been found persuasive even by many Dissenters, perhaps because Spencer otherwise had no persecuting zeal against them. Charles Morton, head of the famous Dissenting Academy at Newington Green before fleeing to Massachusetts in 1686, referred favorably to Spencer's disbelief in comets as prodigies in the physics textbook Morton produced for use at Harvard, "Compendium Physicae" (in use there by 1687). Increase Mather had been alerted by an English correspondent around the time he was finishing his own book on special providences in 1683 that many people found Spencer's arguments convincing.[19]

Increase was sufficiently struck by those arguments to visit Spencer in Cambridge, England, in 1689. He asked Spencer whether he still held to the same disbelief in prodigies that he expressed in his treatise. Spencer answered, according to Cotton Mather, that "hee believed the Divels had pramotions of many things and caused strange prodigies, and that hee did not know, Whether he might not err in Something of an Extreme, on one side, as others did on the other."[20] Cotton recorded Spencer's answer in 1692, the year Increase returned to Massachusetts and the year Cotton first expressed his own skepticism about prodigies. One can only speculate that the effect on Cotton of Morton's approval of Spencer and Spencer's moderate discussion with his father was to make him reexamine his confident, insular dismissal of the Anglican perspective.

Certainly, Cotton Mather was aware that Spencer could not be dismissed as no "gentleman." In the "Biblia Americana," he cited Spencer often on Leviticus, although not always with approval, and he elsewhere referred to him as "Learned and Famous" and praised him as a Latin stylist.[21] In addition, Spencer's allowance for demonic prodigies was close enough to Mather's experiences with witchcraft in 1692 to allow Mather to adopt what could only seem like a more up-to-date attitude toward prodigies. He had authority to retain his belief in prodigies, combined with a warning against indulging in it, and this is precisely what he did. He avoided interpreting prodigies, and he used Spencer as his scholarly vindication on two of the three further occasions in which he referred to his belief in them in print.[22] Henceforth, for Mather the status of prodigies was to be not so much an issue within learned culture itself; now prodigies largely served as a marker of the boundary between genuine knowledge and superstition, between the educated classes and the vulgar masses.

Conspicuously backtracking from his earlier treatment of prodigies, Mather at times made great efforts to indicate that he came down on the correct side of the new boundary. In a communication to the Royal Society in 1712, he included a description of a parhelion (false suns around the sun) he and his father had recorded and sent to Europe in 1685. He made clear to the Society that he did not mistake the phenomenon for a prodigy (at least in hindsight). Although a parhelion seen in Boston in 1645 had been considered ominous by many, including Governor John Winthrop, Mather mockingly referred to "our people of a more prognosticating and superstitious temper" who interpreted the 1685 parhelion to "be ominous, of something or other, if they could have told, what! . . . And you may be sure, Something did happen after them!" Similarly, in 1726, Mather advised ministerial candidates not to entertain "Superstitious Fancies" about eclipses or comets.[23]

Despite pronouncements like the above, Mather never entirely abandoned his faith in prodigies. However, from the 1690s onwards, his conviction ringed itself with defensiveness. In the *Magnalia*, when reporting on the sounds of armies heard in the sky before King Philip's War, Mather asked the readers not to consider him struck with "superstition in reporting *prodigies*, for which I have such incontestible assurance."[24] He was as discreet and defensive in his two communications to the Royal Society on monstrous births as he had been in the *Magnalia*. In his communication of 1716, for example, he stressed that monstrous births were chiefly of interest to natural philosophers because they shed light on the obscure processes of generation and that "the reasonable philosopher will not be too ready to imagine that monsters carry omens in them." Only after having made it clear that he had the same priorities as the reasonable philosophers did Mather feel free to caution that "Monsters may no doubt be sometimes attended with such circumstances that they who are more nearly concerned may do well to be sensible of a voice from Heaven therein unto them."[25]

Mather had learned and adapted to the new priorities of learned culture, but he was not comfortable with them. He walked a narrow line between the requirements of the new natural philosophy and his inherited religious culture. Just how narrow that line was, and just how difficult it was for him to keep his balance on it, became clear when on 11 December 1719 the aurora borealis spectacularly illuminated New England's skies and inspired his last writing on prodigies.

The aurora borealis had been rarely seen in the seventeenth century in America or Europe, and it could produce considerable wonder and fear in that transatlantic world. A prominent display in 1716 in England inspired divines to preach on its ominous character and Jacobites to predict God's wrath against the Hanoverian succession. However, in the eighteenth century, traditional use of prodigies ran into sharp reactions, and use of the aurora borealis proved no exception. Religious interpretations met with ridicule, and Whigs did not counter the Jacobites with alternative ominous interpretations but dismissed attempts to turn natural phenomena into prodigies. Alexander Pope claimed that the aurora borealis (along with an eclipse in 1714 and "Nine Comets seen at once over *Soho Square*") presaged an outbreak of punning, and the Royal Society left unprinted a paper sent to it trying to demonstrate that the aurora borealis had prodigious implications.[26]

Three years later, when the aurora borealis appeared in New England, Mather wrote a pamphlet, A Voice from Heaven, to calm the "Agitation in the Minds of people throughout the Countrey." Whatever his intention, the pamphlet was primarily addressed not to the country people, but to the "learned," since the topic "has been accounted a Subject worthy to be . . . pondered by the most consummate Philosophers of the Age."[27] Mather, while portraying himself as one of those consummate philosophers, was not entirely prepared to abandon his belief in the prodigious nature of the aurora borealis. Therefore, he found himself in the uncomfortable position of addressing the philosophers out of a religious culture whose assumptions were no longer reconcilable with the dominant ones of learned culture.

Mather knew that it was not only the learned culture of England itself that would view a defense of prodigies skeptically. By the 1710s, Boston had a number of people well versed in the priorities and techniques of the new science.[28] Mather's was one of three contemporaneous Boston pamphlets on the aurora borealis. The others were written by men a quarter of a century or more younger than Mather, Thomas Robie and Thomas Prince, and in neither would Mather find much support for his lingering attachment to prodigies.

Thomas Robie, Harvard tutor in mathematics, future Fellow of the Royal Society, and scientific associate of Mather, spent most of his pamphlet on the aurora borealis of 1719 speculating on its natural causes. At the pamphlet's end he dismissed any thought of it as a prodigy: "As to Prognostications from it, I utterly abhor and detest 'em all . . . no Man should fright himself by supposing that dreadful things will follow, such as Famine, Sword, or Sickness." Lest he had seemed too dismissive, Robie added that he did not mean to imply that there would not be signs in the heavens before the Day of Judgment.[29]

Earlier in 1719, Mather's friend and evangelical associate, the minister Thomas Prince, published a pamphlet on the 1716 English appearance of the aurora borealis, which he had seen. The pamphlet consisted of a letter Prince had written at the time to a relative, a letter, he claimed, that the great scientist Edmond Halley read with approval and considered publishing. In the letter, Prince made it clear that he did not believe in prodigies, although he admitted that his conviction momentarily wavered when he first saw the display. Despite his skepticism about prodigies in general, Prince did consider that the wide visibility of the aurora borealis and its dramatic nature surely meant that God intended it as a sign of some sort, most likely as a reminder of the Last Judgment. However, it was explainable by mechanical causes. In other words, a young sophisticated evangelical like Prince was still prepared to see the hand of God in the aurora borealis, even while speculating on its natural causes, but only because it was both spectacular and widely visible. Even so, unlike traditional prodigies, it referred to no mundane events, but only to the indisputable Second Coming. Prodigies per se, Prince dismissed.[30]

Robie's skepticism about the prodigious nature of the aurora borealis and Prince's pronounced restraint indicated that in the learned circles of Boston itself Mather could expect no great sympathy for interpreting the aurora borealis in the manner of his youth. Given his desire to disseminate a universal evangelical message, Mather was in a dilemma. Respecting and employing the cultural power of the new science as he did, Mather did not lightly challenge it, and yet he was still not prepared to abandon the traditional treatment of prodigies. If Mather expounded on the borealis in the old fashion, simply as a heavenly alarm to a drowsy world, the message would be received with skepticism by those attuned to the new science, and in the process Mather's own pretensions to respectability would be impaired. But clearly the borealis carried a divine message, and Mather could not ignore his responsibility to spread it.

Faced with such a conflict, Mather moved cautiously. He had his father review his pamphlet before its publication, and Increase unsurprisingly approved it. Mather then sent the pamphlet on to Thomas Prince, leaving it entirely up to Prince's judgment, he claimed, whether to suppress the interpretive part and only publish the description of the aurora borealis. Prince, in spite of his own skepticism, evidently made no objections—unsurprisingly, in view of Mather's touchy ego, as well as the ambiguity of his effort—and the pamphlet was published.[31]

The result was a tortuous and revealing publication, partly a description of the aurora borealis, partly an evangelical call to awakening, and partly an attempt to justify Mather's own resistance to the naturalistic interpretations of the groups to which he was drawn. Like Prince and Robie, Mather described the appearance of the aurora borealis in the neutral and objective fashion favored by the Royal Society, and he speculated on its possible natural causes. Thereafter, however, he parted ways with Robie and Prince. Mather noted, accurately enough, that natural philosophers, for all their speculation, knew little about what actually created the aurora borealis: "Still the Old Philosophers ingenuous cry of, *Darkness, Darkness!* will return upon us."[32] This darkness was crucial for Mather. In it he found a discursive space into which he could inject his inherited "natural philosophy" and still feel that he retained his intellectual respectability.

Since the "known Principles of Mechanism" seemed not to operate in instances like this, Mather claimed, "some that are little enough tinged with *Enthusiasm* or *Fanaticism*" were "compelled to consider the Operations of *Angels*" in order to account for the aurora borealis. Mather's rhetorical movement here was critical. Nature was mysterious, and that mysteriousness compelled unfanatical gentlemen to resort to their Bibles to fill in the gap in their knowledge. New England itself had offered proof enough that there were evil spirits, Mather asserted, and all ages had believed that the atmosphere had "angelic tribes" in it. "The *Invisible World* has an astonishing share in the Government of ours."[33]

However, with his talk of angelic tribes, Mather knew that he was approaching the limits of acceptable scientific language. He covered himself by adding that "as *Unphilosophical* as it may seem, to talk at this rate, the further our Improvements in Philosophy are carried on, the less it would be found *Unreasonable*." In any event, there certainly would be signs in the heavens before the Last Judgment, and "all Sober Men" look for that particular day. What is more, John Spencer had said that there was something to prodigies. With that authority behind him, Mather spoke for his convictions in the most noncommittal way he could muster: "I will not utterly deny, but that something may be *Read* sometimes by the *Light* of those *Fires*. There is *not* always *Nothing* in them."[34]

Thus Mather tried to assert his belief in the prodigious nature of the aurora borealis, however tenuously, while assuring the learned that he was not enthusiastic, irrational, unphilosophical, or lacking in sobriety. Yet Mather was not entirely sure that he had accomplished his aim. Had not Spencer, Mather's lifeline to respectability on this subject, sneered that "the multitudes" believed in prodigies "especially owing to those two credulous and superstitious principles *Fear and Ignorance* which usually manage and deprave their affections and conclusions"?[35] To avoid being lumped with the fearful and ignorant multitudes, Mather had to show that he could trace and police the new boundaries of legitimate knowledge as well as anyone else.

He therefore took care to state that he was quite aware that "people are never more fanciful and whimsical . . . than when they have *Uncommon Occurrences* in the *Clouds* to work upon." Given the new optimism of the English ruling classes regarding their ability to manipulate the natural world, Mather, unlike his forebears, knew that "it becomes not Serious Christians to be *Dismayed at the Signs of Heaven, as the Heathen are dismayed at them.*" He was ready to concede that comets were no prodigies—especially since pious English scientists had ingeniously reintegrated them into a supernatural economy in a mechanical fashion[36]—and he loftily dismissed traditional wonders like aerial armies and navies as the "prepossessions of a strong Imagination." Indeed, Mather, some thirty years after he had been scrutinizing cabbages, was moved to a "compassion for the miserable world," like all "Men of a Superior Wisdom & Goodness," when he saw "the *Terrors of Death* so generally seizing and frightning People, upon any *Uncommon Occurrences.*"[37]

Having clearly differentiated his position on prodigies from the "vulgar" position, Mather was reluctant to jeopardize it by hazarding a reading of the meaning of the aurora borealis as a prodigy: "I can do little by way of *Prognostic.*" He confined himself to pious reflections on the phenomenon. The aurora borealis's fiery appearance should make us consider the fires of contention among us, he told his readers; its bloody appearance should quicken our prayers for those fighting the Indians on the frontier; its heavenly location brings to mind the necessity of focusing our gaze more heavenward; and such a sight should cause us to reflect on the Last Judgment. How could one argue with such piety, especially since Mather deliberately avoided the question of whether there was any intrinsic relationship between the aurora borealis and these contemplations? Having threaded his way through the tortuous reefs of his inherited sensibility and the new climate of intellectual opinion to arrive at what felt like a culturally unassailable message, Mather could say with a justified sigh of relief at his conclusion, "Whether the *Aurora Borealis* were a *Prodigy* or no, the *Man is One*, who shall ridicule such an improvement of it."[38] He had found a way, however unhappily, to cobble together the aurora borealis and religion that sidestepped entirely the issue of whether the aurora borealis really was a prodigy.

Mather's equivocation in *A Voice from Heaven* marks the distance he had traveled since his discussion of prodigies in 1689. His association of skepticism about prodigies with politics, heresy, and vulgarity had vanished. The traces of a fairly evenly matched cultural struggle, so visible in his text of 1689, were absent from A Voice from Heaven. Now it was Mather, not the skeptics, who had to defend himself against vulgarity if he wished to retain his status as a "consummate philosopher." Although unprepared to abandon prodigies, he clearly, and correctly, considered them to be outside the mainstream of Enlightenment learning.

Mather's retreat from prodigies was not compelled by his understanding of the implications of mechanism per se; he had no problem occupying a universe filled by both active "angelic tribes" and Newtonian laws of physics. Mather could be in this sense both a Newtonian and a Puritan, but he was painfully aware that the natural philosophers whose good opinion he craved were contemptuous of such a combination. In that awareness lay the source of his anxiety about science. Under its pressure, he did not change his mind about prodigies so much as about what constituted correct speech for a learned person.

*

The history of Mather's writings on prodigies makes more intelligible one of his best-known books, The Christian Philosopher, an attempt to demonstrate the harmony of science and religion. In 1712 Mather started sending accounts of American phenomena to the Royal Society, and his efforts won him membership in 1713. Perhaps encouraged by this acknowledgement, Mather began cobbling together an essay from various sources that would demonstrate the unity of religion and natural philosophy. He sent the manuscript to London in 1715, and there The Christian Philosopher was finally published in 1721.[39]

Ostensibly, Mather wrote The Christian Philosopher simply to "demonstrate, that Philosophy is no Enemy, but a mighty and wondrous Incentive to Religion."[40] He was quite aware that he wrote in a well-worked genre of physico-theology, acknowledging a special indebtedness to two recent English authors, "Industrious" John Ray and "Inquisitive" William Derham.[41] Ray and Derham both attempted to show how a study of natural philosophy revealed a universe of benevolent, orderly providential design in which all things worked together to further humanity's existence. Mather took freely from their examples, as well as from other sources, and he confined his original contribution (which itself drew heavily on his own previous work) primarily to religious glosses on the phenomena he discussed.[42]

Mather began *The Christian Philosopher* with a description of the different bodies in the heavens, moving through various atmospheric phenomena to the earth, to arrive at the animal kingdoms and "MAN." Mather's physical framework was Newtonian. The laws of nature he cited were mechanical, not teleological, but they were satisfactory evidence of God's continuing presence in his creation. Although the world was a great machine, Mather, like Ray, saw a vitalistic principle at work in the animal kingdoms. After considering the human soul, Mather, citing the logic of the Great Chain of Being with its gradations of intelligence, discreetly said "there may be *Angels*."[43] From the angels, Mather rose to the highest point of created intelligence, the human soul of Christ as it is united to the Son of God. He ended the book with a meditation on Christ as savior and source of the archetypes of the created world and with an account of the Newtonian mystic William Cheyne's speculation as to the way in which the Trinity was reflected in the Creation.

Superficially, with its Newtonian framework and its ostensibly seamless and optimistic links between science, reason, and religion, *The Christian Philosopher* seems effortlessly to glide into the new century, and that is how scholars tend to read it.[44] However, *The Christian Philosopher* is a more complex and interesting book than a simple derivation from the English physico-theologians would have been. Mather still had a strong streak of Puritanism within him, and his universe on occasion wandered quite far afield from that of his avowed models. *The Christian Philosopher* was an attempt to appropriate the authority and learning of the new science while resisting the ideological framework within which that science developed.

If the mechanical and benevolently commodified universe newly in favor in England dominated *The Christian Philosopher*, it still had to share space with the unpredictable and fearful universe of the Puritans in a way that Mather's English models did not. Mather may have focused largely on the benign aspects of the world order, where even pain had its positive function, but he also stressed that there are "*wild Beasts crying* in its *desolate Houses, Dragons* in its most *pleasant Palaces.*" Mather could wax enthusiastic about the remarkable accomplishments humanity had made, exclaiming after a list of these, "O *my Soul*, what a wondrous Being art thou! How capable of astonishing *Improvements!*" However, he was also emphatic about humanity's fallen and depraved nature. We are crippled in our perceptions by the "*natural Imbecility* of REASON, and the *moral Depravations* of it . . . and the Ascendent which a corrupt and vicious *Will* has obtain'd over it."[45]

Our world might have been described by Mather as an "immense *Machine*" guided by regular laws in *The Christian Philosopher*, but it was a machine in which higher powers were constantly intervening.[46] God withheld rain as punishment, sent earthquakes as judgments, and poisonous snakes and noxious insects as chastisements: mariners whose ship hulls had been riddled by worms "ought to consider *what Rebuke of Heaven upon their Dealings or Doings may lie at the bottom of such a Calamity.*" Furthermore, evil spirits, "thro a just Judgment of God," could possess people, and ravens, seized with a divine afflatus, could cite Saint Paul. Indeed, only the dramatic supernatural intervention of Jesus preserved this sin-drenched, wretched globe: "This *our World* has been by the *Sin of Man* so perverted from the *true Ends* of it, and rendred full of such loathsome and hateful Regions, and such *Scelerata Castra,* that the Revenges of God would have long since rendred it as a *fiery Oven,* if our beloved JESUS had not *interceded* for it."[47]

A world of judgments, possessions, and spirits, a world of desolate places inhabited by a fallen humanity, a world that would have been burnt to a crisp long ago by its creator had not Jesus interceded, a world, moreover, whose finest piece of divine workmanship remained a *"Principle of Grace* infused into [the Soul]"—a close reading of *The Christian Philosopher* makes Mather's engagement with natural philosophy more ambiguous than first meets the eye. Reformed orthodoxy was not going altogether gently into this brave new benign and mechanical universe. Where cracks appeared in the veneer of the Early Enlightenment's discursive formulas in *The Christian Philosopher,* what appeared was a world remaining highly unstable and subject to formidable and unpredictable supernatural interventions.[48]

But the glimpses of a contingent, fallen, and supernaturally dominated world that appear in *The Christian Philosopher* give only a partial view of Mather's "natural philosophy" at the time of writing his book. His declaration that his senses had been convinced of the reality of the invisible world as fully as they had been of anything in the sensible world did indicate that he was holding back on the details of his own "natural philosophy." However, one would never guess from reading *The Christian Philosopher* that Mather still believed in prodigies and the demonic efficacy of witchcraft and charms, or that demons and angels had a part in storms and thunder.[49] Nor would one ever guess from *The Christian Philosopher* that Mather's main intellectual preoccupation in the years that the book was being written was the impending Second Coming. Mather left copious amounts of his "natural philosophy" out of *The Christian Philosopher.* His omissions strongly suggest that he knew when writing *The Christian Philosopher*—as his father had not thirty years earlier when writing his own attempt at natural philosophy, *An Essay for the Recording of Illustrious Providences*—that he needed to tailor his expression of how the supernatural and natural realms interacted for the educated audience that he wished to reach; the universe of Puritanism now fell largely outside the boundaries of legitimate knowledge.

The Christian Philosopher is better seen as a strategic document than as a map of Mather's mind. It represents an attempt to draw wide attention to certain important themes rather than a totalizing statement about the nature of the physical universe and the place of humans in it. The year 1716 was approaching when Mather wrote this document, a year Mather, from his study of Revelation, considered fraught with apocalyptic significance. The Christian Philosopher differs from earlier attempts in physico-theology, as Mather himself stated on a later occasion, in its emphasis on "a Glorious CHRIST, and the consideration due to him in our Philosophy." It is an evangelical document, and perhaps a millennial one, a part of Mather's unceasing attempts at developing a broadly based Christian unity beyond sectarian dispute in preparation for the coming end of history. "Behold, a Religion, which will be found without Controversy," Mather proclaimed at its beginning.[50]

Thus hardly a simple hymn to the power of carnal reason and to a clockwork universe, The Christian Philosopher used the framework of the new natural science to disseminate a religious message. Unlike Mather's models in physico-theology, however, in that message he tried sporadically to preserve the sense of the perilous contingency of the world on which Puritan evangelism drew. Just as he had done in The Wonderful Works of God Commemorated, Mather attempted to accommodate science to his inherited providential sensibility at least as much as he did the opposite. Twenty-five years after Wonderful Works, however, the attempt had become fraught with difficulties.

There is no reason to believe that Mather himself saw any contradiction between his rationally illuminated Newtonian framework and his possessions, judgments, talking crows, and general depravity of reason, and there is no indication that Mather was consciously trying to make a subversive reading of Newtonianism. In fact, the only positive evidence in the book suggests just the opposite. Just as he had done elsewhere, in The Christian Philosopher Mather indicated that he was aware that his traditional Puritan evangelical universe had become problematic within learned and polite society. It was up to him to demonstrate that one could be an evangelical and still a member of that society.

Accordingly, in the preface to The Christian Philosopher, Mather expressed the hope that the physico-theology to which he was trying to confine himself would be one that "the more Polite Part of Mankind, and the Honourable of the Earth, will esteem it no Dishonour for them to be acquainted with . . . a Reli-

gion which will challenge all possible Regards from the *High*, as well as the *Low* among the People . . . a PHILOSOPHICAL RELIGION: and yet how *Evangelical*."[51] Here Mather opposed the high and polite part of mankind to the low just as he opposed a philosophical religion to an evangelical one. In other words, it required a deliberate effort, and not a little self-censorship, on the part of evangelicals to reach out to the more polite part of mankind now that the relationship between the universe of natural philosophy and the universe of Puritan evangelism had grown structurally problematic.

✳

Mather's involvement in the transatlantic world of science had led him on a long and difficult journey. He never lost his commitment to the culture of wonders of the godly community into which he had been born, but his commitment to the learned culture into which he had also been born taught him that much of the "natural philosophy" of the godly community had become socially and intellectually problematic. Puritans lost control of the definition of respectability at the Restoration, and since then that definition had been steadily moving away from their assumptions. The "Biblia" with its shuffling of incompatible sources demonstrates that Mather was attracted to science as much for its cultural authority as he was out of any probing curiosity. As prodigies demonstrate, Mather, to remain within the aura of that authority, had to engage in an elaborate reclassifying of intellectual, social, and religious categories and largely abandon to the "vulgar" much that he had regarded as unproblematically religious. *The Christian Philosopher* speaks of the gap between the Puritan universe and the universe of the early Enlightenment and of the self-censorship in which Mather had to engage to bridge that gap.

Historians sometimes claim that Mather never really understood the essence of science, for with his religious preoccupations he failed to grasp it as an autonomous system.[52] Certainly Mather in his scientific practice never went much beyond unmethodical observations and collection of anecdotes, but neither did many other contributors to the *Philosophical Transactions* of the Royal Society. Scholars have recently and rightly grown skeptical of essences and autonomous systems of discourse, and from the new skeptical perspective it can be argued that Mather understood science accurately enough, insofar as he had use for it. Besides the intellectual stimulation it afforded, science simultaneously legitimated Christianity and learned culture itself. Science magnificently displayed the ontological truth of religion and in the process confirmed the importance of the learned culture in which Mather was steeped. Mather gladly used it for those purposes, locating himself both as a "priest of nature" and as a member of the transatlantic republic of letters, positioned "above the contempt of envious Men." A very useful and powerful structure of knowledge, indeed, but like all structures it defined boundaries even as it offered power, and Mather paid for his access to science's cultural power by abandoning much of his Puritan universe to the fringe of legitimate knowledge.

CHAPTER SIX

✳

Cotton Mather
and the
True Power of Devils

Puritan ministers derived a great deal of their authority from their ability to interpret God's communications. Yet God was not the only impressive supernatural force leaving signs and arguments scattered through the providential theater of the world, as Cotton Mather knew well. "The Divels now and then . . . show their *Powers* in tremendous Instances," he wrote in 1690s. But it was God who permitted those powers, "partly . . . to bespeak and quicken our *praises* of Him, as our *preserver* . . . As men are kept in *Safety*, from the power of *Divels*, by His Restraining of, not their *Dispositions*, but their *Operations*. And our *Safety* from this *Power*, administers no little Occasion of *Glory to God in the Highest*." Given that the Devil's powers derived from God, it followed for Mather that for "man to *Deny* the true *Powers* of the *Divels*, is for him to *Defraud* the Almighty God of his *Glory*."[1]

The true powers of devils and the true power of God, Cotton Mather was saying, were inseparable; deny one and you deny the other. The Puritans' ability to interpret the true power of God drew them inextricably into conflict in the seventeenth century; unsurprisingly, their similar ability to discern the true powers of the Devil had similar results. The Devil was a valuable prize within the politics of wonders, but not until the 1690s did disputes about the powers of the Devil begin to clearly sort themselves out along Puritan/non-Puritan lines. In these disputes Cotton Mather was to play a large role.

Historians usually contextualize Mather's concern about the demonic in the late seventeenth century in terms of Massachusetts's crisis-laden atmosphere. If they refer to a contemporary English context, they link him with efforts to put the reality of witchcraft on a solid evidential basis that were made by Anglican members of the Royal Society like Joseph Glanvill and Robert Boyle.[2] But while Mather appreciated and in some respects emulated those efforts, he interpreted the "true powers of the Divels" as manifested in illicit divinatory technologies, witchcrafts, and possessions in a traditionally Puritan way. In his interpretation, Mather, like the other participants in the debates about witchcraft in Massachusetts, was not caught in provincial isolation or the peculiarities of his own personality. He conspicuously, and rightly, aligned himself with contemporary Dissenters in England. His and their encounters with the demonic and their use of its true powers for partisan evangelical ends generated the last burst of publicity for the wonder-working Providence of the Puritans. Their efforts also help explain why the discourse of the demonic was growing evermore constricted in Anglo-American learned culture.

✳

As has been often pointed out, the concern of evangelical Protestant ministers with diabolical activities wonderfully demonstrates the way that interests of learned reformers and popular culture overlapped. Even in New England, people resorted to charms for illnesses, practiced folk protections against witchcraft, sought lost goods with a sieve or key, and determined marriage partners with mirrors and brooms. Ministers hardly dismissed these forms of divination, but their interpretation of the technologies involved clashed with that of the insufficiently pious. The ministers tried to encourage the population to see such activities as temptations from the Devil that needed to be rigorously avoided. Cotton Mather's complaint in the 1680s and 1690s was not that some who called themselves educated engaged in these practices, but that some "that make a profession of Christianity" did so. He did not draw a secular dividing line, between the learned and the vulgar masses, he drew a religious one, between the godly and the ungodly.[3]

Particularly ungodly in this gallery of devilish divinatory practices was astrology. New England Puritan orthodoxy, like learned opinion in general in the seventeenth century, was divided in its opinions of the effects of the heavens on earthly matters. Some writers allowed that the heavens influenced civic events, some that they were of use in medicine, and everyone accepted that they influenced the weather. However, they all drew the line at the attempt to tell individual destinies from the stars; "judicial" astrology, to give it its full title, was a usurpation of God's prerogative and, as such, blasphemous.[4] In at least two witchcraft cases in New England, dabbling with judicial astrology added to the sinister quality of suspects.[5]

Judicial astrology stood as a learned challenge to the Puritan conception of Providence. Like Providence itself, judicial astrology offered a comprehensive system of explanation that had a basis in learned culture and reached deeply into popular concerns and practices. The resemblance was close enough that it threatened to usurp the omnipotence of God and the drama of salvation with a form of astral determinism: "It were blasphemous to say [Providence] is determined by the Government of the Starres," the second-generation Massachusetts minister Jonathan Mitchel fumed. With its parallels to the universe of the Calvinists, this form of astrology could exert a strange lure on the godly; eminent Saints like William Perkins and Cotton Mather and his father-in-law, Samuel Lee, studied it carefully, and one can only wonder if Mitchel knew of New England cases when he warned that people must not use astrology to determine whether they were "good and godly?"[6] From Calvin onward, Reformed divines had constantly attacked judicial astrology, and in England, most attacks came from Puritans. The Devil instigated astrology, and therefore one could surely assume an implicit contract between the Devil and its practitioners. Its predictions occasionally came true in a way that could not be ascribed to lucky guessing, but such accuracy simply demonstrated that Satan would now and then inspire its practitioners with correct answers.[7]

Whatever Cotton Mather's private curiosity about the subject, in the 1680s and 1690s he publicly and vehemently maintained the Puritan position on the diabolical nature of that form of astrology. Judicial astrology was demonic in inspiration. "Men consult the Aspects of Planets . . . till the *Infernal Dragon* at length insinuate into them, with a *Poison of Witchcraft* that can't be cured." Astrological predictions might come true, but only with Satan's aid, and as lures for Christians. "The *devils* which *fortel* many *true* things, do commonly *fortel* some that are *false*, and, it may be, propose by the things that are *true* to betray men into some fatal misbelief and miscarriage about those that are *false*." The snares of judicial astrology were such that Mather in the *Magnalia* wondered why "no English nobleman or gentleman signalizes his regard unto Christianity" by "promoting an Act of Parliament" against it.[8] In the 1690s, the intensity of Mather's distaste for judicial astrology was such that he was moved on at least two occasions to caution that its pursuit would bring down the judgments of God upon the land.[9]

There is no reason to think that Mather in his fear and loathing of judicial astrology and in his perception of it as a direct demonic threat to piety lagged behind learned Boston opinion. Almanac writers in New England, for example, had long toyed with astrological concepts, like the influence of the signs of the zodiac on the body and the effect of the planetary positions on the weather, and they even occasionally speculated on the probable effect of the heavens on future public events.[10] None of this activity crossed over the boundary into clear-cut impiety. But one Boston almanac writer grew rash enough to publish the first birth horoscope (of Louis the XIV) in 1694. This was an incontrovertible transgression, and the writer got roundly abused for his offering of such "dark Stuff" in this "Land of Light." He later issued an apology in which he unconvincingly blamed all upon his printer.[11]

The "purity" of the New England almanacs throughout the seventeenth century is perhaps the clearest example of how New England's educated classes kept public discourse bounded by traditional piety.[12] In England itself, astrology was one of the first victims of the reaction within learned culture to the exuberance of the mid seventeenth century, and by the end of the century that culture largely regarded astrology as neither a science nor a tool of the Devil: it was nothing but ignorant foolishness. In England, by this time, only the occasional Dissenting divine fulminated in print against the "impiety" and diabolical nature of astrology.[13] In New England, however, astrology still edged up too close for comfort to a learned providentialism immersed in wonders.

✳

Divination was a fairly mild form of diabolic activity compared to witchcraft, but one thing Mather's Puritan heritage did not include, contrary to popular stereotype, was an especially active interest in the hunting of witches. Witches were confederates of Satan and, as the Bible commanded, deserved death; Puritans were usually prepared to hang properly convicted ones. Beyond emphasizing that stricture, however, Puritans manifested no great prosecutorial zeal.[14] Indeed, English Puritan writers on witchcraft in the first half of the seventeenth century usually presented themselves as moderates attempting to calm the witch-hunting eagerness of a superstitious populace, or at least, as more interested in spiritual solutions to witchcraft than in temporal ones.[15] New England stood out among the American colonies in terms of the prosecution of witchcraft, but that exceptionalism is probably more attributable to the fact that New England, far more than any other colonies, reproduced the traditional English village structure within which witchcraft thrived than to any connection with Puritanism.[16] Were it not for the Salem trials in 1692, a mass witch-hunt at a time when executions, although not prosecutions, for witchcraft had come to an end in England, there would be no reason to seek any special connection between Puritanism and prosecution of witches in a Massachusetts context.[17]

If Puritan ministers did not place themselves at the forefront of prosecuting witches, they certainly had a professional interest in them. Puritans wrote the bulk of the treatises on witches. Witches shadowed forth for them, albeit by negative example, the vast providential drama within which the godly hoped to find salvation. The sin of witchcraft was the ultimate heresy, "the greatest apostacie from the faith," as Richard Bernard put it. "As God makes a Covenant of Grace with his: so doth the Devill with his a Covenant of Death," John Gaule explained. Witchcraft was the ultimate magnification of ordinary sin. As John Cotton said, "When a man wittingly and willingly commits any knowne sinne, he doth as actually give his soule to the Devill, as a Witch doth her body and soule; we thereby renounce the covenant of God, and Satan takes possession of us."[18]

Not only did witchcraft serve as a cosmic intensification of ordinary sin, but the victim of witchcraft underwent a kind of cosmic intensification of the afflictions that God habitually sent sinners to test them and therefore should be more concerned with God's motives than the witch's. Bernard neatly laid out the proper balance between soul-searching and prosecution when one was confronted with witchcraft:

> Seeing God's hand upon us . . . this must draw us to a searching of our waies . . . to the acknowledgment of our sinnes, and to confesse God to be just: and so humble our selves in fasting and prayer, leaving our ill courses, and labouring to be reformed and so remove Gods hand: And afterwards, if there be evident proofe, and just cause, then to proceede; yet with charity, against wicked instruments, seeking to have them punished, for their amendment.[19]

If witchcraft had mainly symbolic significance for Puritan ministers, another manifestation of the Devil offered considerably more practical use. Possessions, where the godly could almost directly encounter the Devil face to face, had long had a special appeal for them.[20] Since the beginning of Elizabeth's reign, Church of England ministers had been performing dispossessions. Besides being a public service, dispossessions served the political aim of proving against Rome that the Church of England was a legitimate church. But around the end of the sixteenth century, the Church hierarchy began to associate the activity with Puritan agitation, chiefly because of the dispossessions of the Presbyterian John Darrell. Darrell, in the best Puritan fashion, found the Book of Common Prayer unhelpful in dispossession and relied instead on the power of spontaneous prayer. Just as the Church of England had found the theater of dispossession a powerful tool against Rome, so too did the Puritan wing of the Church of England find it a powerful tool for the glorification of its own style of piety.[21] As a consequence, in 1604 the Church forbade dispossessions without a license from a bishop, a license that was virtually impossible to obtain. With its new quasi-outlaw status, dispossession became an activity, like refusing to make the sign of the cross and refusing to wear a surplice, that labeled a minister a Puritan.[22]

In the second half of the seventeenth century Dissenters on both sides of the Atlantic continued to pray and fast in order to drive out evil spirits, and from Samuel Willard exclaiming that with the possession of Elizabeth Knapp in 1672, Groton, Massachusetts, had become a "Beacon upon a Hill," to Dissenting ministers in Lancashire exulting in the "Burning and Shining Light" manifested in the dispossession of a nineteen-year-old gardener in 1689, they continued to exploit these activities for traditional evangelical/political purposes.[23] Two of the best-known English cases of possession were dealt with by ministers with whom Mather was personally acquainted, Samuel Petto and Thomas Jollie. Both cases are worth examining for they allow the re-creation of a transatlantic Dissenter providentialism in which Mather's treatment of the demonic approaches normative status.

Like Mather, Petto and Jollie were Congregationalists and fervent Calvinists; they had both been ejected from their livings in 1662, and both had connections to Massachusetts. Both Englishmen corresponded with Increase Mather. Petto offered help for Increase Mather's project on the recording of illustrious providences, and Jollie, who termed himself an "old Puritan" and had been involved in seditious activities in the unsettled period after Charles II returned to the throne, made suggestions to Increase that may have provided the impetus for the 1679 Synod in Massachusetts. Petto shared his correspondence with Mather with Jollie.[24] Cotton Mather called Jollie his "Reverend Friend," and compared the criticism Jollie received for his involvement with the supernatural to that which Mather himself received.[25]

Petto interpreted his case of witchcraft and possession from the early 1660s completely within the framework of God's trying the graces of one of His Saints through the hand of Providence. The victim, Thomas Sprachet, had been "one, whom the special Providence of God hath watched over for good, even from his Childhood."[26] He survived a few nasty accidents in his youth to become a devout Christian and a member of a Dissenting congregation. In 1660 he started to have severe fits and convulsions, which, among other things, made it impossible for him to pray audibly or attend services. A poor neighboring woman confessed to bewitching Sprachet after the Dissenters had prayed for such a revelation. But although she had confessed and even had a witch's teat, the local magistrates would not intervene, saying she should not be hanged as long as she limited her activities to Dissenters. The woman (who to a modern reader seems to have had no dealings with devils except internal ones) died a few years later, with skin horribly scratched and torn, and two cudgels beside her bed to fight off Satan. Sprachet's fits had been diminishing, and from that period they remarkably diminished further, although they never completely went away.

Although the Dissenters had been interested in prosecuting the witch involved, Petto focused his attention on the affliction as a teaching sent by Providence for Sprachet's spiritual growth.[27] In publishing it many years later, he stressed its evangelical usefulness, hoping that this story would "be blessed to the awakening of some to seek a freedom from the Dominion of Satan over their Souls, by observing how he exerciseth his Cruelty upon the Bodys of Men."[28]

At about the time when Cotton Mather was dealing with the possessed Goodwin children in 1689, his "Reverend Friend" Thomas Jollie, remembered later as one of the most important Dissenting ministers in the English northwest, dealt with a similar case of possession in Lancashire, and one that generated a similar amount of publicity.[29] On the morning of 29 April 1689, a nineteen-year-old gardener, Richard Dugdale, shortly to gain notoriety as the Surey Demoniack, presented himself at Jollie's home. Dugdale's family had been Catholic, and although they had converted to the Church of England, they were not noted for their piety. Dugdale complained to Jollie of fits and strange symptoms, and Jollie suspected possession. Dugdale's story, as it developed, was that at a festival in a drunken state he offered himself to the Devil on condition of his being made a good dancer. He acquired his skill but subsequently fell into fits.[30]

Jollie, together with other Dissenting ministers in the Lancashire area, spent the better part of a year trying to dispossess Dugdale. The ministers had to deal with interference by Catholics, familiar spirits and moving shapes under Richard's clothes, and flashes of precognition and second sight on his part. Richard came to their meetings, and they attended him in his fits, fasting and praying with him. A young, not yet ordained Presbyterian minister, John Carrington, engaged in verbal duels with the Devil speaking through Richard until restrained by the other ministers, and it was probably Carrington who angered some of the others by directly addressing Satan in his prayers over Dugdale. By January of 1690, Carrington and a few others, frustrated by their lack of progress in curing Richard, suspected that the family was involved in witchcraft and subjected them to traditional tests. Finally, ten months into the struggle, the Lord answered the ministers' prayers, and the Devil departed, under somewhat ambiguous circumstances. Dugdale returned to health and enjoyed "in part at least . . . the Reformation of his Conversation."[31]

Throughout the efforts with Dugdale, the faithful servants struggling with him did not lose sight of their larger evangelical purposes. Tales of their efforts made a "great noise in the country," and upwards of a thousand spectators sometimes watched them at their work.[32] The ministers preached sermons to the multitudes who flocked to watch their struggles with Dugdale "to shew that many are under the Power of Sin and Satan, in a less sensible, and therefore in a more dangerous manner [than Dugdale]."[33] The combination of "the Lord working by Providence [Dugdale's possession] and Ordinance [the ministers' preaching] together" could be powerful: "The People still flocked to the meeting very much, and many were much convinced, and wrought upon all along." Just as the possessions in Massachusetts in which Cotton Mather got involved were to prove, this "tremendous, astonishing Providence" was a "Burning and Shining Light . . . whereof such Multitudes were awaken'd." Even Richard, poor candidate for godliness that he was, at one point delivered a godly exhortation.[34]

✳

Cotton Mather's involvement with the demonic clearly fits in this transatlantic, traditional Dissenter pattern. His first encounter with the working of the Devil came in 1688 when he was called upon to help the possessed young daughters of John Goodwin, a member of his congregation. The children had the reputation of being religious and guileless, and their possession was remembered years later for the consternation it created in the neighborhood.[35] Mather's help led to the girls' cure. As with the Surey Demoniack, witchcraft was suspected, and with the Dissenters in charge of the legal machinery in Massachusetts, an elderly neighbor was tried and executed as a witch. The evidence for her guilt seemed overwhelming at the time, but when one of the possessed children wanted to name more witches, Mather discouraged her. Four assisting ministers in their prefatory address to Mather's account of the possessions, *Memorable Providences, Relating to Witchcrafts and Possessions*, pointed out the evangelical benefits of demonic judgments for believers: "Their Graces are hereby *tried*, their Uprightness is made *known*, their Faith and *Patience* have their perfect work."[36]

In *Memorable Providences* Mather himself continued in the preface's vein of reading Satan's activities as part of a spiritual continuum in which every human participated. Witchcraft itself was the "furthest Effort of our *Original*

Sin," but no one totally escaped its stain. "All that leave the *way everlasting*, and take a *way of wickedness*, they are *bewitched*; a grievous *Witchcraft* has seiz'd upon them."[37] In publications of the early 1690s, Mather assured sinners that they, as well as witches, had a covenant with the Devil. The Devil had a "*Book* wherein he writes the *Names* of all that carry on his Interests in the World," and Mather exhorted sinners to "Tear and Break your Covenant with Satan."[38]

Witchcraft for Mather did not merely serve as a dramatic symbol of humanity's larger league with the Devil, it also figured directly in God's plot of discovering his free grace. When recording in *Memorable Providences* a story of a witch who seemed to have a genuine conversion before her execution, Mather exclaimed, "But that the *Grace of God* may be admired, and that the *worst* of Sinners may be encouraged, Behold, *Witchcraft* also has found a *Pardon* . . . From the *Hell* of *Witchcraft* our merciful Jesus can fetch a guilty Creature to the *Glory of Heaven*."[39]

Like the Surey Demoniack case, the Goodwin possessions had a favorable evangelical outcome. Mather included in *Memorable Providences* a testimony from the Goodwin father about how much spiritual development he had made under his affliction. His children all eventually became church members, and they credited their possessions with helping to awaken them to piety.[40] Other possessions with which Mather was involved in the early 1690s met with similarly happy evangelical results.[41] Had the court hearing the cases in the Salem witchcraft outbreak of 1692 allowed Mather's request to take the afflicted to his house for intensive prayer and counseling, perhaps Mather's record with the infernal world would have consisted of an unbroken succession of evangelical successes, as well as evidence of supernatural approval of Puritanism. It would have been a rousing "awakening" event, leading to the conversion of souls and demonstrating again the success with which Puritan ministers appropriated popular concerns to their own ends.

❋

If Cotton Mather followed a traditional Puritan mode in his evangelical use of Satan, he helped initiate a contemporary transatlantic Puritan trend in writing about it. Mather's relation of the suffering of the Goodwin children was published in England in 1691 with an evangelical preface by the great Dissenting minister Richard Baxter, and the book marked the beginning of a unique cluster of London publications by Dissenters.[42] Baxter followed in the same year with his *Certainty of the World of Spirits*, a motley collection of tales of supernatural agents, mostly diabolical. He stressed that the purpose of this collection was evangelical, to encourage "those great works that Faith had to do, and to overcome the World, the Flesh, and the Devil."[43]

More Dissenter publications followed. Cotton Mather's account of the Salem trials was published in 1692. His father's *A further Account of the Salem Trials* (actually *Cases of Conscience* with Deodat Lawson's brief relation of Salem attached) came out in London at the beginning of 1693 with an announcement (erroneous, as it turned out) that Jollie's account of the Surey Demoniack was shortly to be published. Samuel Petto then belatedly in 1693 published his account of Sprachet's possession incident "as being seasonable in this juncture of time."[44] A variety of problems and delays held up publication of an account of the Surey Demoniack until 1697, even in spite of spectral voices at one point warning the ministers to get on with it and a letter from a prominent Dissenting minister to Jollie, citing Mather's book as an example to be emulated.[45]

While the Dissenters produced these works primarily for the encouragement of evangelism, that was not their only intention. They also hoped to offer irrefutable proof to skeptics who doubted the reality of the spiritual world. If you could prove possessions and witches, the argument went, you had proved the existence of the Devil, and therefore you had proved the existence of God. This goal of the Dissenters intersected with the goal of a small Restoration Anglican campaign to prove the existence of witchcraft. Restoration Anglicans like Joseph Glanvill, Robert Boyle, and Henry More showed interest in witchcraft and spirits. Their motivation, the desire to combat the spread of "atheism" and refute "Epicurean Sadducees" by proving the existence of spiritual agents, was pious, and the Dissenters heartily approved of it.

However, the demonic realm these Anglicans wished to validate seriously conflicted with that of the Dissenters. The Dissenters constructed an intensely intrusive supernatural realm that vindicated and reinforced the power of godliness (mostly theirs); the Anglicans with their "scientific" accumulation of stories of apparitions and witches avoided that immediate interaction. As one historian of science has expressed it, "There was clearly lacking by this stage any sense among the scientists that witchcraft posed a great social danger. They approached the problem in the ethos of latterday scientific devotees of spiritualism, hoping that the labour of sorting through bizarre ghost stories would in some way confirm the existence of hierarchies of immortal spirits."[46]

These Anglicans' concern with witchcraft was "rational," even as Restoration Anglicanism was rational.[47] Just as Anglican Restoration rationalism constructed itself against the religious "enthusiasm" of the Puritans, so too did the Anglican rationalists of the demonic attempt to exclude the Dissenters' claims to it. The atheism the Anglicans combatted was inexorably linked with political anarchy—a perspective More summed up in a famous pronouncement: "That Saying is not more true in Politicks, *no Bishop, no King*; than this is in Metaphysick, *no Spirit, no God*"—and in the eyes of these Anglicans, political anarchy thoroughly stained the Dissenters.[48] Glanvill blamed the Puritans for creating the climate in which the atheism he was combatting was possible, while More seriously considered as an objection to a story the fact that its relator had become a Dissenter. Possessions being the property of the Dissenters, Glanvill used no possession stories, and the only one More included was the tale of a deluded Quaker.[49] The Anglican pursuit of an "objective" demonic realm, like the Anglican pursuit of an "objective" scientific realm, thoroughly intertwined itself with partisan politics.

The Anglicans were not the only ones to politicize the demonic, however. The Dissenters indulged as well, and it is arguable that they were a great deal better at it. Quite apart from the publicity and converts they generated through their dispossessions, even into the 1690s they still showed a remarkable ability to have their own sectarian stance vindicated by the demonic. Baxter, for example, wrapped his interest in the demonic in the politics of Restoration England. In the preface to *Late Memorable Providences*, it was only a short step in logic for Baxter to move from considering the Devil's involvement with the Goodwin children of Boston to his less overt involvement with the Anglican formalists of England:

> I must with grief say of thousands in this Land, that while the Devil can get them to use the Words and Forms of Christianity, against the thing, the Life and Power . . . he will get more this way than by the frightful way of Witches . . . He will lead men in crying up the Church, the Ministry, and Unity, if thereby he can tear and tread down, the Church, and Ministry, and Unity.[50]

Nor could Baxter resist pointing out in his *Certainty of the World of Spirits* that a minister hanged for witchcraft in Essex, England, in 1646 was an "old *Reading* parson," making clear by the italics that he was a Conformist, not a Puritan.[51] With his personal memories of persecution in the Restoration period, Baxter had no doubt that "were but the History of Witches and Apparitions well considered, it would help Men to understand, that Devils make no small number of the Laws and Rulers that are made in the World and have no small number of honoured Servants . . . So that the Phrase, *Rev. 3. (The Devil shall cast some of you into Prison)* should not seem strange."[52]

Similarly, Thomas Jollie, while exulting in the power of God that made it possible for the Dissenting ministers to dispossess Dugdale, graciously con-

ceded that "there have been many, and we hope are some of the Episcopal Per-
swasion who are sound." Cotton Mather, more than the other Dissenters, approached the spirit of the Anglicans by making numerous "experiments" with
his possessed subjects to test the powers of devils. Nevertheless, he contributed
to the politics of wonders with his discovery in the late 1680s, while an appointed Anglican governor tyrannized Massachusetts, that demons liked the
Book of Common Prayer.[53] Mather's eschatological revelation of the enormous
conspiracy against Massachusetts in the early 1690s, in which Quakers, Indians, opponents of Massachusetts's liberties, and Salem witches all were tools in
the hand of Satan, forming a supernatural plot against a divinely inspired
polity, was only the logical, if hysterical, conclusion of this politicized view of
the demonic.

✳

    With Dissenters so ready to appropriate the demonic to augment their
own influence, as well as to attack the Church of England, it is not surprising
that most Anglicans finally chose not to compete with them on their own
terms. Already at the beginning of the seventeenth century, the church hierarchy had fostered skepticism about possessions, driven by concerns about the
politicized use of wonders, and James I eventually adopted that outlook, for the
same reason.[54] But what had been a trickle of doubt in the first half of the century became a general flood in the second. English learned culture was designifying and thereby depoliticizing prodigies, wonders, and judgments, partially
as a response to the intense Puritan party use of these phenomena, and inevitably that meant designifying the atmosphere within which the demonic
flourished. Not only did Christ and the Holy Spirit become more inaccessible,
but things that went bump in the night in general became more objects of
entertainment than of fear or awe.[55] Encounters with the Devil were increasingly described as metaphors for states of mind or the results of bodily distem-
pers. Even if most educated religious English people did not doubt the theoretical existence of witchcraft and possessions, they tended to become more
skeptical about the reality of any given incident, or about framing specific phenomena in that context. Unsurprisingly, convictions for witchcraft plum-
meted in the second half of the century, although concern with witchcraft was
still too broadly spread among educated English people to be specifically associated with Dissenters for polemical purposes.[56] While non-Puritans had never
looked on astrology with quite the same horror as Puritans, astrology became
implicated with radicalism during the Civil Wars and Interregnum, and it

became subjected to the same kind of aggressive designification as other areas of the world of wonders. Thus, in the area of the demonic, as in so many other areas, the general weight of English learned culture was shifting slowly against the presuppositions of Puritanism. Massachusetts, a Dissenter stronghold, was slow in feeling the shift, but its turn was to come.

CHAPTER SEVEN

✳

Cotton Mather
and the
Decline of the Demonic

"I was born in the year 1666, in a small Cottage at *Salem*," the man claimed, an ominous confession, given that 1666 had been widely anticipated as a year of great supernatural changes and Salem had an evil name. "People have sometimes suspected me for a conjurer . . . I am no wizard." In a courtroom the protestation might have sounded defensive, but it unashamedly blazoned itself on the front page of a new Boston journal in 1727, the *New England Weekly Journal*, dedicated to furthering both piety and politeness. Its source was Cotton Mather's nephew, Mather Byles, in the persona of a comic *Spectator*-styled character, Proteus Echo. Echo immediately took away the force of his denial of wizardry by adding, "that being only my own private Opinion, I shall not presume to palm it upon others," and he went on to talk of other humorous quirks of his personality.[1] Such frivolity on such a deadly topic by a member of the Mather family points to a major shift in sensibility among the learned of Massachusetts.

That shift would have been inconceivable thirty years earlier. Byles's uncle, for one, came out of the Salem disaster with his theoretical framework of the demonic intact. It is not that Cotton Mather did not find Salem traumatic. He was extremely sensitive to the confusions it unleashed, and by 1696 he was interpreting a series of family misfortunes as manifestations of God's anger at him for failing to have spoken out more forthrightly against the legal proceedings there. Nevertheless, Mather's growing uneasiness about the judicial process at Salem did not lead him to question the nature of witchcraft itself, let alone the physical activities of demons. Witchcraft still appeared prominently in the *Magnalia*, finished in 1698, in passages quite extraneous to

Salem, as did attacks on astrology.[2] Thus, in spite of the trauma of Salem, the demonic fitted quite comfortably in Mather's providential sensibility.

There is no reason to consider Mather unique among the Massachusetts elite in his reluctance to rethink basic assumptions in the wake of Salem. Increase Mather, in *Cases of Conscience*, the book usually credited with bringing the proceedings to a halt, merely reiterated William Perkins's standard of proof in a witchcraft proceeding, a standard the Salem court conspicuously ignored. John Hale, in *A Modest Enquiry*, wrote the most open admission of error at Salem and most overt challenge by a member of the Massachusetts elite to the legal procedures used to convict witches. But Hale fully accepted the reality of malignant witchcraft, along with conjuring and demonically inspired astrological predicting (he knew people who had experienced all three), and he did not question that some of the witches executed in New England were guilty. Thomas Brattle's contemporaneous letter about Salem is the most scathing criticism of the trials by a member of Boston's elite, but the letter focused on the quality of the trials, not witchcraft per se. Brattle did not question the reality of witchcraft and possessions. While he vacillated on the question of whether witchcraft itself in some form really was occurring at Salem, he had no doubt that the Devil lay at the bottom of the incident; it clearly was a "hellish design to ruin and destroy this poor land."[3] Salem may have curtailed the willingness of the Massachusetts legal system to deal with witchcraft, but, as the eighteenth century dawned, witchcraft had a respectable if shaken place in the providentialism of Massachusetts's elite.

However, the respectable place of the demonic in Puritan religiosity did not go unchallenged, either in England or Massachusetts. Attacks on belief in witchcraft and attacks on Puritans playing politics with the demonic went back to the end of the sixteenth century. But what distinguished the new criticism from earlier attacks is that in the new criticism, those lines of attack merged, and witchcraft and the Puritans' conception of a wonder-working Providence were linked together for the first time, both undesirable hangovers from an earlier era. Critics implied that the activities of the Dissenters were at best irrelevant to the important issues of religion, and at worst, marked their practitioners as enthusiasts, people outside the circle of respectable learned culture. Criticism came not only from Anglicans but from Dissenters themselves as they continued to withdraw from the partisan exploitation of Providence. Cotton Mather had been at the center of the last significant group of publications asserting the traditional Puritan attitude to the demonic, and he shared in the vigorous, newly contoured criticism those publications received, both in Massachusetts and in England. It is through Cotton Mather's reactions to those criticisms that an otherwise almost invisible transition in attitude toward witchcraft and other related demonic activities can be traced among the learned in Massachusetts, a transition that ultimately would permit postures like his nephew Byles's.

✳

In England, the affair of the Surey Demoniack attracted much attention, and partisan criticism quickly emerged. A local Anglican cleric, Zachary Taylor, rector of Wigan and chaplain to the Bishop of Chester, preached against the reality of the Surey Demoniack while the alleged possession was occurring. In a published response in 1697 to Carrington's account, Taylor challenged the Dissenters' affidavits with ones of his own, claimed that Dugdale disagreed with their pamphlet, accused them of pressuring witnesses, asserted that "there was never such Whoring heard of, as whilst the Ministers kept up their Meetings," and offered his own explanation of the affair. Taylor argued that the affair had resulted from a variety of factors: Jesuit duplicity working on superstitious Dissenting ministers, deliberate Dissenter falsehoods, and a mixture of imposture and epilepsy on Dugdale's part.[4]

Whatever the accuracy of Taylor's explanation, he had no doubt of the damage the Dissenting ministers caused by using such episodes for evangelical purposes: "I beseech You, Gentlemen, consider the Evil you have done in Publishing a wild Story, for a Religious Truth, in this Sceptical and Irreligious Age."[5] Alleged extraordinary manifestations of Providence only hindered religion, according to Taylor. Unsurprisingly, he was dismayed by the account of the spectral night voices that told the ministers to get on with publication: "Gentlemen, if you have any sense of Sobriety in Religion, how could you suffer such a shatter'd piece of Enthusiasm to Preface the Narrative."[6]

Taylor gave a new twist to the linkage between Puritanism and the world of wonders. He implied that only enthusiasts troubled themselves with manifestations of the Devil. A century earlier, the critics of the Puritan exorcist John Darrell called him a fraud, implying at the least that he had some rational control over his activities, and they argued with him within a discourse of wonders. While his chief critics, for example, denied that demons could take on bodily form, they had no doubt that angels could, which was "made apparent unto us by often experience." Their substantial criticism of Darrell was not that he made religion look ridiculous, but that he obscured the way the Devil really operated.[7]

Taylor argued that the Dissenting ministers were not simply frauds like

Darrell, but enthusiasts, outside the bounds of rationality altogether, outside the circle of "gentlemen's" discourse. Taylor was particularly cutting about a section in the narrative of the Surey Demoniack in which a minister, in time-honored fashion, had a helpful verse of scripture come to his mind, offering appropriate guidance: "You use that Holy Book, as Wizards do."[8] The assimilation of Dissenters to other groups in the process of elite marginalization had been going on since the Restoration. Earlier Anglican critics in the 1660s had linked Puritans to Rosicrucians, alchemists, and astrologers; now Taylor was giving the Puritan and the witch a common definition: both were enthusiasts, both unaware that the supernatural did not manifest itself in such an overt manner.[9]

Unlike earlier critics, Taylor regarded not only the possession as fraudulent, but the whole concept of immediate supernatural intervention as distasteful and incompatible with "Sobriety" in religion. Such events had ended with the New Testament. Taylor worried that by claiming that their exorcism was as real as any made in Gospel times, the Dissenting ministers had only allowed "nimble Disputants, to call in question the Truth of what our blessed Saviour did."[10] It was not just possession, but wonders in general, that Taylor was trying to exclude from the boundaries of legitimate discourse.

Thomas Jollie made a blistering reply to Taylor. While stressing that Carrington's account was published without his knowledge or approval and that he would not defend it in its details, Jollie insisted that it was true in its broad outlines. As for Taylor's accusations of "enthusiasm," Jollie broadly hinted that Taylor was reserving himself a place in hell by such labeling.[11]

Not only partisan Anglicans were dubious about the Surey Demoniack, however. Some uneasy Dissenters supplied Taylor with Dissenter correspondence concerning the affair and informed him of a conversation with a leading moderate London Presbyterian minister, Vincent Alsop, in which the latter recommended burning the manuscript. It was reported that many "Sober, Grave, Dissenting Ministers" tried to have the account suppressed.[12]

Nor was Jollie the only Dissenter to enter the pamphlet fray. Another Dissenter identifying himself only as "N.N." replied to Taylor in 1698.[13] This Dissenter avoided Jollie's and Carrington's impassioned, evangelical, and partisan language. Significantly, he claimed he had suspected from the beginning that the Demoniack might be an imposture, although he considered that the far-fetched attempts of Taylor to explain the phenomenon away had given it more plausibility. But N.N. was not so much concerned with the question of the reality of the Surey Demoniack as he was with Taylor's accusations of deliberate falsehood and his attacks on the Dissenters as schismatic and superstitious.[14] The Dissenter N.N. made it clear that he had no great investment in the world of wonders and the divisive spirit it engendered, whether that divisiveness came from the partisans of the Surey Demoniack or from its detractors. For N.N., the issue of special providences was not nearly as important as the issues of tolerance and reasonable discussion. Therein, according to N.N., Taylor conducted himself no better than the people he attacked, and N.N. distanced himself from both sides.[15] The contours of Dissenting discourse were beginning to take on a distinctly post-Puritan mold: Dissent would justify itself by a noncoercive reason, not by manifestations of the supernatural. Jollie's traditional authoritarian discourse of wonders was as alien to N.N.'s approach as it was to Taylor's.

✳

It was not only Dissenters in England who were rejecting a concern about demonic technologies in the context of a rejection of an authoritarian discourse of wonders. On the North American side of the Atlantic, Robert Calef adopted that position in his clash with Cotton Mather over witchcraft and possessions. Calef, who immigrated to Boston from England sometime in the 1680s, was a weaver and merchant. He served in various minor town offices, including that social bulwark of the Sabbath, tithing-man. Despite Calef's denominational orthodoxy, he was tolerant enough in his outlook and indifferent enough to the opinions of Boston's elite to go bail for the Quaker Thomas Maule in 1696, when the latter was prosecuted for his book *Truth Set Forth and Maintained* (1694).[16]

Calef carried on a running debate about witchcraft with Mather in the 1690s. The debate possibly began with the trial of Jane Glover for the enchantment of the Goodwin children in 1689, which would indicate that Calef brought his skepticism with him from England.[17] Calef published much of this debate in London as *More Wonders of the Invisible World* (1700). *More Wonders* exemplifies the impact of the new rationalism on Dissent, for Calef's attack was on not just the belief in witchcraft but also the link between religion and special providences and wonders.

Calef in his book made the usual arguments of the "witch advocates" that scripture passages referring to witches had nothing to do with the modern variety. He was even reluctant to concede that biblical references to the appearance of devils or angels alluded to physical or intellectual appearances.[18] With such a rationalistic approach to the scriptures, it might be expected that Calef had little patience for the partisan use of wonders in general, and indeed he did not, turning the full force of his considerable wit on the concept. Referring to the proposal made by the overseers of Harvard College in 1694 that another collection of special providences be made, Calef offered his own tongue-in-cheek list of remarkable divine judgments that he claimed had befallen those involved in the Salem persecution.[19]

Levity aside, Calef found the attempt to bind religion to the interpretation of an intrusive supernatural order and special and remarkable providences, as Puritanism had always done, a dangerous mistake:

> [Remarkable providences cannot be] more sensible demonstrations of the Existence or Agency of the *Invisible World*, than the scriptures of Truth afford . . . for this were Treacherously and Perfidiously to quit the Post to the Enemy; the *Sadducee, Deist*, and *Atheist* would hereby be put in a condition so Triumphantly to deny the Existence and Agency thereof. As that a few Stories told (which at best must be owned to be fallible and liable to misrepresentations) could not be thought Infallibly sufficient to demonstrate the truth against them.[20]

Calef disliked not just witchcraft, but the legible, intrusive, supernatural order of which witchcraft was a part. In a manner similar to Taylor's, Calef suggested that Mather's propensity to interpret "impressions" on his mind as supernatural in origin "savoured so much of Enthusiasm."[21] Calef offered the earliest surviving expression in New England of a religious sensibility that no longer regarded as self-evident the vindication of religion by supernatural intrusions, demonic or otherwise, and in which the old providential sensibility seemed mere enthusiasm. In short, he expressed a religious sensibility that was not Puritanical; as such, it had no use for witchcraft or possessions.

Although Calef spoke in line with cultural trends in England, he hardly cowed Mather by his attack. Mather asserted in his response published in 1701 in Boston that all the ministers in the world he knew, of any persuasion, believed in witchcraft, and, furthermore, that the Bible clearly stated that the Witch of Endor had a familiar spirit, given by the Devil after the witch made her pact with him. Thus, she was the same sort of person as those accused at Salem.[22] Mather saw no reason to obfuscate his beliefs when responding to Calef, something at which, as seen in previous chapters, he was quite competent. Thus, for almost a decade after Salem, there is no evidence that Mather saw any need to revise his views on witchcraft.

Mather might dismiss Calef as a "weaver," but in England concern about witchcraft was growing ever more inappropriate for those who desired to be "gentlemen." Just as one had to be on one's guard now if one wished to talk about prodigies, so did one have to be reserved in talking about witchcraft. In

the early eighteenth century, English writers did not hesitate to put the believer in a wonder-working Providence and the witch exactly on the same
plane, with neither to be taken very seriously.

The emergent English providential sensibility, in which the steady course
of Providence was juxtaposed to both Puritans and witches, may be seen in the
Whig journalist John Trenchard's comments in his *Natural History of Superstition* (London, 1709). Trenchard, writing after the stir created by the Calvinist
French Prophets, attacked those who think they

> attribute more Honour to the Divine Omnipotence, when they suppose he . . .
> accommodates his Providence to each single Actor and Emergency, than in
> believing that his eternal Wisdom hath so contrived . . . Nature, and in its origi-
> nal Constitution implanted such Causes, as by their own Energy shall produce
> all the Events in the World, (unless for some particular Reasons he thinks fit to
> interpose his immediate Providence).[23]

Trenchard then linked together the old providentialism, witchcraft, and religious enthusiasm, in what could almost be a critique of Mather's providential
sensibility:

> How many Nations formerly, and even at this Day, believe Eclipses and Comets
> to be supernatural, and to denounce the Anger of the Gods? How many mistake
> the Stagnation of their own Blood for being Hag-ridden? How many Enthusiasts
> take their own Prejudices and Whimsies for divine Impulses, and the Struggles
> of their Reason for Temptations of the Devil?[24]

Trenchard, together with Thomas Gordon, continued in this vein of analysis when writing "Cato's Letters" in the early 1720s. Here, in a characteristic
early-eighteenth-century Whig line of polemic, he forthrightly associated the
authoritarian discourse of the supernatural with the "priestcraft" of the High
Church party among the Anglicans, loathed and feared by Whigs and Dissenters. "Cato's Letters" were quickly reprinted in Boston, and some in New
England drew delicious polemical parallels between Cotton Mather and the
High Church men.[25]

The new taxonomy of the supernatural, in which the Puritans found
themselves undistinguished from the forces of darkness they so valiantly combatted, with no supernatural distinction accorded to either party, found a rich
politicized expression in Francis Hutchinson's widely translated and reprinted
An Historical Essay Concerning Witchcraft (London, 1718). Hutchinson, a Whig
and an Anglican latitudinarian minister and future bishop, accounted for the
most celebrated witchcraft cases of the previous century, including Salem and

the Surey Demoniack, wholly in naturalistic terms, and he rewrote Restoration intellectual history by crediting the decline of witchcraft to the influence of the Royal Society.[26] Remaining belief in witchcraft he attributed to "dark superstitious Tempers, that usually form their Religion suitable to their own Complexion," and such tempers were "in the main" not found in "our Church of *England* and its Clergy."[27]

Lest readers have any doubt where dark superstitious tempers could be found, in the main, Hutchinson made an exegesis of the scriptural passages that seemed to support the reality of witchcraft. In the process, he sounded the death knell among the English learned elite for the broad respectability of Puritan providentialism.[28] To whom, according to Hutchinson, did the Old Testament refer when it spoke of idolaters and witches?

> By these texts we learn . . . what kind of Men were deepest in that Guilt, and by what Means they were deluded . . . They were not *Atheists* that denied Providence but they were such Providential Men, as pretended to understand the divine Mind and meaning in all sudden Calamities, monstrous Births, Voices in the Air, Strange Birds, Comets, Eclipses . . . They were not cold and careless in their Devotions; but made use of vehement, and as they thought powerful Invocations . . . and they had so many Relations of Facts that seem'd to verify their Predictions, that many Princes were fond of them, and grave Nations enquired of them . . . You will think I aim . . . at the ringleaders of our own Sects . . . But it will be a juster Thought, if you take occasion to observe from it, how very steadily Nature, and even the Imitations of it, keep their Course.[29]

The witches of the Old Testament, according to Hutchinson, were Puritans! The "Providential Men" had assumed that scripture took a steady course throughout the ages, the constant backdrop against which the story of their present time could be interpreted, while nature was subject to interruptions and violations. The new providential sensibility applied that stability to nature itself. It had no need in its outlook for phenomena like witches and certainly no need for religious enthusiasts such as Cotton Mather was trying to demonstrate himself not to be. To drive the point home, Hutchinson laid the blame for the Salem prosecutions on the books on witchcraft and Providence by the Dissenters Richard Baxter and Increase and Cotton Mather (while charitably saying of Cotton, "My business is not to expose him").[30]

Hutchinson elsewhere in his book acknowledged reluctantly that backward-looking Dissenters were not the only ones to believe in witches, but his jabs against the Dissenters indicate what the only lasting effect of the flurry of Dissenter publications on witchcraft in the 1690s had been. By putting themselves out on such a visible limb at a time when English learned culture was withdrawing from an active interest in witchcraft, Dissenters like Mather, Baxter, and Jollie succeeded in providing a polemical binding between their wonder-working Providence, itself already problematic in English learned culture, and belief in witchcraft, also in the process of going out of fashion in that culture. They left themselves vulnerable to Hutchinson's propulsion of the witch and the Puritan together into the dark backward and abysm of time, the decline of magic and the decline of Puritanism.

$$*$$

Detailed studies of Mather's involvement with witchcraft and the demonic end with his debate in the 1690s with Robert Calef. However, Mather's development in the eighteenth century is of considerable interest, both for the light it sheds on him, and for the indication it offers of otherwise largely invisible trends in Massachusetts. In the eighteenth century, Cotton Mather grew increasingly aware that the elite intellectual groups with which he wished to be associated did not take phenomena like witchcraft and astrology too seriously. While never losing his belief in the psychological efficacy of the Devil, Mather cautiously began to distance himself from more overt phenomena like witchcraft and astrology in a manner reminiscent of his retreat from belief in prodigies.[31] He began to make secular distinctions where previously he had made only religious ones.

The clearest evidence of Mather's retreat from the traditional conception of witchcraft comes in his biblical exegesis. One of the strongest biblical supports for the reality of covenanting witches was the Witch of Endor. She was said to possess a familiar spirit, and her possession of this familiar spirit could be taken to imply at least an implicit contract between her and the Devil. That contract meant that the Bible offered proof not just for witches, but for the covenanting witches of contemporary times. Crucial to that interpretation was a translation of the Hebrew word "ob" as "familiar spirit." The "witch advocates" from Reginald Scott onwards had been claiming that this was an incorrect translation, and that the correct one was more like "bottle."[32]

Mather in the 1690s used the traditional translation of the word "ob" and drew from it the traditional conclusion in his debate with Calef: "[The Witch of Endor] was, as you read it, *Baqualath-Obh*, or, *The Mistress of a Spirit*. So then there was a *Contract* between *Her*, and that *Spirit*, and that *Spirit* must bee in some sort subject unto her *Command*."[33] Mather repeated that interpretation in his exegesis on 1 Samuel 28 in the "Biblia Americana," and he flung it again at Calef in his published response to him of 1701. But at some later point he returned to 1 Samuel 28 in the "Biblia Americana," inserting a folio leaf after his first exegesis, with a prefatory remark indicating that his old interpretation now troubled him: "The affair of *Saul* consulting the Witch of *Endor*; an illustration that shall sett it in a new light, is now asked & hoped for."[34]

Why a new reading was asked and hoped for, Mather never explained, but the reading itself is suggestive. Mather now decided, encouraged by the authority of the Huguenot minister Pierre Jurieau, that "ob" was more fittingly translated as "bowl." According to Mather's new reading, the witch caused an image of Samuel to appear in a bowl while a demonic voice spoke from the ground (Mather knew of several instances of comparable magic in his neighborhood). While Mather remained far from the position of the "witch advocates," who claimed that the Witch of Endor was simply a fraud, his new translation still eliminated the familiar spirit and its implicit contract. In doing so, he quietly tore down the strongest biblical sanction for the traditional religious conception of the covenanting witch.

Witches still communicated with demons in Mather's cosmology, but he dismantled the scaffolding of witchcraft as the inverse parallel of organized religion. In a 1712 communication to the Royal Society on monstrous births, he mentioned Mary Dyer (referred to only as the wife of William Dyer) and her infamous birth, but now he referred to her midwife, who was an accomplished and sinister witch in the *Magnalia*, merely as a fortune-teller.[35] In the unlikely event that Mather changed his biblical exegesis within only a few years after defending it in 1701, it may not be coincidental that in a publication of 1704, *The Armour of Christianity*, outlining the various psychological snares of the Devil, Mather made no mention of Satan having a book of sinners' names or of sinners having a covenant with him. The biblical authority for such imagery had vanished, and with the disappearance of that authority witchcraft lost much of its religious significance for Mather.[36]

What induced Mather to revise his conception of witchcraft? It can be assumed that learned gentlemen of Boston like Mather learned of the new attitudes to witchcraft, and of the desirable sociological location of those new attitudes, through their reading, conversations, and communications with England. Mather of course read the skepticism about Salem and his role therein expressed by English Dissenting historians of New England like John Oldmixon and Daniel Neal, and his English correspondents gave him a less than ringing endorsement of his version of that event. He would have encountered a general skepticism about witchcraft in the *Spectator*, and he probably got wind of the fact, known by others in Massachusetts, that already in the first decade of the eighteenth century his publications expounding a traditional

Puritan Providence had given him a reputation for credulity among some of
the most prominent Dissenting ministers of London.[37]

Mather responded once in print to the new English attitude, and that
response demonstrates how much of his belief in witchcraft he surrendered in
the eighteenth century. While discussing the Salem witchcraft in his biography of his father, *Parentator*, published in 1724, Mather answered Francis
Hutchinson. He praised Hutchinson for having the laudable goal of saving
innocent lives but regretted that he resorted to ridicule of Dissenters while
doing so. He considered Hutchinson's explanation of the Surey Demoniack (a
simplified version of Taylor's, making reference to "deluded" Dissenters) an
"Abominable Exhibition," while sputtering almost into incoherence at the accusation that he, his father, and Richard Baxter were responsible for Salem.[38]

But the times bewildered Mather. In spite of Hutchinson's attacks on Dissenters and the Puritans' wonder-working Providence, Mather knew that he
did not speak even for all Dissenters. A Whig "vital center" of Low Church
men and Dissenters was forming in England that dismissed serious witchcraft
belief as belonging only to fanatics, be they indifferently High Church crypto-
Jacobites or Dissenting enthusiasts.[39] Just as he had to wonder at English Dissenters drifting off to Socinianism and Arianism, so must he "wonder what sort
of *Dissenters* they should be, that can applaud a Book, so liable to be by *them* at
least Complained of."[40]

With Dissenters not firmly resisting what appeared to Mather as a blatantly partisan attack, it is not surprising that Mather did not defend belief in
witchcraft itself in his response to Hutchinson. While resolutely claiming that
Salem was caused by an "Extraordinary Descent of *Wicked Spirits*" (an opinion
held by at least some of Massachusetts's learned through the end of the eighteenth century), he added that it "was then generally thought" that the descent "had been introduced by *Witchcrafts*, or the Arts and Acts of such as had
made Compacts with *Daemons*." Mather had already rejected the reality of
that kind of witch in the "Biblia Americana," and he suggested that not
witches but the "Irritated Vengeance of Heaven" had unleashed those demons
as a punishment for the "little and foolish *Soceries* . . . of too many rash People."[41] There may have been people dabbling in magic at Salem, according to
Mather (something few historians would disagree with), but there were no
witches there; only in a past climate of opinion would anyone think otherwise.
On just how fully Mather himself had participated in that bloody discursive
mirage, *Parentator* was silent.

Thus by the last years of his life, the place of witchcraft in Mather's Providence had clearly diminished, and astrology and divination shared in that

shrinkage. Mather displayed markedly less hostility to astrology in *The Christian Philosopher* than in the *Magnalia*. In the former, astrology was simply "foolish."[42] As demonstrated earlier, Mather's opinions in *The Christian Philosopher* are not necessarily to be taken at face value, but at a minimum, he was recognizing that the intellectual elite with which he wished to be associated did not take astrology seriously, demons or no demons. In 1705 an almanac heavily slanted toward astrology appeared in Boston without appearing to have drawn down the wrath that greeted earlier efforts, suggesting that Mather was not alone in no longer perceiving astrology as a religious threat.[43]

It was dawning on Mather that astrology and divination were no longer as much signs of heresy as they were signs of a social location a "gentleman" would avoid. In 1712, for example, the year Mather considered sending material to the *Spectator*, that journal said of astrology and divination, "Notwithstanding these Follies are pretty well worn out of the Minds of the Wise and Learned in the present Age, Multitudes of weak and ignorant Persons are still slaves to them."[44] Four years later, Mather expressed his overt acceptance of this substitution of a sociological location of divination for a religious one.

In 1716 Mather cautioned his auditors at the Thursday lecture to shun various divinatory practices, including astrology. The list of practices to be avoided was quite similar to one he had itemized in 1689, but the reasons for avoiding those practices had changed significantly. Whereas in 1689 he had expressed his surprise that Christians would engage in divination, now he expressed his surprise to his audience, which included the new royal governor, Samuel Shute, that "some who count themselves above the Common People" would do so. A religious categorization of the occult had become a sociological one. Just as Mather was realizing that "gentlemen" should not be concerned with fearful prodigies, he was learning that they should not be concerned about divination. One can hear the cracking as a new fissure formed between popular and learned cultures. While still regarding fortune-telling techniques as "sorceries," Mather was less forward in introducing diabolical agents and denouncing these practices as witchcraft than he had been in the 1680s and 1690s. He simply cautioned that such activities brought on the "Rebukes of God." Neither in that lecture nor elsewhere in his publications of the eighteenth century did Mather make any more references to astrology bringing the judgments of God on the land.[45]

The transformation in Mather's outlook on the demonic can be best seen not so much as a change of mind, but as a change of emphasis and tone. To the end of his life, Mather believed in possession, the demonic efficacy of charms, and sorcery, and that astrology, when it did work, did so through a "*Satanic*

Impulse."[46] He never shied away from proclaiming his belief in possessions, perhaps because both scripture and Massachusetts experience so clearly vindicated it—a quarter of a century after Mather's death, the authenticity of the Goodwin possessions was still generally accepted.[47] In one of his manuscripts, *The Angel of Bethesda*, which Mather claimed to have completed by 1724, he mentioned his old hope of being able to put such activities within a "scientific" framework, and his aim in doing so was still religious, the confutation of "*Epicurean Sadducees.*"[48] He never ceased to caution people that resorting to fortune-tellers was "a crime that will ripen People for the punishments which use to come upon Sinners when they have quite *fill'd up the measure of their Iniquity.*"[49]

But a sin that merely ripens sinners is less severe than one that threatens immediate judgments on the whole land. That lessening of intensity sums up the progression of Mather's thought on the demonic in the eighteenth century. Mather had stripped witchcraft of much of its religious importance. While he still believed in possession, he did not try to use it for the partisan evangelical purposes he had in the past; while he still believed in the diabolical efficacy of divination, he had learned to condemn it as much in secular as in religious terms. Mather had not changed most of his beliefs about the demonic, but the social meaning of those beliefs had undergone considerable alteration. Just as gentlemen no longer showed concern about prodigies in public, whatever their private thoughts, so did they not worry overmuch about diabolical magic and divination.

✳

Evidence about attitudes in Massachusetts toward matters like witchcraft and divination in the first two decades of the eighteenth century is scarce. Ministers had not totally abandoned the politicized use of the demonic; however, it is clear that by the 1720s, a significant "Anglicization" had taken place in educated circles, often expressed with far less ambiguity than Mather showed.[50] A week after Mather Byles treated witchcraft as a source of humor in the *New England Weekly Journal*, another "Proteus Echo" contributor, Matthew Adams, created for the paper an imaginary discussion group that combined with no sense of incongruity a quack astrologer and two eminently pious and respectable divines.[51] Thirty years earlier such wit would have seemed blasphemous, but Adams, like Byles, clearly did not regard his creation as violating religious proprieties.

So far had the pendulum swung that in 1728, the year of Cotton Mather's death, a Massachusetts minister and Benjamin Colman's son-in-law, Ebenezer Turrell, dismissed the whole genre of authentic accounts of encounters with the supernatural such as had preoccupied Mather forty years earlier: "There are some books in the world, filled with stories of witchcrafts, apparitions, trances, &c. to which we owe no more faith than to the tales of fairies and other idle romances." Turell called, instead, for a book of "authentick accounts" of witchcraft fraud.[52] To the learned religion of the early Enlightenment, Dissenting and Conformist alike, the great dark polemical dramas of possession and witchcraft had fallen to the same level of relevance as tales of fairies. Astrology was to have a long future in popular culture, and belief in witchcraft remained widespread in the Massachusetts countryside.[53] However, given that by the eighteenth century within learned culture even so firm a believer in the demonic as Cotton Mather had smoothed off something of that belief's theoretical and experiential edge, it is not surprising that the Salem trials marked the last legal executions for witchcraft within the English "nation."

CHAPTER EIGHT

✳

A Farewell to Wonders

P rovidence for Cotton Mather in the seventeenth century had been the manifestation of a capricious, involved, and fearsome deity. It left its "argumentes and sygnes" in abundance both in the external world and the human soul for the Saints to decipher, just as it had done in Calvin's times. Much of Mather's illuminatory providentialism changed very little in the eighteenth century. The God of temporal judgments and communications never strayed too far from his consciousness, rational religion made little impact on his own piety, and to the end of his life he scrutinized stray Bible leafs he found in the street to see if they bore him personal messages.[1] He never lost his belief in magic and sorcery, nor his belief that those who quested after that sort of illicit knowledge and power were turning themselves over to the Devil. It has even been argued that far from adapting to new cultural trends, Mather's reaction to the early Enlightenment was to plunge into subjectivity and irrationality.[2] The evidence does not support that conclusion; Mather was no more irrational or subjective at the end of his career than he had been at its beginning.

Yet Mather clearly knew by his career's end that more people were prepared to describe him as irrational than had been at its start. Polite society had different standards than the ones Mather had grown up with. Political stances had become culturally normative ones, and cultural hierarchies themselves had been rearranged. As a result, popular technologies of divination were no longer the concern, horrified or otherwise, of educated ministers. One risked being labeled a melancholy visionary should one preach too fervently on God's wrath, risked cultural isolation if one stood too firmly on theological niceties, and risked being labeled credulous by one's co-religionists if one asserted too strongly a wonder-working Providence. One could only hope nervously that the more the pensive and polite part of mankind examined evangelical religion—however uneasily that religion could be fitted into the new, benevolent, stable providential world order—the more they would justify it. If Mather preserved the emphases of seventeenth-century Puritan providentialism much of the time, still he noted the new pressures by increasingly yielding up discursive space in his sermons and treatises to various strategies of compromise and adaptation, spatial marks of the process by which those pressures broke up the seventeenth-century community of the godly.

That was just the effect those cultural pressures had been intended to have, and changing political and social configurations in England and Massachusetts only reinforced them. Mather lived out the consequences. In the *Magnalia*, he acted as the spokesman for a godly culture of wonders that he regarded as codeterminous with the Massachusetts polity, but thereafter, he began to lose faith in Massachusetts as a supernaturally defined community, and coeval with that loss of faith was a loss of faith in the political power of prophecy. Mather could no longer find in his cultural, political, and social surroundings authorization for seventeenth-century-styled close and extensive readings and applications of God's arguments and signs.

On one occasion, Mather rhetorically threw up his hands entirely over his traditional oracular role. In 1715, while enumerating the "clouds of darkness" obscuring Providence, he admitted his inability to understand God's intentions: "It is our Duty to *wait with Patience until the Time of the End*; and bear *patiently* what is done by our God, tho' as yet we *know not*, why he does it."[3] No earlier Puritan would have ever made such an admission, at least not without following it with a discourse on the wonders and power of God's sovereign will, but no earlier Puritan had to deal with such a bewildering context. In his struggles, Mather offers a valuable glimpse into the pressures at work on a vigorous and sensitive, albeit not particularly original, thinker as he tried to make his way through the early Enlightenment's new sites of cultural power with an old map.

✳

Cotton Mather is unique among Massachusetts ministers in the breadth of his interests and in the amount of documentation about him that has survived. But the same cultural pressures that affected him resonated in the province at large, although presumably without the same intensity in the hinterland as in cosmopolitan Boston.[4] Indeed, it is somewhat misleading to present Mather simply as a sufferer of the Enlightenment at the expense of neglecting his role as its transmitter. When Cotton Mather, D.D., F.R.S., possessor of the largest library in British North America and correspondent with many members of Great Britain's learned elite, equivocated on prodigies, scoffed at magic, fudged on witches, praised reason, hedged on the sufficiency of grace, and retreated from the jeremiad, he sent powerful signals to his brethren about what constituted legitimate areas of religious concern for cultured ministers. He pointed out a path of cultural accommodation that others, less rooted in their Puritan traditions, gladly followed. Ministers who were Mather's age and younger joined in his complicated process of accommodation to new providential configurations.

The Massachusetts election sermons from 1701 to 1728, the year of Mather's death, exemplify that process of accommodation. Those sermons were the most important civic sermons given in Massachusetts, delivered every year toward the end of May to the assembled government of Massachusetts, as the House of Representatives made its selections for the Governor's Council. The impact of the sermons increased by their publication, with three copies distributed to each town, in order that the towns' representatives, clergyman, and leading gentlemen stay abreast of the province's self-representation.[5] At the very least, the sermons indicate the state of acceptable religious discourse within Massachusetts orthodoxy.

In the period from 1701 to 1728, a wide range of ministers delivered the sermons. Leading figures from the second generation of ministers like Increase Mather and Solomon Stoddard preached, as did lesser known contemporaries, ministers like Jeremiah Shepard, who had led the countryside into Boston in the Andros uprising, and Jonathan Estabrooks, whose family had migrated to New England at the time of the Restoration. Younger prominent "catholick" Boston ministers like Benjamin Colman and the future president of Harvard Benjamin Wadsworth preached, but the rulers of Massachusetts also heard from the extraordinary frontier evangelist Samuel Moodey.[6] The very oldest preachers might have heard the great Puritan preachers Thomas Shepard or John Cotton as children; the youngest had at most only the dimmest memories of Old Charter Massachusetts. Thus, the sermons represent a cross section of the varieties of Massachusetts preaching and experience.

In the seventeenth century, the providential framework within which ministers delivered their election sermons remained constant. God was omnipotent, overpowering, often bad-tempered, and dramatically at work in His creation. He led the Puritans to New England, was in a covenantal relationship with them analogous to that which he had with ancient Israel, and looked after them. He rewarded them, punished them, and determined the health of their venture according to how faithfully they carried out the duties of the Two Tables of the Law. The providentialism of the first settlers remained intact in the election sermons of the seventeenth century.[7]

What happened to the seventeenth-century divinatory providentialism in the election sermons of the early eighteenth century? Did the preachers retain the old conception of Providence in these sermons in a new guise? If not, to what extent did the new clothes make for a new doctrine? The election sermon was not a place to discuss witches, cabbage roots, or even the reading of stray Bible leaves. Nevertheless, through it, the development of the providentialism within which those phenomena were contained can be traced.

In the early eighteenth century the oldest ministers giving election sermons carried on in the traditional manner. All ten ministers born before 1660 framed their sermons in the language of high supernaturalism and New England's divine guidance, the same strange mixture of exaltation, abasement, and supernatural agency that prevailed in the seventeenth century. The older ministers were almost entirely united in perceiving God as being in a controversy with Massachusetts. They praised the glorious works the Lord had done for His People in New England, and they lamented the terrible decline in piety those people had subsequently manifested. The supernatural realm was still close and overpowering in their sermons.[8] Given the immediacy and involvement of the supernatural world, it is not surprising that the older ministers scrutinized their province and their times for the "argumentes and synges" of their angry deity, using the time-honored techniques of providential divination.

John Russell's extended jeremiad of 1704, to take one example, displayed the techniques in their fullness. His guiding assumption was that Massachusetts remarkably resembled ancient Israel. Therefore, God's present work and His words clarified each other, as the Restoration providential treatise writers had maintained, and Russell had no inhibitions about elucidating their relationship: "That has been in some remarkable manner accomplished upon us which was spoken of Israel of old, *Lo, the People shall dwell alone, they shall not be reckoned among the Nations, Numb. 23.9.* And that also, Chap. 24.9. *Blessed is he that blesseth thee, and cursed is he that curseth thee.*"[9] But God was angry with Massachusetts, and the form of that anger was also foreshadowed in the scriptures: "God has done by us, as he speaks, *Ezek. 7.24. Wherefore I will bring the worst of the Heathen upon them.*"[10]

God was chastising Massachusetts not only with external enemies but also with internal conflict: "We have had our Errors and Evils; our Sins and Follies, both personal and Publick." It was possible that through those internal sins "hereby God accomplishes upon us the threatening denounced, *Isa. 3.1, 2, 3. For behold the Lord the Lord of Hosts doth take away from Jerusalem and Judah, the Stay and the Staff.*" Divination through scripture verse even allowed Russell a certain amount of prophecy: "There are some Prognosticks so apparent upon us, that . . . there's reason to look upon our case as brought to this sad *dilemma, That either we must be put into some hotter furnace than we have yet known . . .* or expect to undergo a Divine but woeful dereliction, as they did *whom God gave up to their own hearts lust, Psal. 81.12."* [11]

In other words, the Bible offered for Russell, as it did for the earlier Puritans, a technology for interpreting contemporary events and divining their outcome. All the older ministers but Belcher used motifs of the jeremiad in their sermons, and most of them offered general axioms for providential interpretation. [12] The older ministers had no problem evoking out of their cultural framework a wrathful, active God, leaving His ominous marks on the theater of the world for those with the techniques to read them. They were at home in the divinatory culture of the Renaissance out of which Reformed orthodoxy emerged.

Appropriately enough, the last of those old ministers, Jeremiah Shepard, youngest son of Thomas Shepard, preached an election sermon in 1715 that he intended as a "Memorial" to "the mercies shewed by the God of *Israel* to his People in the Wilderness." Shepard was closely attuned to a wonder-working God. He said of rainfall at the end of the previous summer's drought "God did secretly and unaccountably (I had almost said miraculously) Reserve a blessing for us." As his father had done in the election sermon of 1638, Shepard exulted in "the many sweet returns of Prayer we have had! . . . God hath made his Arm Glorious, and Glorified that Title among us that he is, *A God hearing Prayer.*" [13] He sounded a familiar refrain when speaking of the settlement of Massachusetts:

> And oh the powerful calling voice of God to gather his People into the Wilderness! And they were a choice select Number, whom God with his Glorious Arm did bring hither to lay the foundations of the Everlasting Gospel . . . and God has granted Prosperity to these blessed Enterprizes . . . Oh how hath God prospered our small Beginnings, and given us Towns and Buildings, and Blessings of all sorts, and hath sown our Land with the Seed of Man and Beast. [14]

Shepard's exultation in the supernatural guidance of New England can stand as a mark of the distance in sensibility between older and younger ministers. When Cotton Mather's occasional antagonist, the liberal Benjamin Colman (b. 1673), pitched on the same theme of the Great Migration in 1723, he struck a significantly altered tune:

> Altho' God has *never* . . . since [the Old Testament] . . . assayed to go and take him a Nation from the midst of another nation, by temptations and signs and wonders, by a stretched out arm and great terrors, as he did for the *Children of*

Israel; yet the presence of God with our *Fathers* . . . was very remarkable in bringing them into this Land, making room before them, and drawing out the Nation that before possess'd it . . . Indeed we cannot say, that God gave them a subdued and improved Land for which they did not labour . . . But God it was that gave them Wisdom and Courage and Strength, a heart to subdue a waste Wilderness, and to fill it with Towns and Villages.[15]

For Colman, God did not subdue the land, English people did, and God's signs and wonders were limited to sending diseases among the Indians and fortifying the resolve of the English. In Colman's variation on the errand into the wilderness, he accomplished two ends. One was to discourage the conceptualizing of an actively overwhelming God and a correspondingly dependent generation of "fathers," the other was to suggest God's Providence was no less real for flowing quietly through the ordinary channels of cause and effect. Colman, in the manner of the Restoration Anglicans, carefully qualified the power of Providence, subdued its off-balancing wonder, and made it more overtly operative through ordinary second causes.

Colman was far from alone in his recasting of Providence. Peter Thatcher (b. 1677) was to say in 1725, "GOD gives as really & truly . . . in the *Ordinary* Methods of Providence, as in the *Extraordinary*." If the people set up a good government and good men served in it, Thatcher explained, that was as much the activity of Providence as if God accomplished the same ends through "the most miraculous Operations and Appearances." Providence was to be found in the ordinary and regular, not in the wondrous. God, according to Ebenezer Pemberton (b. 1672) in 1710, "governs not by unaccountable Will, or incontested humor . . . but by *Stable Measures*." It was not the younger ministers but the older ones who filled their discourses with references to "Gods wonderworking Providences," or Providence's "Mysteries," "so wonderful and sometimes so amazeing."[16]

What was to take the place of the disruptive, mysterious, and wondrous was the natural and reasonable, as these had been conceptualized by the Restoration Anglicans. Nine sermons by the fifteen ministers born after 1660 made significant appeals to reason and/or nature.[17] Six of the sermons accenting reason or nature placed little or no stress on supernatural intervention, and most of those that did stress this theme mingled it with others in a new fashion. Authority was becoming literally disenchanted. For example, Colman in 1718 thought it worthwhile to go on at length to prove "our Obligation to a General Kindness and Public Spirit from the light of Nature," and he appealed to his auditors' love of country as a "kind of Instinct in Nature which is unaccountable and irresistible." In 1719, Nathaniel Stone (b. 1667) demonstrated that the public support of ministers was "reasonable from the very light of Nature and usage of Nations."[18]

Moreover, a number of ministers, speaking out of the commodified providentialism of the early Enlightenment, observed that nature and reason coincided nicely with self-interest, not just for ministers but for the entire province. Robert Breck (b. 1682) stated it most baldly when he claimed in 1728 that "Happiness is what all Mankind are in eager pursuit of, in this there is an unanimous agreement . . . The acquiring of this Happiness is what every Rational Being will endeavour." Furthermore "there is another desire . . . in which Men almost universally agree; *scil*. the Good and Welfare of their Posterity."[19] How to reach such sensible goals?

The answer, as Breck and others observed, was religion. "Living obediently to God's preceptive will . . . has a direct *natural* tendency in many regards, to promote the outward good & welfare," Benjamin Wadsworth (b. 1670) announced to his auditors in 1716. Religion "would in a Natural way serve to increase the Welfare of a People," William Williams (b. 1665) claimed in 1719. "Religion has both a *natural* and *moral* tendency to promote the Prosperity of a People," John Hancock (b. 1671) said, "If Religion flourishes the country will flourish; Our *Merchandize* will flourish . . . our *Fishery* will flourish . . . Our *Husbandry* will flourish." Indeed, so natural was religion, Robert Breck claimed in 1728, that "The Law of Self Preservation leads to it, which is not impressed on the Rational, but the Brutal World too."[20] Older ministers had not condescended to argue about the natural benefits of religion: a country prospered because its people's activities were acceptable to God. "They sought and Served God, God prospered them," as Norton put it. While earlier ministers did not deny the value of the "light of Nature," they kept it clearly subordinate to divine guidance. As Stoddard said, "We should attend the light of Nature, search the Scriptures, and beg the teachings of the Spirit of God."[21]

A few of the younger ministers in this most ceremonial and public of sermons in the Massachusetts year continued to speak in an undiluted language of high supernaturalism.[22] But for most of them, nature, the realm of second causes, was covering over the direct experience of Providence. Although no one questioned the reality of a God of judgments, many of the sermons of the younger ministers lacked precisely the ominous and portentous sense of Providence. The doctrine remained unchanged, but the application was much altered. "Catholicks" Pemberton, Colman, Hancock, and Wadsworth mentioned the possibility of judgments and divine responses to human behavior, but as possibilities, not as ongoing situations, and only in passing asides.[23] Stone did not mention them at all. The wrath of God was scarcely to be seen in those ministers' sermons. Only Danforth made a broad axiomatic statement about the working of Providence in the manner of the older ministers, and Ebenezar Thayer (b. 1689) delivered a jeremiad using only the close scriptural techniques of the older ministers and invoking a thoroughly angry God.[24]

Even when ministers did resort to jeremiad-type approaches and oracular stances, they often betrayed Anglican influences. Not infrequently they regarded the authoritarian appeal to the scriptures for their providential divination as insufficient. Two of the ministers, while not overtly questioning old formulas about God's interventions in temporal matters, made appeals not to the intrinsic authority of the Bible, but to reason. Peter Thatcher in 1726, for example, assured his audience of the empirical and nonpartisan basis of the jeremiad: "I suppose upon the strictest search and the best Judgment, it will be found, that generally, and for the most part, these Blessings are given, when a People in Covenant are Upright and Faithful in it. Were it at all needful here, I could for Proof draw together very many Instances from the most unquestionable Records, Sacred & Common."[25]

In 1719 the Connecticut Valley evangelist William Williams struggled to swath an old-style authoritarian jeremiad within the new-style talismanic protection of reason. God had a reasonable controversy with Massachusetts, he explained to his distinguished audience, and he demonstrated his claim with a thoroughly reasonable chain of logic. "Every Man's reason must . . . acknowledge it to be fit that GOD should govern the World," he began. Anticipating no dissent to that proposition, he asked, "Is there any reason to question, whether the *Laws* we profess to be govern'd by, *be from* GOD," and therefore, "have we any reason to *except against the Laws* which GOD *hath given us?*" Moving onward, he said, "If we acknowledge any part of the Word of GOD to be true, we have reason to acknowledge His Promises and Threatenings to be so," which claim brought him to the completion of his edifice: "It is then highly Reasonable that a Declining People should put a stop to their Degeneracies, and be obedient to the Voice of GOD." Williams threw in for good measure that no one could "reasonably object" against wanting to go to heaven and behaving in a way that might offer hope of the possibility of that goal.[26]

If the younger ministers in general emphasized human authority and played down overt irruptions of the supernatural, it is not surprising that some ministers went beyond tacit shifting of providential priorities and assumptions and searching for new sources of authority. Two of them openly indicated dissatisfaction with the old tight providential formulas for discerning the signs of the times.

John Rogers (b. 1666) in 1706 was the first election sermon minister to

question the scriptural authority for providential interpretations of Massachusetts affairs. God's acts, Rogers argued, were not bound by the scriptures, "nor
can we argue from Scripture examples that the Providence of God towards the
Nations shall in all Circumstances be conformable to his dealings with the
Jews." As a "late Learned PRIMATE of our Nation" (Tillotson, unattributed) had
argued, God punishes and rewards nations for their behavior on earth, not
because of any eternal covenant with his Church, but because nations, unlike
individuals, cannot receive their just deserts in the afterlife.[27] In other words,
according to Rogers, specific parallels between biblical Israel and Massachusetts were invalid.

Like Rogers, Robert Breck in 1728 indicated his doubts about trying to
divine the meaning of current events in New England too strictly within an
Old Testament framework. He noted that "*Divines* of great fame" argued that
"GOD doth observe the same exactness in conferring *temporal Blessings*, and
inflicting *Punishments* under the Gospel, as of old under the *Sinai Covenant*
Administration . . . but it may be questioned whether the Argument, wherewith they endeavour to confirm their Opinion, be forcible." While Rogers was
at least sure that national judgments were in response to national sins, Breck
was not even entirely positive about that. "No reason can be assigned why a
Holy GOD for wise Ends may not bring great distressing Judgments on *Ten
Thousand* Good Men tho' they are formed into Civil Society, as well as upon
Job who was *perfect* and *upright*, by GOD's own acknowledgement."[28] Breck con-
tented himself with a vague and mild formula for interpreting Providence:
"this is the general way of GOD in his Providence, to *Honour those that Honour
Him, and to exalt a Righteous Nation.*"[29]

Both Breck and Rogers were Janus-faced in their providentialism, Rogers
especially so, ambivalent as to whether they were talking out of the old godly
culture or arguing with it. When Rogers came to the jeremiadic part of his sermon, he discarded his cloak of Anglican rationality. Invoking God's wrath and
forgetting his earlier caution about extrapolating from the example of Israel,
Rogers buttressed his case for declension and God's displeasure in the time-
honored manner for providential divining with extensive scripture citation.[30]

Like Rogers, Breck eventually turned, ambiguously, to jeremiadic formulas. That turn was not surprising, given that the province recently had suffered
severe storms, a drought, and an earthquake; if any ministers saw the last as
anything but a message from an angry God, they kept that opinion out of
print.[31] Unlike Rogers, Breck did not linger on the wrath of God, and his suggestion for the appeasement of the Deity further demonstrated the Anglican
influence on his thought. What was needed, according to Breck, disseminator

of the *Spectator* to other rural Massachusetts ministers, was more morality: "To promote practical Religion should be the great end of our Ministers: This is what is worthy to expend our zeal upon, and not in unhappy jangles about speculative Opinions that have no influence on our Morals." Dissenter religiosity itself, according to moralizing Anglicans, amounted to little more than the unhappy jangling of speculative opinions, and Breck, realizing that his discursive borrowing had him skating on thin ice, hastened to relocate himself properly: "I would not be understood to intimate as if Moral vertues were to be insisted upon only or principally in our Preaching & inculcated upon our auditory: No, Faith in JESUS CHRIST and Repentance unto Life are the great Doctrines of the Gospel."[32] Breck got back to the fold of orthodoxy (more easily than his son and namesake a few years later in Hampshire County), but it had been touch and go for a while.

✳

Breck preached his election sermon in the year of Mather's death, and that sermon demonstrates the complexity that Massachusetts providentialism had acquired. For most of the younger ministers, the old divinatory techniques were beginning to be unsatisfactory. Reading the signs of the times became for some problematic, for others more a tradition than a living force, except in exceptional circumstances. The younger ministers were less inclined to vivid personifications of God's agency and less inclined to describe God's relationship with Massachusetts consistently in terms of influx of supernatural power or in intimate emotional terms. Thus by the year of Cotton Mather's death, the Anglican effort to "disenchant" the Puritans' Providence had made significant and general inroads into one of the last bulwarks of Reformed orthodoxy in Christendom.

Do these transformations point to fundamental changes in Massachusetts orthodoxy? Harry S. Stout has recently argued that although ministers in their election sermons may have "embraced new terminologies that enjoyed secular meanings in England," in New England, these were "turned into a traditional defense of inherited religious beliefs and values." For all the integration of new vocabulary, "providential themes and biblical allusions continued to dominate the discourse in terms that could be distinguished from earlier election sermons only by their more expansive literary style."[33]

Doctrinally Stout is correct: All the ministers preaching election sermons considered themselves orthodox. Yet when doctrine is embedded in changed imagery, changed usage, and changed sources of authority, it becomes difficult to regard the result as a traditional defense of inherited religious beliefs. To emphasize generalized morality and repentance rather than the all-sufficiency of Christ and His sacrifice or the intricate stages of conversion and regeneration; to appeal to reason rather than to scripture or the occult literacy conveyed by the Holy Spirit or God's sovereign power; to refer to the natural benefits of religion along with, or in place of, its supernatural benefits; to question the exactitude of providential divination and to back away from the traditional ministerial role of seer—all this was to encourage conceptions of the divine and the human relationship to the divine very different from what earlier generations in Massachusetts, let alone Calvin, would have recognized.

Slowly and ambiguously, without disavowing the formulas of earlier creeds, the ministers of Massachusetts were redefining the nature and boundaries of religion and religiosity. Younger ministers were increasingly accepting their reconstitution as religious subjects within the discursive patterns of the early Enlightenment even as those patterns reconstituted the objects of their religious discourse. If secularization is defined as a diminishment of belief in, and experience of, the frequent and powerful intervention of the supernatural in the natural and human worlds, then Massachusetts ministers were indeed becoming secularized.[34] But it should be noted that the reconfiguration of Providence that they were processing through their Puritan heritage originated as a deliberately chosen religious option, formed to a great extent in response to religious and Puritan provocations.

Ministerial discomfort with the more overt manifestations of the supernatural by the turn of the eighteenth century thus did not emerge out of a presumed dialectical tension in Puritanism, as some historians have maintained.[35] Ministers might have always been, in general, somewhat more resistant to overt signs and wonders than some of the laity, but they held a similar overall conception of the supernatural economy. Puritanism, at least in the second half of the seventeenth century, was far from being an agent of modernization, if modernization is to be identified with a desacralized experience of existence. Its proponents actively resisted Max Weber's "disenchantment of the world." They remained in dialogue, albeit a taut and angry one, with magic and divination.

Nor were Massachusetts Puritan ministers acting in provincial isolation by retaining that dialogue. During the Restoration period, Massachusetts culture indeed went a separate way from English Anglican culture, but it remained largely indistinguishable from English orthodox Dissenter culture. Its isolation was the isolation of the English Dissenters, and that isolation had a large component of deliberate resistance in it. In *An Essay for the Recording of Illustrious Providences* and *Magnalia Christi Americana* Massachusetts produced two of the most important intellectual documents of Dissenting culture. The reluctance of Massachusetts to settle down to imperial authority after the Restoration had its counterpart in the stream of plots hatched by Dissenters in the British Isles. Even so quintessentially American a document as Mary Rowlandson's providentially rich tale of her capture by the Indians was paralleled by English Dissenter tales of captivity and release, also published for the displaying of God's providential power.[36]

When Weberian disenchantment began creeping tortuously into Puritan orthodoxy from the 1680s onwards, in old and New England, it came from cultural impulses alien to Puritanism. It came from the prestige of the new learning and of preachers like Tillotson, prestige that reinforced and helped to define shifting political, institutional, and discursive configurations. Change came about because Massachusetts ministers, like the Dissenting culture of which they were a part, were forced gradually into a dialogue with aggressive external agencies of change. The ministers, besides being in a dialogue with their own godly community, were in a dialogue with a larger changing learned culture in which they shared, whose imperatives they ignored only at the peril of losing much of their own cultural authority. At least in the sphere of providentialism, the progression from Puritan to Yankee in Massachusetts orthodoxy was fueled by external factors, factors outside Massachusetts and outside Puritanism.

It is hardly surprising that Massachusetts ministers responded to English intellectual and social trends powerful enough to break down the resistance of their English brethren. The weakening of resistance on both sides of the Atlantic marked the end of what has long been termed, rightly or wrongly, the "Heroic Age" of Puritanism.[37] Massachusetts's Restoration isolation is usually brought into relief by its contrast with the "Anglicization" of the 1690s. It is more accurate, at least as far as religion is concerned, to look at those ministers as part of a process of Anglicanization, not simply Anglicization, for the ministers of Massachusetts had never ceased being Anglicized. It was only in the early decades of the eighteenth century, as even prominent English Congregationalists started to bid John Calvin goodnight, that New England orthodoxy, in any sense, began to be isolated from English religious developments.[38]

✳

In the eighteenth century, Massachusetts ministers found themselves to be genuinely intellectually provincial, aware of religious developments in England, but reluctant to embrace them as wholeheartedly as many of their Dis-

senting brethren in the home country. Now it would take the cultural politics
of events in Massachusetts itself to tighten that embrace. The Great Awakening of 1740–45, complete with itinerant preachers, broken parishes, no shortage of signs and wonders, and anarchy in interpretive frameworks, repeated as
a provincial coda the social disruptions stemming from the religious creativity
of the English Civil Wars. Its intellectual consequences likewise paralleled on
a provincial level the consequences of that earlier episode. For supporters and
opponents of the Great Awakening alike, the tumult of that event precipitated
redefinition of the boundaries of acceptable providential discourse.

Opponents of the Awakening, some perhaps already with a "soft center"
to their Calvinism, could seize upon interpretive options opened up in the
previous century to refuse the Awakening any legitimacy at all.[39] Charles
Chauncy, in his well-subscribed *Seasonable Thoughts on the State of Religion in
New England* (Boston 1743), conjured up old New England bogeys like Anne
Hutchinson and the Quakers to discredit the Great Awakening. But unlike
ministers a hundred years earlier, he felt no need to invoke diabolic possession
or witchcraft or the wrath of God to explain religious phenomena of which he
disapproved. Instead he used the approach of the Anglican opponents of Puritanism, denying that the revivals required supernatural explanations of any
sort. Chauncy accounted for them almost completely in naturalistic psychological terms, with only a very occasional passing reference to the influence of
Satan. While Chauncy remained an orthodox Calvinist, at least for the time
being, other ministers grew alarmed enough at the social effects of the religiosity of the Awakening to come out as overt Arminians.[40]

But it was not only the opponents of the Awakening for whom the turmoil of that event altered some of the habits of thought of Reformed orthodoxy. As the Great Awakening spun itself out, its foremost defender, Jonathan
Edwards, while ready enough to see the hand of God or Satan in events, grew
increasingly and vocally alarmed at its disruption of New England's hierarchical social order. He traced the root of that disruption to the widespread and traditional belief among those participating in the revival that their saintliness
gave them access to privileged supernatural information, to revelations, "the
error that will support all errors."[41] By 1743 he was attacking revelations of
temporal events unaccommodatingly, and while he admitted, grudgingly, that
God might send scripture verses to the mind in mysterious ways (although the
capacity for self-delusion here was enormous), he denied that those verses
could communicate anything beyond the doctrinal information they signified
on the printed page.[42]

In 1743 he also began presenting accounts of exemplars of Reformed piety that edited out those Christians' reception and transmission of privileged information.[43] In the most famous of his examples, his 1749 biography of the missionary David Brainerd, Edwards stressed repeatedly, and not entirely correctly, that Brainerd's piety lacked entirely "any sudden suggestions of words or sentences, either words of Scripture or any other." Therefore, that piety, with its lack of overt supernatural authorization, also demonstrated that true religion could be "an amiable thing, of happy tendency, and of no hurtful consequences to human society." In a related gesture, Edwards, like earlier Anglicans, dropped the central Reformed conception of Christ's substitutionary atonement because of the perceived supernatural empowerment it bestowed on its beneficiaries.[44] Edwards's followers accelerated his retreat from a providentialism based on close contact with supernatural agents, and the *Life of Brainerd* went on to become one of the formative books for nineteenth-century evangelical culture.[45] Tillotson would have understood.

With Edwards and the Arminians indicating the poles of ministerial enthusiasm for a religion of wonders, the educated discourse of later-eighteenth-century Massachusetts provided only limited room for a seventeenth-century providential sensibility. Those who wished to participate in that discourse had to make the necessary adjustments. For example, Isaac Backus started his career as an unordained itinerant during the Great Awakening, and he eventually became a Baptist minister. Unengaged in a dialogue with learned culture at this time, he knew what it was to have a text supernaturally hurled into his mind, and he recorded God's judgments against persecutors of the Baptists and noted "remarkable providences."[46] By the 1770s, Backus had risen to be the respectable leader of New England Dissent. Like Dissenters in England a century earlier, he discovered the polemical advantages of early Enlightenment rationalism while arguing for religious tolerance. Accordingly, when Backus wrote his history of New England in 1777, he passed over judgments and remarkable providences in silence. While he acknowledged that New England's history was as much like Canaan's as any other place's had been, he plotted his account of the struggles of New England Dissent against oppression not in supernaturalistic language, but rather in the Whig language of the corrupting nature of power.[47]

At the popular level, however, the world remained subjected to intense supernatural irruptions and messages. Evangelical sects perceived the immediate hand of God in the famous "Dark Day" of 1780. People across New England saw armies and battles in the sky in the troubled year of 1787. Popular suspicions of witchcraft were raised against a heretic like Ann Lee at the end of the eighteenth century just as they had been against Anne Hutchinson in the

1630s. Semi-educated popular religious leaders of the early nineteenth century were explicit about the role that dreams, visions, and supernatural encounters played in their spirituality, while a back-country New England farmer in the nineteenth century feared the imminent descent of God's wrath in an approaching storm cloud just as had John Dane two hundred years earlier.[48]

If segments of the laity remained in a world of wonders and close prophecy, that is not to imply by contrast that orthodox learned ministers abandoned providentialism in its entirety. Up through the Civil War, a significant, if shrinking, segment of New England's learned population continued to compare God's Word and His work with varying degrees of intensity at various periods to understand their times.[49] From the mid nineteenth century the very idea of providentialism fell under increasing attack by materialistic scientists, would-be scientists, and social reformers, and by the turn of the twentieth century, providentialism, as well as the doctrine of Providence itself, had largely disappeared from mainstream academic religious circles.[50]

Perhaps unsurprisingly the disappearance of providentialism paralleled the disappearance of Calvinism itself, both vestiges of Renaissance structures of knowledge crumbling before the onslaughts of naturalistic scientism and progressive social reform. Already two hundred years earlier, however, as Massachusetts ministers followed in the wake of English learned culture, they left behind them the close presence and close communication of the providentialism of the earlier Reformed tradition. The God who troubled the growth of cabbage roots, darted scripture verses into people's minds, and brought the Puritans with an outstretched arm across the Atlantic was in retreat from Massachusetts orthodoxy, driven out by the cultural politics of the seventeenth century.

Notes

✳

Introduction

1. To begin, see Keith Thomas, *Religion and the Decline of Magic: Studies in Popular Belief in Sixteenth- and Seventeenth-Century England* (London, 1971), chap. 4. My considerable debt to this work will be obvious to those familiar with it. David D. Hall, *Worlds of Wonder, Days of Judgment: Popular Religious Beliefs in Early New England* (New York, 1989), chap. 2, is also very useful. Paul S. Seaver, *Wallington's World: A Puritan Artisan in Seventeenth-Century London* (London, 1985), is a magnificent re-creation of the providential sensibility of an orthodox Puritan. Blair Worden, "Providence and Politics in Cromwellian England," *Past and Present* 109 (1985), 55–99, is a fine introduction to the intricacies of providential terminology and its practical application; see also ibid., "Oliver Cromwell and the Sin of Achan," in *History, Society, and the Churches*, ed. Derek Beales and Geoffrey Best (Cambridge, 1985), 125–45. For other studies on Puritan providentialism, see Barbara Donegan, "Providence, Chance and Explanation: Some Paradoxical Aspects of Puritan Views of Causation," *Journal of Religious History* 11 (1981), 385–403, ibid., "Godly Choice: Puritan Decision-Making in Seventeenth-Century England," *Harvard Theological Review* 76 (1983), 307–34, and Margo Todd, "Providence, Chance and the New Science in Early Stuart Cambridge," *Historical Journal* 29 (1986), 697–711. John Spurr, "'Virtue, Religion and Government': The Anglican Uses of Providence," in *The Politics of Restoration England*, ed. Timothy Harris, Paul Seawood, and Mark Goldie (Oxford, 1990), 29–47, provides a somewhat simplified overview of Restoration Anglican providentialism. An overview of Restoration Dissenting providentialism does not exist. There is one full-length study of the transformation of Massachusetts providentialism, Peter Lockwood Rumsey, *Acts of God and the People, 1620–1730* (Ann Arbor, 1986). While it has some shrewd readings of texts, Rumsey's book largely demonstrates the perils of trying to write strictly internalist accounts of Massachusetts's intellectual history.

2. Thomas, *Religion*, is the standard introduction to the "culture of wonders." Michael MacDonald, *Mystical Bedlam: Madness, Anxiety and Healing in Seventeenth-Century England* (Cambridge, 1981), is the best introduction to the psychology of the period.

3. See Patrick Curry, *Prophecy and Power: Astrology in Early Modern England* (Princeton, 1989), Brian Easlea, *Witch-hunting, Magic, and the New Philosophy: An Introduction to the Debates of the Scientific Revolution 1450–1750* (Brighton, 1980), James R. Jacob, *Henry Stubbe, Radical Protestantism and the Early Enlightenment* (Cambridge, 1983), ibid., *Robert Boyle and the English Revolution: A Study in Social and Intellectual*

Change (New York, 1977), Margaret C. Jacob, *Newtonians and the English Revolution, 1689–1720* (Ithaca, 1976), James R. and Margaret C. Jacob, "The Anglican Origins of Modern Science: The Metaphysical Foundations of the Whig Constitution," *Isis* 71 (1980), 251–67, Michael MacDonald, "Religion, Social Change, and Psychological Healing in England, 1600–1800," in *The Church and Healing*, ed. W. J. Shiels (Oxford, 1982), 101–25. Ideological interpretations of Restoration science have generated considerable debate, but even one of the foremost critics of such interpretations, Michael Hunter, acknowledges that practices like alchemy and astrology were looked on as potentially subversive and "enthusiastic" in Restoration England and clashed with the dominant culture's standards of reasonableness and clarity, standards to which people attempting to do "normative" science adhered. See Hunter's introduction to his edited volume, *Robert Boyle Reconsidered* (Cambridge, 1994), 14.

4. Thomas also stresses the separation of religion and magic by the end of the seventeenth century in *Religion and the Decline of Magic*, but he basically attributes "the decline of the old magical beliefs" not to the disruptions of the mid seventeenth century but to "the growth of urban living, the rise of science, and the spread of an ideology of self-help" (665). The rise of science itself he treats as unproblematic. While he notes the Restoration campaigns against enthusiasm, he seems to consider an ideology of nonsuperstitious self-help essential to Protestantism, as if reliance on the supernatural somehow "forced [Protestantism] against its own premises" (77). Thomas has had his critics, and historians of early New England have continued the debate about the relationship between Puritanism and magic. For a good recent assessment of the relationship of early Protestantism to magic, see Robert W. Scribner, "The Reformation, Popular Magic, and the 'Disenchantment of the World,'" *Journal of Interdisciplinary History* 13 (1993), 475–94. For New England, see Richard Weisman, *Witchcraft, Magic, and Religion in Seventeenth-Century Massachusetts* (Amherst, 1984), which argues for a sharp dichotomy between magic and religion in Massachusetts, while David D. Hall, *World of Wonders*, argues that the particular circumstances of Massachusetts made them largely inseparable. Richard Godbeer, *The Devil's Dominion: Magic and Religion in Early New England* (New York, 1992) makes magic somewhat more autonomous than Hall does.

5. For example, Harry S. Stout, in his recent synthetic history of colonial New England Congregational preaching, *The New England Soul: Preaching and Religious Culture in Colonial New England* (New York, 1986), claims that Restoration New Englanders had "fashioned an independent identity for themselves that largely ignored England . . . Only at the end of their lives, amidst revolution and royal government, did circumstances force them to take into account the Old World" (123). A notable exception to historians' tendency to portray Massachusetts in the Restoration period as isolated is David Cressy, *Coming Over: Migration and Communication between England and New England in the Seventeenth Century* (New York, 1987). Norman Fiering, *Moral Philosophy at Seventeenth-Century Harvard* (Chapel Hill, 1981), pays no attention whatsoever to the issue of Massachusetts's isolation, with no perceptible harm to his text. Francis J. Bremer, *Congregational Communion: Clerical Friendship in the Anglo-American Puritan Community, 1610–1692* (Boston, 1994) amply demonstrates the continuing ties of Massachusetts and English ministers in the Restoration period.

6. David D. Hall was lamenting twenty years ago that there was no equivalent to

Miller's *The New England Mind* for Restoration Dissent, and the lament remains valid. With the recent growth of scholarly interest in the Restoration period and awareness that religious issues continued to play a crucial role in English political life, the situation will perhaps soon change. In the meantime, for good overviews of Restoration Dissent, see N. H. Keeble, *The Literary Culture of Non-Conformity in Later Seventeenth-Century England* (Athens, Ga., 1987), Isabel Rivers, *Reason Grace, and Sentiment: A Study of the Language of Religion and Ethics in England, 1660–1780*, vol. 1, *Withcote to Wesley* (Cambridge, 1991), Michael R. Watts, *The Dissenters: From the Reformation to the French Revolution* (Oxford, 1978), and C. E. Whiting, *Studies in English Puritanism from the Restoration to the Revolution, 1660–1688* (London, 1931).

7. For the dependence of the seventeenth-century Massachusetts political and social power structure on the authority of learned culture, see Darren Marcus Staloff, "The Making of an American Thinking Class: Intellectuals and Intelligentsia in Puritan Massachusetts" (Ph.D. diss., Columbia University, 1991). On just how closely New England learned culture stayed in touch with English trends, see Fiering, *Moral Philosophy*.

8. Hall, *Worlds of Wonder*, 4. Hall's study is the culmination of a line of argument that has been pursued by a number of historians recently. For studies that emphasize the congruence of lay and ministerial piety, see Charles E. Hambrick-Stowe, *The Practice of Piety: Puritan Devotional Disciplines in Seventeenth Century New England* (Chapel Hill, 1982), Charles Lloyd Cohen, *God's Caress: The Psychology of Puritan Religious Experience* (New York, 1986), George Selement, "The Meeting of Elite and Popular Minds at Cambridge, New England, 1638–1645," *William and Mary Quarterly*, 3d ser., 41 (1984), 32–48, David D. Hall, "Toward a History of Popular Religion in Early New England," *William and Mary Quarterly*, 3d ser., 41 (1984), 49–55, and ibid., "The World of Print and Collective Mentality in Seventeenth-Century New England," in *New Directions in American Intellectual History*, ed. John Higham and Paul K. Conklin (Baltimore, 1979), 166–80.

9. Hall, *Worlds of Wonder*, 106–8.

10. Peter Burke, *Popular Culture in Early Modern Europe* (New York, 1978), 339–42.

11. Thomas, *Religion*, 643.

12. A good starting point for the issues involved in defining Puritanism is Peter Lake, "Defining Puritanism—Again?" in *Puritanism: Transatlantic Perspectives on a Seventeenth-Century Anglo-American Faith*, ed. Francis J. Bremer (Boston, 1993), 3–29.

13. On the use of the terms "Dissenters" and "Nonconformists," see Keeble, *Literary Culture*, 41–45,

14. A satisfactory overview of the dynamic of the early English Enlightenment does not yet exist, but for a start, see John G. A. Pocock, "Clergy and Commerce: The Conservative Enlightenment in England," in *L'Età dei Lumi: Studi Storici sul Settecento Europeo in Onore di Franco Venturi*, 2 vols. (Naples, 1985), 1:523–62.

15. For a discussion of the formal relationship between providentialism and eschatology, see Stephen J. Stein, "Providence and Apocalypse in the Early Writings of Jonathan Edwards," *Early American Literature* 13 (1978–79), 250–67.

16. Andrew Delbanco, "The Puritan Errand Re-viewed," *Journal of American Studies* 18 (1984), 343–60, Theodore Dwight Bozeman, *To Live Ancient Lives: The*

Primitivist Dimension in Puritanism (Chapel Hill, 1988). They both argue convincingly that the "errand into the wilderness" is a historiographical construct based on a very few, and questionably interpreted texts.

17. Francis J. Bremer, *Puritan Crisis: New England and the English Civil Wars, 1630–1670* (New York, 1989) makes no mention of either Delbanco or Bozeman. Avihu Zakai, *Exile and Kingdom: History and Apocalypse in the Puritan Migration to America* (Cambridge, 1992), refers to Bozeman occasionally but does not engage with any of his arguments. In other writings Bremer has been attempting to salvage something of the "errand" motif in the context of Bozeman and Delbanco, most recently in *Congregational Communion*, 107–9.

Chapter One: The Providence of the Massachusetts Puritans

1. John Dane, "John Dane's Narrative," *New England Historical and Genealogical Register* 5 (1854), 155, John Norton, *Three Choice and Profitable Sermons* (Cambridge, Mass., 1664), 26. I inferred the time of year from the presence of geese and the absence of food. The opening of this chapter is adapted from Michael P. Winship, "Encountering Providence in the Seventeenth Century: The Experiences of a Yeoman and a Minister," *Essex Institute Historical Collections* 124 (1990), 27–36.

2. Cotton Mather, *Magnalia Christi Americana*, 2 vols. (1702; reprint, Hartford, 1853), 1:290. Norton left behind him a large estate, valued at 2,095 pounds, including six acres in Ipswich purchased from "Goodman Dane." See "Abstract from the Earliest Wills on Record in the County of Suffolk, Massachusetts," *New England Historical and Genealogical Register* 11 (1857), 344, 343.

3. John Norton, *The Orthodox Evangelist* (London, 1657), 102.

4. Ibid., 110.

5. Thomas Allen, Sermon on 13 John 26, 27, 28, Russell Family Sermons and Sermon Notes, 1649, American Antiquarian Society, fols. 364v, 364r, 364v.

6. Dane, "Narrative," 155, 156.

7. J. G. A. Pocock, *Politics, Language and Time: Essays on Political Thought and History* (New York, 1971), 82. See also Jean Delumeau, *Sin and Fear: The Emergence of a Western Guilt Culture in the Thirteenth to Eighteenth Centuries*, trans. Eric Nicholson (New York, 1990), 153–68, and D. R. Woolf, *The Idea of History in Early Stuart England: Erudition, Ideology, and 'The Light of Truth' from the Accession of James I to the Civil War* (Toronto, 1990), 5–7. Both astrology and fortune could be assimilated, more or less convincingly, to Providence.

8. Michel Foucault, *The Order of Things: An Archeology of the Human Sciences* (New York, 1970), 33. That Renaissance thought was analogical in nature has been a scholarly commonplace at least since E. W. Tillyard, *The Elizabethan World Picture* (London, 1943). Foucault, *Order of Things* (chap. 2), has aggressively updated the argument and wreathed it in a mysterious archeology. For all of its scholarly shoddiness and its refusal to deal with the question of historical change, Foucault's book remains one of the most useful introductions to patterns of thought in the early modern period. See the comment in John Bossy, "Some Elementary Forms of Durkheim," *Past and Present* 95 (May 1982), 12–13. As a cautionary modification of too sweeping generalizations about a monolithic structure of Renaissance thought, see the careful distinction be-

tween rational and participatory thought processes by Debora Kuller Shuger, *Habits of Thought in the English Renaissance: Religion, Politics, and the Dominant Culture* (Berkeley, 1990), 19–20.

9. Calvin, *Treatises against the Anabaptists and Libertines*, trans. Benjamin Wirt Farley (Grand Rapids, 1982), 244, ibid., *Institutes of the Christian Religion*, ed. John T. McNeil, trans. Fred Lewis Battles, 2 vols. (Philadelphia, 1960), I.xvi.2. Although Calvin did not tend to define and distinguish between his terms with the scholastic rigor of his followers, he once defined special providence as "the manner in which God operates in His creatures [to] cause them to serve His goodness, righteousness, and judgment according to His present will to help His servants, to punish the wicked, and to test the patience of His faithful, or to chastise them in His fatherly kindness." Ibid., *Treatises*, 243–44.

10. Calvin, *Institutes*, 1.xvi.2.

11. Ibid.

12. Ibid., I.xvi.7.

13. Ibid., I.xvi.8.

14. Ibid., 1.xvii.10.

15. Ibid., I.xvii.1.

16. Ibid., I.xvii.10. William J. Bouwsma, *John Calvin: A Sixteenth-Century Portrait* (New York, 1988), interprets Calvin's theology as driven, ultimately unsuccessfully, by the need to overcome anxiety.

17. Keith Thomas, *Religion and the Decline of Magic: Studies in Popular Belief in Sixteenth- and Seventeenth-Century England* (London, 1971), 79.

18. Late-medieval nominalists rejected the earlier scholastic formulation that God had imparted an "inherent motion" in second causes (a motion that accounted for the efficacy of the sacramental means of salvation) in favor of a covenantal conception of God's sovereignty with striking similarities to Reformed conceptions of Providence. See Heiko Augustinus Oberman, *Masters of the Reformation: The Emergence of a New Intellectual Climate in Europe* (Cambridge, 1981), 166, and Francis Oakley, *Omnipotence, Covenant, and Order: An Excursion in the History of Ideas from Abelard to Leibniz* (Ithaca, 1984), 63. The doctrine of double predestination had been expounded occasionally from the patristic period onward but was not an element of late-medieval debates. For a survey of late-medieval conceptions of predestination, see Heiko Augustinus Oberman, *The Harvest of Medieval Theology: Gabriel Biel and Late Medieval Nominalism* (Cambridge, Mass., 1963), 185–215. Providence and predestination were discussed in the same chapter in all but the last edition of the *Institutes of the Christian Religion*, and Calvin never lost sight of the parallel between the two. See Francois Wendel, *John Calvin: Origins and Development of His Religious Thought* (Durham, 1987), 178. Later theologians made the connection between Providence and predestination explicit. See Heinrich Heppe, *Reformed Dogmatics set out and illustrated from the Sources*, trans. G. T. Thomson (London, 1950), 252. For a brief, lucid discussion of pre-Reformation conceptions of predestination and soteriology, see Alister E. McGrath, *Justitia Dei: A History of the Christian Doctrine of Justification*, vol. 1 (Cambridge, 1986), 128–45.

19. Calvin, *Institutes*, III.xxiv.14.

20. Ibid., III.xxiii.7.

21. John Calvin, cited in John Stachniewski, *The Persecutory Imagination: English Puritanism and the Literature of Religious Despair* (Oxford, 1991), 22.

22. Calvin, *Institutes*, III.ii.39, III.xiv.18,19.

23. Ibid., III.ii.17, III.ii.24.

24. John Calvin, *Sermons of Maister John Calvin, upon the Booke of Job* (London, 1584), 584.

25. John Calvin, cited in Stachniewski, *Persecutory Imagination*, 23. On the hypocrite's faith, see Calvin, *Institutes*, III.ii.12.

26. Calvin, *Institutes*, I.xvi.9, ibid., *Commentaries on the Book of the Prophet Jeremiah and the Lamentations*, trans. John Owen (Edinburgh, 1852), 297.

27. A recent influential article has suggested on the basis of statements of Calvin's like the above that such a gulf existed. Ronald J. VanderMolen, "Providence as Mystery, Providence as Revelation: Puritan and Anglican Modifications of John Calvin's Doctrine of Providence," *Church History* 47 (1978), 27–47, has claimed flatly that Calvin did not consider Providence readable, except in the stories of the Bible. But that claim comes from taking statements by Calvin like the ones cited above completely at face value and overlooking numerous examples of a more complex relationship to Providence. Scholars of seventeenth-century English providentialism have tended to accept uncritically VanderMolen's assertion. See Paul S. Seaver, *Wallington's World: A Puritan Artisan in Seventeenth-Century London* (London, 1985), 46–47, 219n. 1, Barbara Donegan, "Providence Chance and Explanation: Some Paradoxical Aspects of Puritan Views of Causation," *Journal of Religious History* 11 (1981), 390n. 9, Margo Todd, "Providence, Chance and the New Science in Early Stuart Cambridge," *Historical Journal* 29 (1986), 700n. 14, and Winship, "Encountering Providence," 30n. 12.

28. John Calvin, *Commentaries on the Four Last Books of Moses, Arranged in the Form of a Harmony*, trans. Charles William Bingham (Edinburgh, 1854), 223, ibid., *Sermons of Maister John Calvin*, 343.

29. Calvin, *Commentaries on Moses*, 256, ibid., *Commentaries on Lamentations*, 295, ibid., *Sermons of Maister John Calvin*, 625.

30. *Letters of John Calvin Compiled from the Original Manuscripts and edited with Historical Notes by Dr. Jules Bonnet*, 4 vols. (Philadelphia, n.d.), 4:408, 160, 414, 1:245, 4:314, 1:367.

31. Ibid., 4:405–7, Delumeau, *Sin and Fear*, 136. On the reverberations of the pope-ass through the Reformation and Counter-Reformation, see Konrad Lange, *Der Papstesel: Ein Beitrag zur Kultur- und Kunstgeschichte des Reformationszeitalters* (Göttingen, 1891).

32. *Letters of Calvin*, 2:190, 4:32, 1:417, 1:376.

33. The quotation is from a citation in Stuart Clark, "French Historians and Early Modern Popular Culture," *Past and Present* 100 (1983), 84. Clark is concerned with ritual and magic, not religious doctrines; my point is to stress their relation.

34. The most apt comparison is with the priestly magus, for which see Frances A. Yates, *Giordano Bruno and the Hermetic Tradition* (London, 1964).

35. John Calvin, *Commentaries on the First Book of Moses called Genesis*, trans. John King (Edinburgh, 1847), 479. "God . . . hath a book of his resolved decrees, and a book of his acted providences; this latter is but a transcript, or a copy of the former,"

as the English Puritan Isaac Ambrose put it. See *Look unto Jesus* in *The Compleat Works of Isaac Ambrose* (London, 1673–74), 34.

36. Thomas Allen, Russell Family Sermon Notes, 292r, American Antiquarian Society.

37. John Miller, Notes of Ipswich Preachers, 1645–1646, Massachusetts Historical Society, 95, Thomas Shepard, *The Parable of the Ten Virgins Opened & Applied*, 2d ed. (London, 1695), 2d pag., 5.

38. *Letters of Calvin*, 2:112.

39. A long historiographical controversy that began with the claim of William Haller, since largely repudiated, in *The Elect Nation: The Meaning and Relevance of John Foxe's Book of Martyrs* (Evanston, 1963) that sixteenth-century English thought considered God to have singled England out for His favor can be traced through the bibliography given in Theodore Dwight Bozeman, *To Live Ancient Lives: The Primitivist Dimension in Puritanism* (Chapel Hill, 1988), 89n. 15. The most lucid discussion and summary of the various usages of the Israel/England comparison can be found in Patrick Collinson, *The Birthpangs of Protestant England: Religious and Cultural Change in Sixteenth and Seventeenth Century England* (New York, 1988), chap. 1.

40. On the primacy of religious motivation for the English migrants to Massachusetts, see Virginia DeJohn Anderson, *New England's Generation: The Great Migration and the Formation of Society and Culture in the Seventeenth Century* (New York, 1991).

41. Thomas Hooker, *The Application of Redemption, by the Effectual Work of the Word* (London, 1657), 129, 79.

42. John Norton, *Abel being Dead yet speaketh* (London, 1658), 5.

43. John Cotton, *Gods Mercie Mixed with his Justice* (London, 1641), 10. For fine discussions of the role of afflictions in mid-seventeenth-century English religiosity, see J. Sears McGee, *The Godly Man in Stuart England: Anglicans, Puritans, and the Two Tables, 1620–1670* (New Haven, 1976), chap. 2, and Peter Lake, *Moderate Puritans and the Elizabethan Church* (Cambridge, 1982), 123–25.

44. Shepard, *Parable*, 107.

45. John Davenport, *The Saints Anchor-Hold, in All Storms and Tempests* (London, 1667), 4.

46. Ibid., 11.

47. Hooker, *Application*, 299.

48. Peter Bulkely, *The Gospel-Covenant*, 2d ed. (London, 1651), 299.

49. William K. B. Stoever, *'Faire and Easie Way to Heaven': Covenant Theology and Antinomianism in Early Massachusetts* (Middletown, Conn., 1978), has argued that the inclination to divine God's intentions through His created order, as opposed to the immediate revelation of the Spirit, is what distinguished Massachusetts orthodoxy from sectarianism in the antinomian crisis of the late 1630s, at least in the realm of the quest for personal salvation. See also Philip F. Gura, *A Glimpse of Sion's Glory: Puritan Radicalism in New England, 1620–1660* (Middletown, Conn., 1984).

50. John Brinsley, *The Third Part of the True Watch* (London, 1622), sig. Gr. For Puritans acting on Brinsley's predictions, see Increase Mather, *The Life and Death of that Reverend Man of God, M. Richard Mather* (Cambridge, Mass., 1670), 18, and John Allin and Thomas Shepard, *A Defence of the Answer Made unto the Nine Questions* (London,

1648), 21. See Stephen Foster, *The Long Argument: English Puritanism and the Shaping of New England Culture, 1570–1700* (Chapel Hill, 1991), 108–13, for an analysis of the similar way in which John Winthrop was reading the signs of the times in England in the 1620s.

51. Cotton's prophecy, not too risky to make about a boat attempting a late autumn crossing, and its outcome are discussed in Robert Emmet Wall, *Massachusetts Bay: The Crucial Decade, 1640–1650* (New Haven, 1972), 186–89. Jonathan Mitchel, A Continuation of Sermons upon the Body of Divinity (lib. 4), Massachusetts Historical Society, 33.

52. John Hull, "Diary," American Antiquarian Society *Transactions* 3 (1857), 218, Mather, *Magnalia*, 2:519–20.

53. Davenport, *Saints Anchor-hold*, 35, John Cotton, *A Practical Commentary, or An Exposition with Observations, Reasons, and Uses upon the First Epistle General of John* (London, 1656), 197, Shepard, *Parable*, 74, 88. For an introduction to the Puritans' conception of the Holy Spirit, see Geoffrey F. Nuttall, *The Holy Spirit in Puritan Faith and Experience* (Oxford, 1947).

54. John Cotton, *Christ the Fountain of Life* (London, 1651), 35.

55. Mather, *Magnalia*, 1:283, 1:314–16, 1:295. For Puritan dismissal of dreams, see Thomas, *Religion*, 128. For double-mindedness, see John Winthrop, *Winthrop's Journal, "History of New England," 1630–1649*, ed. James Kendall Hosmer, 2 vols. (1908; reprint, New York, 1953), 1:121, and Thomas Shepard, *The Works of Thomas Shepard*, ed. John A. Albro, 3 vols. (Boston, 1853), 3:465. Thomas Hooker, *Writings in England and Holland, 1626–1633*, ed. George H. Williams, Norman Pettit, Winfried Herget, and Sargent Bush (Cambridge, Mass., 1975), 244. Protestants generally agreed that extraordinary gifts of the Spirit like revelations at least in some sense ended in the early days of the Church. That belief could create a bounded skepticism about contemporary divinely inspired revelations. Shepard, in the example cited above, accepted that God sent an Indian a prophetic dream because the Indians lacked a gospel ministry at the time. Other sticklers might give contemporary phenomena euphemistic titles like illuminations of the Spirit, while others simply called them revelations, at the risk, perhaps, of theoretical inconsistency. For a general discussion of what constituted the boundaries of tolerance for revelations by Puritans, see Nuttall, *Holy Spirit*, chaps. 1 and 3. The Quakers transgressed those boundaries by erasing altogether the difference between the work of the Holy Spirit in the New Testament and the work of the Holy Spirit in seventeenth-century England. See ibid., chap. 7.

56. "The Notebook of the Reverend John Fiske," ed. Robert G. Pope, Colonial Society of Massachusetts *Collections* 97 (1974), 52–55, quotation from 53.

57. John Breck, "The Autobiographical Memoranda of John Breck, 1636–1659," ed. Clifford K. Shipton, American Antiquarian Society *Transactions* 53 (1943), 98, Francis Johnson, *The Wonder Working Providence of Sion's Saviour in New England*, ed. J. Franklin Jameson (New York, 1910), 243. John Winthrop reserved judgment on this and other contemporaneous prodigies, but he did not always practice such restraint, having no doubt that Ann Hutchinson's and Mary Dyer's monstrous births were related to their no-less-monstrous doctrines. See *Winthrop's Journal*, 2:264, 1:266–69, 277. For a range of contemporaneous responses to the same atmospheric phenomenon in Eng-

land, see William Lilly, *The Starry Messenger, or, An Interpretation of Strange Apparitions* (London: 1644).

58. William Hubbard, *A General History of New England*, 2 vols., Massachusetts Historical Society *Collections*, 2d. ser., 5 & 6 (1815, 1816), 2:516–17.

59. The classic statement of this position is Edmund S. Morgan, "The Case against Anne Hutchinson," *New England Quarterly* 10 (1937), 635–49. For recent examples, in the context of larger analyses not hinging on the point, see Gura, *Glimpse of Sion's Glory*, 259–60, David S. Lovejoy, *Religious Enthusiasm in the New World: Heresy to Revolution* (Cambridge, Mass., 1985), 75–76, and Marilyn J. Westerkamp, "Anne Hutchinson, Sectarian Mysticism, and the Puritan Order," *Church History* 59 (1990), 485. But see Michael Schuldiner, *Gifts and Works: The Post-Conversion Paradigm and Spiritual Controversy in Seventeenth-Century Massachusetts* (Macon, Ga., 1991), 82–88, for a very different interpretation of Hutchinson's revelations.

60. Hutchinson presented her revelations to the Court in the perfectly orthodox form of scripture verses that darted into her mind (the same method by which John Fiske, cited above, obtained his). John Cotton reminded the Court that Hutchinson had in fact not claimed any new matter of doctrine from her revelations (the only form of revelation unanimously condemned by the orthodox), but the Court was not in the mood to listen to such fine distinctions. However, even in spite of their desire to convict her, her examiners had to grope for a while to determine what precisely the unorthodox nature of her revelations was. John Eliot, for example, was rebuked by Winthrop when he asserted that one could not have a "particular revelation of things that shall fall out." Winthrop called Hutchinson's revelations "desperate enthusiasm," but not because she had scripture verses darting into her mind but because "then an application is made which is nothing to the purpose." The determination of what constituted appropriate purpose was of course Winthrop's. Winthrop, in other words, was primarily upset with the way Hutchinson interpreted the scriptures she received, not with her receiving scriptures per se, although he also disapproved of her relying so heavily on them, and perhaps thereby encouraging others to do so likewise, without seeking the guidance of ministers, the "ministry of the word." See *The Antinomian Controversy, 1636–1638: A Documentary History*, ed. David D. Hall (Middletown, Conn., 1968), 336–43. The Winthrop quotes are from p. 342, the Eliot quote from p. 343.

61. Jonathan Mitchel, Notes of Sermons, 1654–1655, Massachusetts Historical Society, Boston, Massachusetts, unpag. [second sermon in manuscript]. Wheelright, whose relationship with the Massachusetts authorities had not always been smooth, had recently been certified as orthodox by the General Court; see Mather, *Magnalia*, 2:512. Edward Taylor, *Harmony of the Gospels*, ed. Thomas M. and Virginia L. Davis with Betty L. Parks, 3 vols. (Delmar, N.Y., 1983), 1:67.

62. Shepard, *Parable*, 144, 203, Davenport, *Saints Anchor-Hold*, 6–7, Shepard, *Parable*, 14. The most extensive account of the place of Satan in ministerial discourse in seventeenth-century New England can be found in Edward K. Trefz, "A Study of Satan with Particular Emphasis upon His Role in the Preaching of Certain New England Puritans" (D.D. diss., Union Theological Seminary, 1952). See also Richard Godbeer, "The Devil's Dominion: Magic and Religion in Early New England" (Ph.D. diss., Brandeis University, 1989), 97–120.

63. Hubbard, *General History*, 2:646, 648, 648, 644–45, 649.

64. The common historiographical interpretation of Hubbard was set by Samuel Drake's praises of his rationality scattered in the footnotes of Drake's edition of Hubbard's *The History of the Indian Wars in New England from the First Settlement to the Termination of the War with King Philip*, in 1677, 2 vols. (1677; reprint, Roxbury, Mass., 1865). See for example, 1:12 n., 63 n. Modern historians have kept to this theme with lesser or greater fidelity, mostly when referring to the *History*. See Kenneth B. Murdock, "William Hubbard and the Providential Interpretation of History," American Antiquarian Society *Proceedings* 52 (1943), 15–37, Richard S. Dunn, "Seventeenth-Century English Historians of America," in James Morton Smith, ed., *Seventeenth-Century America: Essays in Colonial American History* (Chapel Hill, 1959), 213, Anne Kusener Nelsen, "King Philip's War and the Hubbard-Mather Rivalry," *William and Mary Quarterly*, 3d ser., 27 (1970), 628, David D. Hall, *The Faithful Shepherd: A History of the New England Ministry in the Seventeenth Century* (Chapel Hill, 1972), 240, and Michael G. Hall, *Increase Mather: The Last American Puritan* (Middletown, Conn., 1988), 118, 119. E. Brooks Holifield, *Era of Persuasion: American Thought and Culture, 1521–1680* (Boston, 1989), 59, contests the usual reading of Hubbard and correctly notes that Hubbard's providentialism is that of a "conventional Puritan," but Holifield leaves unanswered the question of how his colleagues have wandered so far astray in their interpretations.

65. The source for assuming Hubbard was in favor of religious tolerance is a passage in *The Happiness of a People In the Wisdome of their Rulers* (Boston, 1676), where he called for the "indulgence, or connivance" of those who did not differ from the Congregationalists in "fundamentals" (41). That, in context, seems a call for toleration of Baptists. However, in his *General History*, Hubbard displayed a conventional hostility toward them, calling them, among other things, the "*materia prima* of all the corrupt opinions that christian religion hath of late days . . . been besmeared withal" (2:626), and elsewhere stating that the difference between them and Congregationalists was one of fundamentals (2:374), while complaining that their continued existence was against the order of the civil authorities (2:676). One way of resolving the two publications is to assume that in *Happiness* Hubbard was not talking about Baptists at all, but about dissension among the Congregationalists over the Halfway Covenant, although the passage is hard to read that way. Another is that he was talking about toleration for the Baptists, but only because it would bring unity among the Congregationalists, who were split on the issue. Later, as internal divisions among Congregationalists lessened in the face of the threat from the Crown, he could go back to a position more comfortable for him. A third possibility, of course, is that he changed his mind.

66. Hubbard, *General History*, 2:640–41, 2:626, 1:81, 2:580.

67. Ibid., 2:325, 2:574, 2:313, 2:325.

68. Ibid., 2:646.

69. "I would not be too forward in obtruding uncertain Reports upon the Belief of the far distant Reader, especially considering how much the World hath oft been abused with false Coyne of the like Nature." Hubbard, *History of the Indian Warrs*, 2:262–63. For the partisan Dissenter accounts, see chap. 2.

70. Hubbard, *General History*, 2:342, 1:194, 199.

71. Hubbard, *Happiness*, 51.

72. Hubbard, *History of the Indian Warrs*, 2:249, 254, 253–54.

73. Ibid., 2:258.

74. Ibid., 2:257.

75. Hubbard, *Happiness*, 51.

76. Hubbard, *History of the Indian Warrs*, 2:248.

77. For a convenient collection of examples, see Francis J. Bremer, *The Congregational Connection: Clerical Friendship in the Anglo-American Puritan Community, 1610–1692* (Boston, 1994), 237. In addition, see *The Works of John Owen*, ed. William H. Goold, 16 vols. (1850–1853; reprint, London, 1967), 14:524, *Hutchinson Papers*, 2 vols. (Albany, 1865), 2:205.

78. Massachusetts Historical Society *Collections*, 4th ser., 8 (1868), 576, Hubbard, *History of the Indian Warrs*, 1:xxii.

79. Hubbard, *Happiness*, 54–60, ibid., *The Benefit of a Well Ordered Conversation* (Boston, 1684), 98.

80. Hubbard, *History of the Indian Warrs*, 1:110–11, Increase Mather, *A Brief History of the Warr with the Indians in New-England* (Boston, 1676), in *So Dreadful a Judgment: Puritan Responses to King Philip's War, 1676–1677*, ed. James K. Folson and Richard Slotkin (Middletown, Conn., 1978), 199.

81. Mather, *Brief History*, 124–25.

82. Ibid., quotation from p. 88.

83. Battles, as Hubbard recorded them, were inevitably won and lost through the interposition of Providence, and the entire course of the war was dependent on God's good pleasure. While Hubbard analyzed at length the weaknesses and strengths of the English forces, he also firmly asserted that the fortunes of the war did not change until God was ready to have them change, and strategies counted for nothing against God's overarching intentions. See Hubbard, *History of the Indian Warrs*, 259–61, Increase Mather, *An Historical Discourse Concerning the Prevalency of Prayer* (Boston, 1677), 4–11.

84. Hubbard, *History of the Indian Warrs*, 1:247, ibid., *General History*, 2:604.

85. Mather, *Brief History*, 198. For Mather's and Hubbard's roles in the politics of Restoration Massachusetts, see Nelsen, "King Philip's War," and Foster, *Long Argument*, chap. 5.

86. Mather, in *Kometographia* (Boston, 1683), 113, referred to the connection, obvious to him, between a comet that appeared in 1662 and the subsequent ejection of nonconforming ministers in England. "The *Fanaticks* say that the like is not to be paralleled in any History, that five and twenty hundred Ministers should be silenced in one day. It is also said, that these Stars which were thus cast down, were some of them of the first magnitude. And therefore a Comet might well precede an event so remarkable. But this must pass for a *Phanatick* notion."

87. Massachusetts Historical Society *Collections*, 4th ser., 8 (1868), 581, 376, 576–77.

88. Increase Mather, *A Relation of the Troubles which Have Hapned in New-England* (Boston, 1677), "To the Reader," Perry Miller, *The New England Mind from Colony to Province* (Cambridge, Mass., 1953), 31–33. Miller's excellent analysis of *A Brief History* is marred only by his claim that Mather did not place the war within a larger cosmological framework, a claim consistent with Miller's desire to portray an isolated, tribal New England. Mather specifically placed the war within the struggles of the Last Days, of which it was but one episode.

89. From Increase Mather's diary, 19 August 1666 (typescript, American Antiquarian Society), 1:121, "At night much troubled to hear that many of the ministers wished I would make an end of preaching de [regarding] the Jews &c [referring to the conversion of the Jews that was to precede the Second Coming]." Samuel Willard, perhaps Mather's equal in the esteem of his contemporaries, might have spoken for more of his brethren when he said regarding eschatological predictions, "In what year and day this appearance of Christ shal commence is not for us to know; the father hath kept times and seasons in his own hands: but that it is not far off, and will in a short time come to pass, is certain." Willard was dubious about one of Mather's favorite themes, the thousand-year reign of the Saints. See Samuel Willard, *The Child's Portion* (Boston, 1684), 96, 95. For a summary of Willard's eschatology, see Seymour Van Dyken, *Samuel Willard: Preacher of Orthodoxy in an Era of Change* (Grand Rapids, 1972), 188–91. See Bozeman, *To Live Ancient Lives*, chap. 6, and 338–39, for a discussion of the limited extent to which millennial concerns occupied the psyches of ministers of the first and second generation.

90. Mather conveniently summarized the most prominent prophecies of doom given by first-generation preachers in "To the Church and Inhabitants of Northampton in New-England," his preface to Eleazar Mather, *A Serious Exhortation* (Cambridge, 1671).

91. Increase Mather, *Some Important Truths about Conversion* (London, 1674), sig. Av, ibid., *The Day of Trouble is Near* (Cambridge, Mass., 74), 26.

92. Increase Mather to John Cotton, 13 December 1676, Massachusetts Historical Society.

93. Mather, *Life and Death*, 28.

94. "The Autobiography of Increase Mather," ed. Michael G. Hall, American Antiquarian Society *Proceedings* 71 (1962), 282.

95. T.H., *The Life and Death, of the Eminently Learned, Pious, and Painful Minister of the Gospel, Dr. Samuel Winter* (London, 1671), sigs. Air–Aiv, 41–56.

96. The exceptional nature of Winter's abilities can be easily ascertained by comparing the epitome of Winter's life that appears in Samuel Clark, *The Lives of Sundry Eminent Persons in this Later Age* (London, 1683), 95–103, with the rest of Clark's far more prophetically and prayerfully subdued biographies.

97. Cotton Mather, *Parentator* (Boston, 1724), 195. Cotton Mather, whose "particular faiths" stemmed directly out of this tradition, exempted himself and his father from his warning. Richard F. Lovelace, *The American Pietism of Cotton Mather: Origins of American Evangelicalism* (Grand Rapids, 1979), 183, has also located the term in the writings of the English Independent divine Thomas Goodwin.

98. Hubbard's few printed works were more topically oriented than devotional. On the basis of an ambiguous passage in one of them, David D. Hall, *Faithful Shepherd*, 259, has even labeled Hubbard a legal moralist, one who stressed morality over piety, and so again a harbinger of the eighteenth century. But it is far from clear that such a stress in that passage was Hubbard's intention. The one sermon from the John Hull sermon notebooks, vol. 1 (of 2), Massachusetts Historical Society, unquestionably by Hubbard (on John 10, 28) is evangelical.

99. Charles Morton, "Compendium Physicae," Colonial Society of Massachusetts *Collections* 33 (1940).

100. William Brattle in John Hancock's Sermon notebook, 1687, Houghton Library, Harvard, MS Am 121.1, 18, John Leverett, Hancock's notebook, 30, Edward Thompson, Samuel Thompson Notebook 1678–1695, American Antiquarian Society, sermon on Luke 2:29.

Chapter Two. Providence Besieged

1. On miracles, see Paul H. Kocher, *Science and Religion in Elizabethan England* (San Marino, Calif., 1953), 104–14, D. P. Walker, "The Cessation of Miracles," in *Hermeticism and the Renaissance: Intellectual History and the Occult in Early Modern Europe*, ed. Ingrid Merkel and Allen G. Debus (Washington, D.C., 1988), 111–24.

2. D. P. Walker, *Unclean Spirits: Possession and Exorcism in France and England in the Late Sixteenth and Early Seventeenth Centuries* (Philadelphia, 1981), 66–73, Kocher, *Science and Religion*, 111–13, 108.

3. Samuel Willard, *A Compleat Body of Divinity* (Boston, 1726), 144, Ambrose Paré, *Des Monstres et Prodigies*, ed. Jean Céard (Geneva, 1971), 4.

4. Margo Todd, "Providence, Chance and the New Science in Early Stuart Cambridge," *Historical Journal* 29 (1986), 703.

5. Sarah C. Dodson, "Abraham Fleming, Writer and Editor," *Texas Studies in English*, 34 (1955), 51–66, R. Mark Benbow, "The Providential Theory of Historical Causation in Holinshed's Chronicles: 1577 and 1587," *Texas Studies in Literature and Language* 1 (1959), 264–76, Henry Ansgar Kelly, *Divine Providence in the England of Shakespeare's Histories* (Cambridge, Mass., 1970), F. Smith Fussner, *The Historical Revolution: English Historical Writing and Thought, 1580–1640* (London, 1962), chap. 7, D. R. Woolf, *The Idea of History in Early Stuart England: Erudition, Ideology, and 'The Light of Truth' from the Accession of James I to the Civil War* (Toronto, 1990), chap. 1. For the "subversiveness" of the Jacobean theater's treatment of Providence, consider, with some grains of salt, Jonathan Dollimore, *Radical Tragedy: Religion, Ideology and Power in the Drama of Shakespeare and his Contemporaries*, 2d ed. (Durham, 1993). On a more erudite level, see William R. Elton, *King Lear and the Gods* (San Marino, Calif., 1966), and Frederick Kiefer, *Fortune and Elizabethan Tragedy* (San Marino, Calif., 1983).

6. Thomas Gataker, *Of the Nature and Use of Lots*, 2d ed. (London, 1627), passim.

7. Ibid., 24.

8. William Fulke, *A Goodly Gallerye with a Most Pleasaunt Prospect* (London, 1563), sigs. 10v, 45r–45v.

9. John Harrington, cited in Howard Dobin, *Merlin's Disciples: Prophecy, Poetry, and Power in Renaissance England* (Stanford, 1990), 111.

10. Nicholas Tyacke, *Anti-Calvinists: The Rise of English Arminianism, c. 1590–1640* (Oxford, 1987). Recently Peter White has been launching a revisionist attack on Tyacke's thesis about Calvinism and Arminianism, arguing that (a) the period of Calvinist influence in the English church was only a late-sixteenth- and early-seventeenth-century aberration in a longer history of reformation, (b) the extent of that Calvinist influence has been greatly exaggerated, and (c) the issues of the 1630s did not revolve primarily around theology, and there was certainly no aggressive Arminian attack on Calvinism. For a full statement of the thesis, see Peter White, *Predestination, Policy, and Polemic: Conflict and Consensus in the English Church from the Reformation to the Civil War*

(Cambridge, 1992). For a collection of essays by Tyacke, White, and others covering the current state of debate about the English Church in this period, see Kenneth Fincham, ed., *The Early Stuart Church, 1603–1642* (Stanford, 1993).

11. G. J. R. Parry, *A Protestant Vision: William Harrison and the Reformation of Elizabethan England* (Cambridge, 1987), 191, 197–98, John Morrill, *The Nature of the English Revolution* (New York, 1993), 127, Joseph Hall *Contemplations Upon the Principal Passages of the Holy Scriptures* (London, 1614), 262–63. In the Old Testament, both Samuel and Amos, among others, were called "seers"; for examples, see 1 Chron. 9:22 and Amos 7:12.

12. John Standish, *A Sermon Preached before the King at White-Hal Septem. the 26th 1675* (London, 1676), 23, referring to Richard Hooker, Thomas Jackson, and William Chillingworth. For the extent to which Hooker strayed from Reformed orthodoxy, see Peter Lake, *Anglicans and Puritans? Presbyterianism and English Conformist Thought from Whitgift to Hooker* (London, 1988), 145–97, 229, and Deborah Kuller Shuger, *Habits of Thought in the English Renaissance: Religion, Politics, and the Dominant Culture* (Berkeley, 1990), 26–44, 69–90.

13. Keith Thomas, *Religion and the Decline of Magic: Studies in Popular Beliefs in Sixteenth- and Seventeenth-Century England* (London, 1971), 90, Barbara Donegan, "Providence, Chance and Explanation: Some Paradoxical Aspects of Puritan Views of Causation," *Journal of Religious History* 11 (1981), 390n. 10.

14. *The Works of the Reverend and Learned Divine Dr. Thomas Jackson, D.D.*, 3 vols. (London, 1673), 2:394. For Jackson's theology, see White, *Predestination*, chap. 13.

15. Mary Ellen Bowden, "The Scientific Revolution in Astrology: The English Reformers (1558–1686)" (Ph.D. diss., Yale University, 1974), chap. 2.

16. H. R. Trevor-Roper, *Catholics, Anglicans, and Puritans: Seventeenth Century Essays* (London, 1987), chap. 4.

17. See Frances A. Yates, *Giordano Bruno and the Hermetic Tradition* (London, 1964), ibid., *The Occult Philosophy in the Elizabethan Age* (London, 1979), ibid., *The Rosicrucian Enlightenment* (Boulder, 1979), and Paolo Rossi, *Francis Bacon: From Magic to Science*, trans. Sacha Rabinovitch (London, 1968). For Rossi's moderate defense of the whig interpretation of history in the light of subsequent contextualist research into the occult roots of modern science, see Paolo Rossi, "Hermeticism, Rationality and the Scientific Revolution," in *Reason, Experiment, and Mysticism in the Scientific Revolution*, ed. M. L. Righini and William R. Shea (New York, 1975).

18. Dobin, *Merlin's Disciples*, 132–33.

19. Francis Bacon, *The Advancement of Learning* (New York, 1899), 48–49 (bk. 2, chap. 2).

20. Christopher Hill, *The World Turned Upside Down: Radical Ideas during the English Revolution* (New York, 1972), 149.

21. Griffith Williams, *The Great Antichrist Revealed, Before this Time, Never Discovered* (London, 1660), 3d pag., 23. See in general Robert S. Bosher, *The Making of the Restoration Settlement: The Influence of the Laudians 1649–1662* (New York, 1951), 47, 80–81.

22. Margaret C. Jacob, *Newtonians and the English Revolution, 1689–1720* (Ithaca, 1976), 42, Peter Lake, "Serving God and the Times: The Calvinist Conformity of

Robert Sanderson," *Journal of British Studies* 27 (1988), 112–13, C. R. Cragg, *From Puritanism to the Age of Reason* (Cambridge, 1950), 21. For a review of Anglican attacks on predestination in the Civil Wars and Interregnum period, see Dewey D. Wallace, Jr., *Puritans and Predestination: Grace in English Protestant Theology, 1525–1695* (Chapel Hill, 1982), 120–30.

23. Williams, *Great Antichrist*, 3d pag., 39. On William's moderation, see "To the Parliament," in *Great Antichrist*, and Samuel Parker, *A Free and Impartial Censure of the Platonick Philosophie*, 2d ed. (London, 1667), 139.

24. Herbert Thorndike, *The Due way of Composing the Differences on Foot* (London, 1660), 16, Joseph Glanvill, *Some Discourses, Sermons and Remains of the Reverend Mr. Jos. Glanvil* (London, 1681), 381. There was no shortage of early-seventeenth-century complaints about Puritans considering themselves the Elect, but in the earlier period the theological basis for those assumptions went mostly unchallenged.

25. William Clagett, *A Discourse Concerning the Operations of the Holy Spirit* (London, 1678), 308.

26. Simon Patrick, *A Friendly Debate Between a Conformist and a Non-Conformist* (London, 1669), 48, George Hickes, *Peculium Dei, A Discourse about the Jews, as the Peculiar People of God* (London, 1681), 29, Patrick, *Friendly Debate*, 48. See also, for example, Glanvill, *Some Discourses*, 59–60, Tillotson, *Works*, 1:132–33, John Moore, *Of Religious Melancholy* (London, 1692). For a discussion of the naturalization of the psyche in Restoration England, see Michael MacDonald, "Religion, Social Change, and Psychological Healing in England, 1600–1800," in W. J. Shiels, *The Church and Healing* (Oxford, 1982), 101–25.

27. Simon Patrick, *A Continuation of the Friendly Debate* (London, 1669), 216. Patrick's Dissenter, in this "friendly debate," replied to his charges about Hutchinson, "There was Witchcraft sure in the business" (218).

28. Tillotson, *Works*, 2:34. On enthusiasm see Umphrey Lee, *The Historical Backgrounds to Early Methodist Enthusiasm* (New York, 1931), Ronald Knox, *Enthusiasm: A Chapter in the History of Religion, with Special Reference to the XVII and XVIII Centuries* (New York, 1950), Susie I. Tucker, *Enthusiasm: A Study in Semantic Change* (Cambridge, 1972), Michael Heyd, "The Reaction to Enthusiasm in the Seventeenth Century: Towards an Integrative Approach," *Journal of Modern History* 53 (1981), 258–80, Attracta Anne Coppin, "Religious Enthusiasm from Robert Browne to George Fox: A Study of Its Meaning and the Reaction to it in the Seventeenth Century" (Ph.D.diss., Oxford University, 1983). These works tend to deal with enthusiasm as a fixed category. For the question of how enthusiasm came to be redefined in this period, see George Williamson, *Seventeenth-Century Contexts* (London, 1960), chap. 9.

29. Protestants needed to make the claim for divine guidance in their reading of the scriptures to explain why they did not need the authority of the Roman Catholic Church to understand the Bible.

30. Coppin, "Religious Enthusiasm," 35–36, 86–88.

31. The godly had always been objects of hostility for their neighbors; I am arguing a question of degree here. For example, Robert Burton's *Anatomy of Melancholy* is the standard pre–Civil Wars book with which secondary studies of attacks on enthusiasm begin. Burton did indeed attack Puritan-like figures such as "giddy heads [who] will take upon them to define how many will be saved and who damned in a parish," as well

as "indiscreet pastors" who "intempestively rail at and pronounce them damned . . . for giving so much to sports and honest recreations, making every small fault and thing indifferent an irremissible offence." But Burton also cited with approval the works of staunch Puritans like William Perkins and Richard Greenham and vigorously defended Calvinism. See Robert Burton, *The Anatomy of Melancholy*, ed. Holbrook Jackson (New York, 1977), "The Second Partition," 370, 399–400, 409, 423–24. William Worship, in a visitation sermon at Boston in the early 1620s, where John Cotton's parishioners had recently decapitated statues and smashed stained glass, claimed that the Puritans were certainly unpleasant "Opinitive heads," but they were not "franticke *Enthusiasts*." See William Worship, *Three Sermons Preached at Three Several Visitations at Boston* (London, 1625), 13. Restoration Anglicans were less disposed, and had less incentive, to make such nice distinctions, and Puritans were institutionally less favorably situated to defend themselves.

32. George Hickes, *The Spirit of Enthusiasm Exorcised* (London, 1680), 41, Patrick, *Friendly Debate*, 15, John Standish, *A Sermon Preached at the Assizes at Hertford, March the 9th. 1682/3* (London, 1683), 17, Burnett, cited in Cragg, *Puritanism to the Age of Reason*, 31. For the Anglican attack on Dissenter extempore praying, see John Spurr, *The Restoration Church of England, 1646–1689* (New Haven, 1991), 338–39.

33. For general discussions of these theological developments, see C. F. Allison, *The Rise of Moralism: The Proclamation of the Gospel from Hooker to Baxter* (London, 1966), and Spurr, *Restoration Church*, 296–330.

34. In the mid-1670s, it could still be assumed that the Anglican as much as the Puritan "expects Salvation by the extrinsical Righteousness of Christ without him, not by any interior righteousness within his own soul," although "some of the Prelatick clergy begin to scoff at the Doctrine." See W[illiam] H[utchinson], *The Puritan Convert* (n.p., 1676), 6. The identification of the author is from Richard Baxter, *Reliquae Baxterianae* (London, 1694), 3d pag., 180.

35. C. John Sommerville, *Popular Religion in Restoration England* (Gainsville, Fla., 1977).

36. A good account of the Montague affair is contained in Tyacke, *Anti-Calvinists*, chap. 6. The degree to which Anglicans had ceased to be concerned about the issue of justification may be seen in the controversy that erupted around the publication by the Anglican William Sherlock, *A Discourse Concerning the Knowledge of Jesus Christ* (1673), in which Sherlock aggressively expounded the new view of justification. He inspired a flurry of responses, most of them indignant, but the only clergy to attack him publicly were Dissenters. The controversy is reviewed in Wallace, *Puritans and Predestination*, 170–73.

37. Samuel Wesley, *Athenian Mercury* 2, no. 26 (1691).

38. Cragg, *Puritanism to the Age of Reason*, 29–30. On moral certainty, see Barbara J. Shapiro, *Probability and Certainty in Seventeenth-Century England: A Study of the Relations between Natural Science, Religion, History, Law, and Literature* (Princeton, 1983), chap. 3, and more generally, Richard W. F. Kroll, *The Material Word: Literate Culture in the Restoration and Early Eighteenth Century* (Baltimore, 1991). See also the various works of Richard H. Popkin, especially *The History of Scepticism from Erasmus to Spinoza*, 2d ed. (Berkeley, 1979), and *The Third Force in Seventeenth-Century Thought* (Leiden, 1992).

39. For a general discussion of the technical meanings and use of reason in Restoration polemics, see John Spurr, "'Rational Religion' in Restoration England," *Journal of the History of Ideas* 49 (1988), 563–85. Spurr concentrates on appeals to reason against deists and Socinians, while ignoring the intense debates about reason between Anglicans and Dissenters. On Anglican rationalism itself, see Gerard Reedy, S.J., *The Bible and Reason: Anglicans and Scripture in Late Seventeenth-Century England* (Philadelphia, 1985), 10, 16, 141, Irène Simon, *Three Restoration Divines, Barrow, South, Tillotson: Selected Sermons* (Paris, 1967), chap. 3, and Phillip Harth, *Swift and Anglican Rationalism: The Religious Background of "A Tale of a Tub"* (Chicago, 1961), chap. 2. The assertion of broad midcentury changes is not intended to negate the pre–Civil Wars history of Anglican rationalism, going back to Richard Hooker, with Puritanism from the beginning the defining "other."

40. For the changes in Anglican preaching in this period, see W. Fraser Mitchell, *English Pulpit Oratory from Andrewes to Tillotson: A Study of its Literary Aspects* (London, 1932), 309–43.

41. Edward Fowler, *Principles and Practices of Certain Moderate Divines of the Church of England* (London, 1670), 106–7, 112–13, John Eachard, *A Free and Impartial Inquiry Into the Causes of that Very Great Esteem and Honour that the Non-Conforming Preachers are Generally in with Their Followers* (London, 1673), 113, and Patrick, *Friendly Debate*, 6, 15–16.

42. Tillotson, *Works*, 2:368–69.

43. Parker, *Free and Impartial Censure*, 94.

44. Richard Ashcraft, *Revolutionary Politics and Locke's Two Treatises of Government* (Princeton, 1986), 54, 64. See also Mark Goldie, "The Theory of Religious Intolerance in Restoration England," in *From Persecution to Toleration: The Glorious Revolution and Religion in England*, ed. Ole Peter Grell, Jonathan I. Israel, and Nicholas Tyacke (Oxford, 1991), 331–68.

45. *Calendar of State Papers, Domestic Series, of the Reign of Charles II, 1661–1662*, ed. Mary Anne Everett Green (London, 1861), 517. On the ways in which the Dissenters coped with the Licensing Act, see N. H. Keeble, *The Literary Culture of Non-Conformity in Later Seventeenth-Century England* (Athens, Ga., 1987), chap. 3.

46. Thomas Sprat, *History of the Royal Society* (London, 1665), 362.

47. Eachard, *Free and Impartial Inquiry*, 77.

48. Robert South, *Sermons Preached Upon Several Occasions*, 4 vols. (Oxford, 1842), 4:339.

49. *Eniautos terastios* (n.p., 1661), *Mirabilis Annus Secundus; or, The Second Year of Prodigies* (n.p., 1662), *Mirabilis Annus Secundus; or, The Second Part of the Second Years Prodigies* (n.p., 1662). On this series and the reactions to it, see C. E. Whiting, *Studies in English Puritanism from the Restoration to the Revolution, 1660–1688* (New York, 1968), 546–52, Thomas, *Religion*, 111–12, and Richard L. Greaves, *Deliver Us from Evil: The Radical Underground in Britain, 1660–1663* (New York, 1986), 139, 211, 213–16, 219, 221, 223–24.

50. *Eniautos terastios*, sig. A2v.

51. *Massachusetts Historical Society Collections*, 4th ser., 8 (1868), 126.

52. Baxter, *Reliquiae*, 1st pag., 432–33, and ibid., *The Certainty of the World of Spirits* (London, 1691), 163–64. Baxter's complaint about the series was that its compilers

mixed in false prodigies with genuine ones, thus allowing the skeptics to ignore the message being sent by the Lord. See ibid., *The Saints Everlasting Rest* (London, 1677), 246.

53. Sprat, *History*, 364.

54. Ibid., 360.

55. Ibid., 363–64.

56. The main documents are Meric Casaubon, *A Letter of Meric Casaubon D.D. to Peter du Moulin D.D.* (London, 1669), Henry Stubbe, *The Plus Ultra reduced to a Non Plus* (London, 1670), and ibid., *The History of the Royal Society As being Destructive to the Established Religion and Church of England* (Oxford, 1670). The controversy is discussed in Richard Foster Jones, *Ancients and Moderns: A Study of the Rise of the Scientific Movement in Seventeenth-Century England*, 2d ed. (St. Louis, 1961), Michael Hunter, *Science and Society in Restoration England* (Cambridge, 1981), chap. 6, James R. Jacob, *Henry Stubbe, Radical Protestantism and the Early Enlightenment* (Cambridge, 1983). Jacob's interpretation of Stubbe has not been generally accepted.

57. John Spencer, *A Discourse Concerning Prodigies*, 2d ed. (London, 1665), 226–27, 238–39, 261–66, 364. Hutchinson's and Dyer's babies seem to have fallen well within the possibilities of nature; twentieth-century scholars have confidently claimed from the hostile descriptions of contemporary commentators that Hutchinson delivered a hydatidiform mole and Dyer an anencephaletic fetus with spina bifida and other abnormalities. See Anne Jacobson Schutte, "'Such Monstrous Births': A Neglected Aspect of the Antinomian Controversy," *Renaissance Quarterly* 38 (1985), 90.

58. Spencer, *Discourse*, sig. A4v, 289–90.

59. In the Galenic medical tradition, melancholy was a delusive condition, resulting in fear, anxiety, and delusions of insight and prophetic power. See Michael MacDonald, *Mystical Bedlam: Madness, Anxiety and Healing in Seventeenth-Century England* (Cambridge, 1981), 150–60. To preserve the connection he was trying to establish between scrutinizing prodigies and Reformed orthodoxy, Spencer explained away the Arminian Thomas Jackson's discussion of prodigies (see above) as attributable to his melancholy, *Discourse*, 30–31. For a discussion and example of the relationship between Reformed orthodoxy and an anxious scrutinizing of Providence, see John Stachniewski, *The Persecutory Imagination: English Puritanism and the Literature of Religious Despair* (Oxford, 1991), 157. On the growing tendency after the mid seventeenth century to define Puritanism as a mental illness, see, with a certain amount of caution (the term "Puritan" becomes broad enough to include Methodists), John F. Sena, "Melancholic Madness and the Puritans," *Harvard Theological Review* 66 (1973), 293–309.

60. Spencer, *A Discourse*, sigs. a3r–a3v.

61. Sprat, *History*, 360, 364.

62. John Gascoigne, *Cambridge in the Age of the Enlightenment: Science, Religion and Politics from the Restoration to the French Enlightenment* (Cambridge, 1989), 34.

63. John Spurr, "'Virtue, Religion and Government': the Anglican Uses of Providence," in *Politics in Restoration England*, ed. T. Harris, P. Seawood, and M. Goldie (Oxford, 1990), 32–35.

64. Benjamin Calamy, *A Sermon Preached before the Lord Mayor, Aldermen, and Citizens of London*, 2d ed. (London, 1682), 3–4.

65. Reedy, *The Bible and Reason*, chap. 4. A general discussion of Restoration

Anglican jeremiads can be found in Spurr, *Restoration Church*, chap. 5. For studies that stress the survival of the England/Israel parallel, see Pascal Covici, Jr., "God's Chosen People: Anglican Views, 1607–1807," *Studies in Puritan American Spirituality* 1 (1990), 97–128, and more generally, Linda Colley, *Britons: Forging the Nation, 1707–1837* (New Haven, 1992), chap. 1. For a lucid discussion of the relationship between national sins and national judgments, see Edward Stillingfleet, *A Sermon Preached on the Fast Day, November 13, 1678* (London, 1678), 13–15. Also relevant in this sermon is Stillingfleet's discussion of the natural advantages of religion to a country (27–28).

66. William Whiston, *Memoirs of the Life and Writings of Mr. William Whiston* (London, 1749), 5.

67. Simon Ford, *A Discourse Concerning God's Judgments* (London, 1678), 22, 21, 22.

68. Ibid., 40, 41, 56.

69. Henry Hesketh, *A Sermon Preached before the Right Honorable Lord Mayor and Aldermen of the City of London* (London, 1678), 41–43, Standish, *A Sermon: 1682/3*, 24, Patrick, *Continuation*, 187. I am only arguing for a trend in Anglican polemics, not an absolute standard. For an uninhibited partisan invocation of God's wrath upon Dissenters in the 1680s, see *The Theological Works of William Beveridge, D.D. Sometime Lord Bishop of St. Asaph*, 12 vols. (Oxford, 1844–48), 4:154–66.

70. On Stubbe, see Jacob, *Henry Stubbe*, on the radical wing of the Puritan Revolution, see Hill, *World Turned Upside Down*. For examples of prominent English scientists rejecting magically tinged natural philosophies because of their radical associations, see Brian Easlea, *Witch-hunting, Magic, and the New Philosophy: An Introduction to the Debates of the Scientific Revolution 1450–1750* (Brighton, 1980), 132–40, and James R. Jacob, *Robert Boyle and the English Revolution: A Study in Social and Intellectual Change* (New York, 1977).

71. Wallace, *Puritans*, 76, 88, 90, 92, Spencer, *Treatise*, 46, Meric Casaubon, ed., in John Dee, *A True and Faithful Relation of What Passed for Many Yeers Between Dr. John Dee (A Mathematician of Great Fame in Q. Eliz. and King James their Reignes) and Some Spirits: Tending (had it Succeeded) To a General Alteration of most States and Kingdomes in the World* (London, 1659), esp. sigs. Ar, Er–Ev, H2v, and Lee, *Historical Backgrounds*, 104n. 3. The classic assimilation of Calvinism to occultism and of both to enthusiasm is Jonathan Swift's *A Tale of a Tub* written around 1696.

72. James R. Jacob and Margaret C. Jacob, "The Anglican Origins of Modern Science: The Metaphysical Foundations of the Whig Constitution," *Isis* 71 (1980), 251–67, Peter Dear, "Totius in verba: Rhetoric and Authority in the Early Royal Society," *Isis* 76 (1985), 145–61. An account of the role of witnesses in the emergent "conventions of generating the fact" and the nature of the experimental community may be found in Steven Shapin and Simon Schaffer, *Leviathan and the Air-Pump: Hobbes, Boyle, and the Experimental Life* (Princeton, 1985), 55–60; see also Simon Schaffer, "Making Certain," *Social Studies of Science* 14 (1984), 137–52. On the logically empty and thus ideologically plastic nature of experience in the context of late-seventeenth-century English science, see Paul K. Feyerabend, *Philosophical Papers*, 2 vols. (New York, 1981), vol. 2, chap. 2. A close relationship between Puritanism and "modern" science in the mid seventeenth century has been recently ingeniously asserted by Charles Webster, *The Great Instauration: Science, Medicine and Reform, 1626–1660* (London,

1975), the bond being providentialism, millennialism, and reform. But see Lotte Mulligan, "Puritans and English Science: A Critique of Webster," *Isis* 71 (1980), 456–49.

73. Sprat, *History*, 362. The degree to which Sprat's book is a statement of the ideology of the Royal Society, and even the degree to which the Royal Society had an ideology is a matter of debate among historians. For a recent minimalist reading of both Sprat's book and the ideology of the Society, see Michael Hunter, *Establishing the New Science: The Experience of the Early Royal Society* (Woodbridge, 1989), chap. 2.

74. For examples of Englishmen so converting in the 1650s, see Easlea, *Witch Hunting*, 132–40, P. M. Rattansi, "The Intellectual Origins of the Royal Society," *Notes and Records of the Royal Society of London* 23 (1968), 136–37. For a controversial study of the changes in a single individual's thought in this period, see Jacob, *Robert Boyle*, chap. 3. A sketch of French responses to enthusiasm can be found in Betty Jo Teeter Dobbs, *The Foundations of Newton's Alchemy or "The Hunting of the Greene Lyon"* (New York, 1975), 51–57.

75. The question of atheism in seventeenth-century England is dealt with in G. E. Aylmer, "Unbelief in Seventeenth-Century England," in *Puritans and Revolutionaries*, ed. Donald Pennington and Keith Thomas (Oxford, 1978), 22–46, and Michael Hunter, *Science and Society in Restoration England* (Cambridge, 1981), chap. 5, and ibid., "Science and Heterodoxy: An Early Modern Problem Reconsidered," in *Reappraisals of the Scientific Revolution*, ed. Robert S. Westfall and David C. Lindberg (New York, 1990), 437–60. For English atheism in a broader European context, see D. C. Allen, *Doubt's Boundless Sea: Skepticism and Faith in the Renaissance* (Baltimore, 1964).

76. For contemporary, horrified reactions to Hobbes and *Leviathan*, see Samuel I. Mintz, *The Hunting of Leviathan* (Cambridge, 1962), Hunter, *Science and Society*, 175. The mechanical philosophy's traditional association with a Greek philosopher who tottered on the edge of atheism, Epicurus, was also a serious liability for its acceptance.

77. For the seventeenth-century history of the mechanical philosophy in England, see Robert Hugh Kargon, *Atomism in England from Hariot to Newton* (Oxford, 1966). The mechanical philosophy was not quite the equivalent of later normative scientific naturalism, but rather, as Richard S. Westfall has said, a "protean idiom" capable of explaining such diverse phenomena as the weapon salve, astrology, alchemy, and the evil eye, Richard S. Westfall, *Never at Rest: A Biography of Isaac Newton* (Cambridge, 1980), 22. Even so, as historians of science have recently pointed out, the mechanical philosophy did not enjoy an uncontested triumph in English elite circles in the Restoration. Even as uncompromising a figure like Boyle had residues of occultism in his philosophy, beyond his interest in witches and spirits. For explorations of the intricacies of the thought of even "mechanical" philosophers of the period, see G. Ross MacDonald, "Occultism and Philosophy in the Seventeenth Century," Simon Schaffer, "Occultism and Reason," in *Philosophy, Its History and Historiography*, ed. A. J. Holland (Dordrecht, 1985), 95–116 and 117–44, Keith Hutchinson, "Supernaturalism and the Mechanical Philosophy," *History of Science* 21 (1983), 297–333, and Charles Webster, *From Paracelsus to Newton: Magic and the Making of Modern Science* (Cambridge, 1982).

78. Henry More, *Immortality of the Soul* (London, 1659), 469.

79. This theological link has been pointed out by Eugene M. Klaaren, *The Religious Origins of Modern Science* (Grand Rapids, 1972), J. E. McGuire, "Boyle's Concep-

tion of Nature," *Journal for the History of Ideas* 33 (1972), 523–42, Francis Oakley, "Christian Theology and Newtonian Science: The Rise of the Conception of the Laws of Nature," *Church History* 30 (1961), 433–57, and Margaret J. Osler, "Providence and Divine Will in Gassendi's Views on Scientific Knowledge," *Journal for the History of Ideas* 44 (1983), 549–60. None of the above deal with the intricacy of Boyle's development. He started out a Calvinist, jettisoned that in the process of adopting a Helmontian, spiritist conception of the universe, and abandoned that before taking up the position that these authors connect with his Calvinist origins.

80. *Works of the Honourable Robert Boyle*, ed. Thomas Birch, 6 vols. (London: 1772), 5:519, 522. On Boyle's conception of himself as a "priest of nature," see Harold Finch, "The Scientist as Priest: A Note on Robert Boyle's Natural Theology," *Isis* 44 (1953), 252–65.

81. On these late-seventeenth-century debates, see John Redwood, *Reason, Ridicule and Religion: The Age of Enlightenment in England* (London, 1976), chaps. 4 and 5, D. C. Kubrin, "Providence and the Mechanical Philosophy: The Creation and the Dissolution of the World in Newtonian Thought" (Ph.D. diss., Cornell University, 1968), Michael Macklem, *The Anatomy of the World: Relations between Natural and Moral Law from Donne to Pope* (Minneapolis, 1958), chap. 3, James E. Force, *William Whiston: Honest Newtonian* (New York, 1985), chap. 2, and Paolo Rossi, *The Dark Abyss of Time: The History of the Earth and the History of Nations from Hooke to Vico*, trans. Lydia G. Cochrane (Chicago, 1984). Charles Blount launched the attack of the English deists with his *Miracles, no Violations of the Laws of Nature* (London, 1682). He quoted Burnet in *The Oracles of Reason* (London, 1693). The idea that Moses had "accommodated" the limited understanding of the vulgar in his writings had long been a widely accepted idea; what was new was the amount of accommodation being claimed. On the history of accommodation, see Scott Mandelbrote, "Isaac Newton and Thomas Burnet: Biblical Criticism and the Crisis of Late Seventeenth-Century England," in James E. Force and Richard H. Popkin, eds., *The Books of Nature and Scripture: Recent Essays on Natural Philosophy, Theology, and Biblical Criticism in the Netherlands of Spinoza's Time and the British Isles of Newton's Time* (Dordrecht, 1994), 149–78.

82. See R. M. Burns, *The Great Debate on Miracles: From Joseph Glanvill to David Hume* (Lewisburg, Pa., 1981), 51–57, for a interesting critique of Richard Westfall's claim that Robert Boyle must have realized on some level that there was a contradiction between his science and his religion.

83. Margaret Jacobs, *Newtonianism*, associated Newtonianism with Whig politics and commercialism. She has left a number of historians of science unconvinced. See Geoffrey Holmes, "Science, Reason, and Religion in the Age of Newton," *British Journal for the History of Science* 11 (1978), 164–71, Michael Hunter, *Science and Society in Restoration England* (Cambridge, 1981), 185–87, and Anita Guerrini, "The Tory Newtonians: Gregory, Pitcairne, and Their Circle," *Journal of British Studies* 25 (1986), 288–311. Newton's acceptance was not universal. High Churchmen, while committed to the mechanical philosophy, sometimes found Newtonianism, which relied heavily on experimentation and insufficiently on revelation, which introduced "occult" terms like gravity, and which tended, they thought, to factionalize the scientific community, in a way reminiscent of the troublesome doctrines of the mid seventeenth century. See Larry Stewart, "Samuel Clarke, Newtonianism, and the Factions of Post-Revolutionary

England," *Journal of the History of Ideas* 42 (1981), 53–72. The High Church in the eighteenth century was even to produce its own natural philosophy, Hutchinsonianism, which offered less room for heretical exegesis than did Newtonianism. On Hutchinsonianism, see C. B. Wilde, "Hutchinsonianism, Natural Philosophy and Religious Controversy in Eighteenth-Century England," *History of Science* 18 (1980), 1–24. Hutchinsonianism in America was propagated by the New England convert to Anglicanism, Samuel Johnson.

84. John Edwards, *Brief Remarks upon Mr. Whiston's New Theory of the Earth* (London, 1697), 28, 41–42.

85. For the early adaptation of Newtonian physics for the "saving" of the providential world order, via the Boyle lectures, see Henry Guerlac and M. C. Jacob, "Bentley, Newton, and Providence (The Boyle Lectures Once More)," *Journal of the History of Ideas* 30 (1969), 307–18. For Newton's own, more complex ideas on Providence, see David Kubrin, "Newton and the Cyclical Cosmos: Providence and the Mechanical Philosophy," *Journal of the History of Ideas* 28 (1967), 325–46.

86. Michael Hunter, "The Crown, the Public, and the New Science, 1689–1702," *Notes and Records of the Royal Society* 43 (1989), 109–11, dates the general acceptance of science's fashionableness in England to Queen Anne's reign. For eighteenth-century Anglican theology and providentialism, see Gregory F. Scholtz, "Anglicanism in the Age of Johnson: The Doctrine of Conditional Salvation," *Eighteenth Century Studies* 22 (1988–89), 182–207, and Jacob Viner, *The Role of Providence in the Social Order: An Essay in Intellectual History* (Philadelphia, 1972).

87. Simon, *Three Restoration Divines,* 274. Simon's book is the best modern source for Tillotson's life. Thomas Birch's account, appended to the third volume of Tillotson's *Works,* is the standard source. Earlier scholars characterized Tillotson and his circle as being semi-deists, but that caricature is disappearing. Simon is the place to start for a study of Tillotson's thought. For an interesting, theologically thoroughly internalist rehabilitation of Tillotson's thought from an orthodox perspective, see Alan C. Clifford, *Atonement and Justification: English Evangelical Theology, 1640–1790* (Oxford, 1990). For a study that mixes an analysis of Tillotson's circle as responding to its historical circumstances and as manifestating an enduring and conservative Christian piety, see W. M. Spellman, *The Latitudinarians and the Church of England, 1660–1700* (Athens, Ga., 1993). See also Roger L. Emerson, "Latitudinarianism and the English Deists," in *Deism, Masonry, and the Enlightenment,* ed. J. A. Leo Lemay (Newark, 1987), 19–48, and Gerard Reedy, S.J., "Interpreting Tillotson," *Harvard Theological Review* 86 (1993), 81–103. For a detailed study of one of Tillotson's close associates, see Robert Todd Carroll, *The Common-Sense Philosophy of Religion of Bishop Edward Stillingfleet, 1635–1699* (The Hague, 1975).

88. Norman Fiering, "The First American Enlightenment: Tillotson, Leverett, and Philosophical Anglicanism," *New England Quarterly* 54 (1981), 323–30, Larzer Ziff, *Puritanism in America: New Culture in a New World* (New York, 1973), 272–78, Silence Dogood [Benjamin Franklin], *New-England Courant,* 14 May 1722.

89. Tillotson, *Works,* 2:368, 2:558.

90. Ibid., 2:558.

91. Ibid., 2:344, 1:131, 2:344, 2:387, 2:388–89.

92. Ibid., 3:455–56, 2:340–41, 3:311, 2:346. Tillotson's fullest statement on the

difference between his soteriology and Calvinist soteriology is to be found a series of sermons, 2:324–49, in which he uncharacteristically went into a great deal of theological detail. Characteristically, he apologized at the end for having "so long insisted upon this argument, and handled it in a more contentious way than is usual with me" (344). But he did so "to undeceive good men concerning some current notions and doctrines, which I do really believe to be dishonorable to God . . . and a cause of great perplexity and discomfort to the minds of men, and a real discouragement to the resolutions and endeavours of becoming better."

93. Ibid., 3:68, 1:268, 2:330.

94. Ibid., 1:132–33, 3:295, 1:132.

95. Ibid., 2:533, 532. Tillotson did believe in witches and ghosts (the thought of seeing an apparition he considered "dreadful and full of terror"). See ibid., 1:261, 2:480.

96. Ibid., 1:80–81.

97. Ibid., 2:144.

98. Ibid., 1:82.

99. Ibid., 1:42–44. The equation of godliness and worldly prosperity was a new theme in Anglican Restoration preaching. Sommerville (*Popular Religion*, 43) has even found it in Anglican devotional manuals of the period. Horton Davies summed up the teaching of *The Whole Duty of Man*, the most popular Anglican devotional manual of the Restoration, as "enlightened self-interest is the sensible man's guide here to get to the hereafter." See Horton Davies, *Worship and Theology in England from Andrewes to Baxter, 1603–1690* (Princeton, 1975), 115.

100. Tillotson, *Works*, 3:630.

101. Ibid., 3:629, 626.

102. Ibid., 2:488.

103. Ibid., 1:36.

104. The one specific sin for which Tillotson was sure the nation had been punished, sure enough even to cite a scriptural text to justify his interpretation, an extremely rare practice for him, was the flirtation of its kings with Catholicism. Ibid., 1:289.

105. Tillotson was not alone in his amazed reaction to the deposing of James and the arrival of William and Mary. For Anglican providential interpretations of the events of 1689: see Gerald M. Straka, *Anglican Reactions to the Revolution of 1689* (Madison, 1962), chap. 6.

106. Tillotson, *Works*, 2:486. The idea expressed here goes back at least to Augustine, and was not alien to the Puritans. What is important is the new way in which it was being contextualized.

107. Simon, *Three Restoration Divines*, 276.

108. N. H. Keeble and Geoffrey F. Nuttall, *Calendar of the Correspondence of Richard Baxter*, 2 vols. (Oxford, 1991), 328–31, Cotton Mather, *Magnalia Christi Americana*, 2 vols. (1702; reprint, Hartford, 1853), 2:248.

109. See Jacob, *Newtonians*, chap. 1. The attempt to identify a coherent body of thought entitled "latitudinarianism" with a coherent group of churchmen has been challenged by John Spurr in a useful, if overstated, article, "Latitudinarianism and the Restoration Church," *Historical Journal* 31 (1988), 61–82. See n. 83 for other reservations voiced by historians about her hypothesis.

110. Thomas, *Religion*, 650–60. Thomas is careful to stress that he does not see these changes as causal for the large changes he is trying to account for.

111. Jürgen Habermas, *The Structural Transformation of the Public Sphere: An Inquiry into a Category of Bourgeois Society*, trans. Thomas Burger (Cambridge, Mass., 1989). Also useful is Peter Stallybrass and Allon White, *The Politics and Poetics of Transgression* (Ithaca, 1986), chap. 2. For an excellent account of the relationship between the public sphere, commerce, and the dissemination of the new science, see Larry Stewart, *The Rise of Public Science: Rhetoric, Technology, and Natural Philosophy in Newtonian Britain, 1660–1750* (New York, 1992).

112. Habermas does not speak of magi or ministers, but the extension seems logical enough.

113. Cited in Aytoun Ellis, *The Penny Universities: A History of the Coffee-Houses* (London, 1956), 258–59.

114. Habermas's account of the formation of a public sphere in England relies heavily on a Marxist-influenced base/superstructure model. For a debate about the appropriateness of that model in relationship to the formation of a public sphere in seventeenth-century England, see the essays by David Zaret and Lloyd Kramer in Craig Calhoun, ed., *Habermas and the Public Sphere* (Cambridge, Mass., 1992), "Religion, Science, and Printing in the Public Spheres in Seventeenth-Century England," 212–35, and "Habermas, History, and Critical Theory," 236–58.

115. Addison called Tillotson "the most eminent and useful author of the age we live in." He used him as a standard of English writing and annotated his sermons. See *Essays of Joseph Addison*, ed. James George Frazer, 2 vols. (London, 1915), 1:28, Peter Smithers, *The Life of Joseph Addison* (Oxford: Clarendon Press, 1954), 423.

116. For an overview of the intertwining of magic and science throughout the late seventeenth century, see Webster, *Paracelsus to Newton*.

117. See Stewart, *Rise of Public Science*, chap. 2, and Viner, *Role of Providence*, for the new conception of Providence.

118. On the French Prophets, see Hillel Schwartz, *The French Prophets: The History of a Millenarian Group in Eighteenth-Century England* (Berkeley, 1980).

119. H. Maurice, *An Impartial Account of Mr. John Mason of Water-Stratford, and His Sentiments* (London, 1695), 27, 29, 39. For more on Mason, see Christopher Hill, "John Mason and the End of the World," in his *Puritanism and Revolution: Studies in Interpretation of the English Revolution of the Seventeenth Century* (New York, 1964), 323–36. Cotton Mather considered Mason "well meaning but Melancholy." See Reiner Smolinskie, "An Authoritative Edition of Cotton Mather's Unpublished Manuscript 'Triparidisus,'" 3 vols. (Ph.D. diss., Pennsylvania State University, 1987), 3:599.

120. Maurice, *Impartial Account*, 12.

Chapter Three. Israel Strikes Back

1. John Collinges, *A Reasonable Account Why Some Nonconforming Ministers in England Judge it Sinful for Them to Perform their Ministerial Acts, in Publick, Solemn Prayer by the Prescribed Forms of Others* (London, 1679), sig. A5r.

2. Michael G. Hall, *Increase Mather, The Last American Puritan* (Middletown, Conn., 1988), 173.

3. On the flow of communication, see David Cressy, *Coming Over: Migration and Communication between England and New England in the Seventeenth Century* (New York, 1987), chaps. 10, 11. See also Francis J. Bremer, *Congregational Communion: Clerical Friendship in the Anglo-American Puritan Community, 1610–1692* (Boston, 1994), chap. 10.

4. Increase Mather, in Notes of Sermons Taken by Cotton Mather 1683, American Antiquarian Society, 133, Samuel Willard, Heads of Sermons by Cotton Mather 1684, American Antiquarian Society, 267, James Allin, Notes of Sermons, 40, 11, Timothy Woodbridge, in Cotton Mather, Notes of Sermons . . . I. Mather and Others 1681–1682, American Antiquarian Society, "XXV Section," no pag., John Danforth, ibid., "XXVII Section," Cotton Mather in Lectures, Notes of Sermons, September 1680–March 1681. See also Increase Mather, *A Sermon Wherein is Shewed that the Church of God is Sometimes a Subject of Great Persecution* (Boston, 1682), Samuel Willard, *The Fiery Trial no Strange Thing* (Boston, 1682), Samuel Willard, *The Child's Portion* (Boston, 1684).

5. Increase Mather, *The Doctrine of Divine Providence Opened and Applyed* (Boston, 1684), sig. A3r. The treatises referred to were Stephen Charnock, *A Treatise of Divine Providence* (London, 1680), John Collinges, *Several Discourses Concerning the Actual Providence of God* (London, 1678), Thomas Crane, *Isagoge ad Dei Providentiam: or, a Prospect of Divine Providence* (London, 1672), and John Flavel, *Divine Conduct: or, The Mystery of Providence* (1678; reprint, London, 1698).

6. Mather's list of Dissenter treatises perhaps should have included William Gearing, *The Eye and Wheel of Providence* (London, 1662). Gearing's book covered roughly the same territory as the others, although not as extensively or rigorously. He appears to have been a conservative Presbyterian, but while the other Dissenters were aware of each others' works, none of them referred to his. The one extended Anglican treatise from this period, Samuel Parker, *Disputationes Deo, et Providentia Divina* (London, 1678), was a philosophical tract. More Anglican treatises were to come in the 1690s, in response to deist and Socinian publications.

7. Mather, *Doctrine*, sig. A3v.

8. For biographical details on these ministers, see A. G. Matthews, *Calamy Revised: Being a Revision of Edmund Calamy's Account of the Ministers and Others Ejected and Silenced, 1660–1662* (Oxford, 1934), under the respective names. The republished work was an abridged version of *Divine Conduct*, discussed below, put out by a Scottish evangelical publishing firm, The Banner of Truth Trust, with a preface recommending its study and application.

9. Collinges, *Several Discourses*, sig. A2v.

10. Crane, *Isagoge*, sigs. A3v–A4r.

11. Collinges, *Several Discourses*, sig. A2r.

12. Flavel, *Divine Conduct*, 14.

13. Mather, *Doctrine*, 42–43, Crane, *Isagoge*, 113, Collinges, *Several Treatises*, 177.

14. Crane, *Isagoge*, sig. A3r.

15. Charnock, *A Treatise*, 373–74.

16. Flavel, *Divine Conduct*, 128.

17. Charnock, *A Treatise*, 179, Collinges, *Several Discourses*, 162.

18. Flavel, *Divine Conduct*, 254–55. Increase Mather, in John Flavel, *An Exposition of the Assemblies Catechism* (London, 1692), sig. A3v.

19. Mather, *Doctrine*, 34, Charnock, *A Treatise*, 293, Flavel, *Divine Conduct*, 32, Crane, *Isagoge*, 486.

20. Collinges, *Several Discourses*, sig. A2r, Flavel, *Divine Conduct*, 155, Charnock, *A Treatise*, 190, Collinges, *Several Treatises*, sig. A2iiv.

21. Very recent history in some instances: an arrest warrant had been issued in 1678 for Collinges in connection with a plot on the life of the Bishop of Norwich. See John T. Evans, *Seventeenth-Century Norwich: Politics, Religion and Government, 1620–1690* (Oxford, 1979), 266–67.

22. Collinges, *Several Discourses*, 148, 266–67. Others were making similar arguments for the economic advantages of tolerating Dissenters at this time, without necessarily invoking Providence. See Nicholas Tyacke, "The 'Rise of Puritanism' and the Legalizing of Dissent, 1571–1719," in *From Persecution to Toleration: The Glorious Revolution and Religion in England*, ed. Ole Peter Grell, Jonathan I. Israel, and Nicholas Tyacke (Oxford, 1991), 34–36.

23. Collinges, *Several Discourses*, 150.

24. Flavel, *Divine Conduct*, 17, Crane, *Isagoge*, 302–3, Charnock, *A Treatise*, 307, 311, Mather, *Doctrine*, 56. Faith that God struck down informers and other enemies of the Saints was as widespread in Nonconformist circles in England as the faith that God struck down the enemies of New England was in Massachusetts. Bunyan's Mr. Wiseman tells Attentive in *The Life and Death of Mr. Badman* (London, 1984), as a matter of fact, that "the judgment of God against this kind of people was made manifest, I think I may say, if not in all, yet in most of the counties of England . . . true stories, that are neither lie nor romance" (217). In the next century the otherwise tolerant and rationalistic Daniel Neal (who provoked the ire of Cotton Mather for both those reasons) was repeating tales of judgments on informers and persecutors in *The History of the Puritans*, 3 vols. (1732–38; reprint, London, 1837), 3:203, 394–96.

25. Collinges, *Several Discourses*, 207, Mather, *Doctrine*, 18.

26. Collinges, *Several Discourses*, 232, Charnock, *A Treatise*, 326, Flavel, *Divine Conduct*, 132, Charnock, *A Treatise*, 344.

27. Mather, *Doctrine*, 37–38, 55–56, quote from 55, Collinges, *Several Treatises*, 170. On experientially derived Restoration Puritan caution about precise eschatological dating, see Christopher Hill, *Antichrist in Seventeenth-Century England* (New York, 1971), 146–47, and *The Miscellaneous Works of John Bunyan*, ed. W. R. Owen, vol. 12 (Oxford, 1994), xxvi.

28. Theophilus Gale, *The Anatomie of Infidelitie* (London, 1672), has an interesting passage on the relationship of the Dissenters to national sins. While noting that Dissenters were not free from their share in the nation's vices he added, "Doth our blessed Lord, who was free from al sin, so much lament the sins of others, wherein he had no share . . . Oh! What a sad contemplation is it, to think how many great Professors make themselves guilty of National, or other-mens sins, by not lamenting over them?" (71–72). It is hard to think of a New England sermon conceiving such a distance between the Saints and the nation. Simon Patrick claimed that Dissenting ministers in their conventicles preached that they were all that restrained God from aban-

doning England entirely. See Simon Patrick, A *Friendly Debate Between a Conformist and a Non-Conformist* (London, 1669), 237.

29. For the covering laws, with their accompanying commentaries, see Collinges, *Several Discourses*, 188–447, Flavel, *Divine Conduct*, 33–104, Crane, *Isagoge*, 73–498.

30. Increase Mather, *An Essay for the Recording of Illustrious Providences* (Boston, 1684), was reissued once more in Massachusetts and twice in London, using the original sheets. See Thomas J. Holmes, *Increase Mather: A Bibliography of His Works*, 2 vols. (Cleveland, 1931), 1: 232–8.

31. The first dated reference to Poole's project comes in a letter to Richard Baxter dated 27 March 1656. See N. H. Keeble and Geoffrey F. Nuttall, *Calendar of the Correspondence of Richard Baxter*, 2 vols. (Oxford, 1991), 1:206. In secondary sources, Poole's project is discussed briefly in Keith Thomas, *Religion and the Decline of Magic: Studies in Popular Belief in Sixteenth-and Seventeenth-Century England* (London, 1971), 94–95, and at more length, with some excerpts from the Cambridge manuscript, in Alan Gauld, "Psychical Research in Cambridge from the Seventeenth Century to the Present," *Journal of the Society for Psychical Research* 99 (1978), 925–37. Gauld claims that the anonymous correspondent of Poole's (see below) was John Beale, but he gives no reason for the attribution.

32. Cambridge University Library (hereafter abbreviated as C.U.L.), MS Dd. iii. 64, fol. 136v. Used with permission of the Syndics of Cambridge University Library.

33. Ibid., fol. 136r.

34. Ibid., fols. 136r, 137r, 137r.

35. Thomas, *Religion and the Decline of Magic*, 95.

36. Peter Dear, "Totius in verba: Rhetoric and Authority in the Early Royal Society," *Isis* 76 (1985), 145–61. The pressure of this mode was such that Newton once faked the details of an experiment to bring it in line with expectations; an account of the role of witnesses in the emergent "conventions of generating the fact" may be found in Steven Shapin and Simon Schaffer, *Leviathan and the Air-Pump: Hobbes, Boyle, and the Experimental Life* (Princeton, 1985), 55–60, Thomas Sprat, *The History of the Royal Society of London* (London, 1665), 362.

37. C.U.L., MS Dd. iii. 64, fols. 138r, 139r. This correspondent includes a wonderful apparition story concerning a Dr. Firth, prebend at Windsor (141v), which bears repeating for two reasons: the story was recorded in Increase Mather, *An Essay for the Recording of Illustrious Providences* (Boston, 1684; reprint, London, 1856, as *Remarkable Providences Illustrative of The Earlier Days of American Colonisation*), sig. Bv, hereafter referred to as *Illustrious Providences*, but in a somewhat different and briefer form, and the story affords, in a section not included in Mather's version, a vivid example of the power of suggestion in a culture of wonders. "[Dr. Firth's] sonn told mee that his Father had seene a Vision representing his owne death & the death of all or most of the rest of his family. The Vision is executed saith hee & the rest are all dead, & my returne is next & at hand. Hee was not then sick, but soone after his Spirit was smitten, & at midnight hee repayrd to the graves & monuments at Eton College. I ofttimes rose at midnight, & for pitty fetcht him thence. But hee refused comfort & said hee must take his habitation amongst the dead. Soe in a short time hee did. And I observd, that the Vision was performed, throughly."

38. C.U.L., MS Dd. iii. 64, fol. 140r. The partisan activities of Sion College in this

period are recounted in Philip J. Anderson, "Sion College and the London Provincial Assembly, 1647–1660," *Journal of Ecclesiastical History* 37 (1986), 68–90.

39. C.U.L., MS Dd. iii. 64, fol. 137r.

40. Ibid., fol. 139r.

41. Richard Baxter wrote enthusiastic letters to Poole about the project and its organization. In a letter to Baxter dated 3 February 1658/9, Poole mentioned that he was still attending to the "business of providences" but that he needed a scribe, someone to collect stories, and funds for expenses. This and other letters relating to Poole's project from the Baxter Papers at Dr. William's Library are satisfactorily abstracted in Keeble, *Calendar*, 1:206, 262–65, 380.

42. For accounts of these shipments by Hartlib to Davenport, see "Correspondence of the Founders of the Royal Society with Governor Winthrop of Connecticut," *Massachusetts Historical Society Proceedings* 16 (1878), 212, "Some Correspondence of John Winthrop, Jr., and Samuel Hartlib," ed. G. H. Turnbull, Massachusetts Historical Society *Proceedings* 72 (1957–60), 55–58, 37–38, and *The Letters of John Davenport, Puritan Divine*, ed. Isabel MacBeath Calder (New Haven, 1937), 141. On Hartlib's collecting of providences, see his letters to John Worthington in *The Diary and Correspondence of Dr. John Worthington*, 2 vols. (Chetham Society, 1847, 1855), 1:292, 350, 2:61. The phrase "histories of illustrious providences" occurs on 1:350. More on the relationship of Hartlib, a Royalist and non-Calvinist of broad reformist sympathies and wide interests, to Davenport, usually considered a fervent Independent, can be gathered from G. H. Turnbull, *Hartlib, Dury and Comemius: Gleanings from Hartlib's Papers* (London, 1947), passim.

43. Michael G. Hall has a thorough review of Mather's scientific activities in this period in *Last American Puritan*, 165–74. But his claim that Mather's interest in science was new at this time (159) has to be weighed against the fact that copies of the Royal Society's *Philosophical Transactions* in the Mather Library at the American Antiquarian Society, the basic contemporary dispenser of information on the work of the Royal Society and related groups, go back to 1667.

44. As much as probably will ever be known or even inferred about the philosophical society can be found in Otho T. Beal, "Cotton Mather's Early 'Curiosa Americana' and the Boston Philosophical Society of 1683," *William and Mary Quarterly*, 3d ser., 18 (1961), 360–72. The advanced nature of Increase Mather's scientific writings at this time can be exaggerated. Robert Middlekauff, *The Mathers: Three Generations of Puritan Intellectuals* (New York, 1971), 141–42, claims that Mather, with his commitment to signs and wonders generated by an unpredictable God, was "appalled" in *Kometographia* (Boston, 1683) by his realization that Robert Hooke was on the verge of mathematically working out the periodicity, and thus the predictability, of comets. In fact Mather did not mention Hooke's speculations at all, only his observations of an earlier comet (16). Mather did discuss (calmly) astrologers' efforts to predict the appearance of comets (such predictions had only a limited validity). Michael G. Hall, *Increase Mather: The Last American Puritan* (Middletown, Conn., 1988), 170–71, has argued that Mather in claiming that comets had natural effects on earth was veering from traditional New England doctrine. But the traditional New England (and Reformed) doctrine was only that heavenly bodies could not affect the minds of humans, and Mather never disputed it. David D. Hall, *Worlds of Wonder, Days of Judgment: Popular Religious*

Beliefs in Early New England (New York, 1989), 107–8, stresses Mather's skepticism about eclipses in *Kometographia* as an indication of his progressivism. However, eclipses, or any predictable and accountable phenomenon, were never taken by the "learned" to be automatically ominous. Mather, *Kometographia*, 20–21, thought that in some circumstances they were and that in most they were not.

45. Increase Mather, *A Discourse concerning the Danger of Apostacy* (Boston, 1679), 71.

46. Perry Miller and Stephen Foster see *Illustrious Providences* as a failed attempt on Mather's part to write his providential history of New England, but the essay's stated intentions and its contents give no reason to think either that it is anything except an attempt to carry on Poole's design or that it represents a retreat from writing a history of New England. See Perry Miller, *The New England Mind: From Colony to Province* (Cambridge, Mass., 1953), 142–45, and Stephen Foster, *The Long Argument: English Puritanism and the Shaping of New England Culture, 1570–1700* (Chapel Hill, 1991), 231–36. The statement of John Higginson to Mather that Foster cites in support of his claim, "Being lately at Mr. Shepard's I understood from him that you do not confine yourselfe in giving Instances of Illustrious Providences to things done in NE" (361n. 4), reads to me simply as a clarification of the prospectus drawn up at the start of the project (for which, see below).

47. Mather, *Illustrious Providences*, "Preface."

48. The following are the studies of *Illustrious Providences* that I found most insightful and accurate. Kenneth Murdock, *Increase Mather: The Foremost American Puritan* (Cambridge, Mass., 1925), 167–76, as part of his larger effort to portray Mather as something other than a reactionary fanatic, demonstrated that *Illustrious Providences* in its assumptions about the supernatural was not abnormally superstitious for the times and in its techniques was up to date for scientific writing. Holmes, *Increase Mather*, 1:232–49, traced the book's literary sources and its bibliographical history. Michael G. Hall, *Last American Puritan*, 167–73, nicely placed *Illustrious Providences* within the context of Mather's scientific interests in the early 1680s. Hall, *Worlds of Wonder*, 82–89, well re-creates the web of traditional beliefs out of which *Illustrious Providences* sprang.

49. Gary Stuart De Krey, *A Fractured Society: The Politics of London in the First Age of Party, 1688–1715* (Oxford, 1985), 84.

50. For Boyle's dread of supernatural phenomena, see Michael Hunter, "Alchemy, Magic and Moralism in the Thought of Robert Boyle," *British Journal for the History of Science* 23 (1990), 387–410; for his providentialism, see Steven Shapin, *A Social History of Truth: Civility and Science in Seventeenth-Century England* (Chicago, 1994), 156–60.

51. Murdock, *Increase Mather*, 264–65. For Boyle as an emblematic figure, see Steven Shapin, "'A Scholar and a Gentleman': The Problematic Identity of the Scientific Practitioner in Early Modern England," *History of Science* 29 (1991), 298–99. For the power of Boyle as a cultural model on at least one New Englander, see Rick Alan Kennedy, "Thy Patriarch's Desire: Thomas and William Brattle in Puritan Massachusetts" (Ph.D. diss., University of California at Santa Barbara, 1987), 48–50.

52. For examples of Boyle's changing prose style over the 1650s, see Lawrence M.

Principe, "Style and Thought of the Early Boyle: Discovery of the 1648 Manuscript of *Seraphic Love*," *Isis* 85 (1994), 257.

53. Robert Boyle, *Works of the Hounorable Robert Boyle*, ed. Thomas Birch, 6 vols. (London, 1772), 1:291–318. These passages are from "A Proemial Essay . . . with Some Considerations touching Experimental Essays in General."

54. Simon Schaffer, "Making Certain," *Social Studies of Science* 14 (1984), 142. See also Ian Hacking, *The Emergence of Probablity: A Philosophical Study of Early Ideas about Probablity, Induction and Statistical Inference* (Cambridge, 1975), 18–33.

55. For Mather's diligence in tracking down information from his correspondents, see Massachusetts Historical Society *Collections*, 4th ser., 8 (1868), 309, 311, 464, 609. Mather claimed in *Illustrious Providences* that most of the ghost stories he investigated proved to be but "phansie and frightful apprehensions, without sufficient ground" (142). Mather left out of his volume, for reasons now impossible to discern, the accounts of monstrous births and omens he received. If he had a philosophical objection to these, it was a late one. He mentioned them in his account of King Philip's War, and noted, "God would have such providences to be observed and recorded; He doth not send such things for nothing." Increase Mather, *A Brief History of the Warr with the Indians in New-England* (Boston, 1676), reprinted in *So Dreadfull a Judgment:Puritan Responses to King Philip's War, 1676–1677*, ed. Richard Slotkin and James K. Folsom (Middletown, Conn., 1978), 125–26.

56. Mather, *Illustrious Providences*, 45, 111, 245.

57. See Peter Lockwood Rumsey, *Acts of God and the People, 1620–1730* (Ann Arbor, 1986), 33, David Paul Nord, "Teleology and News: The Religious Roots of American Journalism, 1630–1720," *Journal of American History* 77 (1990), 35. These authors interpret the lack of a didactic framework in *Illustrious Providences* as a natural outgrowth of the Puritan approach to special providences, which approach, it is said, had tended to assume that providences could, if presented clearly enough, speak for themselves. But providences were never left to speak for themselves by the Puritans when their meaning could be deciphered. They were always presented within a didactic framework. See Foster, *Long Argument*, 232, for a similar observation about *Illustrious Providences* within a very different interpretive framework.

58. Mather, *Illustrious Providences*, 235.

59. Mather, *Doctrine*, 97–103.

60. Increase Mather, *The Later Sign Discoursed of*, bound with Increase Mather, *Heavens Alarm to the World* (Boston, 1682), 27–29.

61. John Oldmixon, quoted in Cotton Mather, *Parentator* (Boston, 1724), ix.

62. Massachusetts Historical Society *Collections*, 4th ser., 8 (1868), 630, 311. George Keith, the unguided missile of late-seventeenth-century Anglo-American religious controversy, who was at this time a Quaker, attacked Mather for the judgments on Quakers that did get into *Illustrious Providences*. Keith denied that the Quakers who had been punished by God were approved of by other members of that sect. He then interpreted God's judgments against New England as punishment for its persecution of Quakers and cited some specific examples of God's revenge on New England. See *The Presbyterian and Independent Visible Churches of New England . . . found to be No True Church of Christ* (Philadelphia, 1687), 220–28. Quaker predictions of God's punishment of New England had some effect on Congregational nerves, already frayed by the

Deity's judgments on their colony. "The *Quakers* in their late Pamphlets presume to foretel, *the utter Removing, Undoing,*and *Destroying of all* our Churches . . . and no doubt, the Devil will turn every stone to accomplish that Prediction." Cotton Mather, *Fair Weather* (Boston, 1691), 17.

63. Cotton Mather, for example, "*Memorandum.* On 7 *d.* 11*m.* Arrives to mee, a Book in *Folio,* this year published in *London,* which professes itself to bee a Collection of *Remarkable Providences.* I find myself often quoted in this Book; yea, very often; and very large Paragraphs from several Books of mine transcribed into it. And I find, the Names and Lives of Nonconformists, therein much magnified, tho' the Book bee written by a Conformist." *The Diary of Cotton Mather,* 2 vols. (New York, n.d.) 1:246–47.

64. Turner, *History,* sig. Br.

65. The prospectus for the project may be found in the *Athenian Mercury,* 22 May 1695.

66. These advertisements seem to have been used to drum up interest in the book as well. Turner's project might be seen thus as forming a bridge between the popular culture of traditional society and the popular culture of a commercial society. For examples, see the *Athenian Mercury,* 20 July 1695, and 4 June 1695.

67. Alexander Pope, *God's Revenge against Punning* (London, 1716), in *The Prose Works of Alexander Pope,* ed. Norman Ault, 2 vols. (Oxford, 1936), 269–72. The attribution is not universally accepted; see Marjorie Hope Nicolson and G. S. Rousseau, '*This Long Disease, My Life': Alexander Pope and the Sciences* (Princeton, 1968), 182–83.

68. Whiston, *Memoirs of the Life and Writings of Mr. William Whiston* (London, 1749), 5, James E. Force, *William Whiston: Honest Newtonian* (New York, 1985), 129–30.

69. Flavel, *Divine Conduct,* 235–36.

70. Collinges, *Several Discourses,* 186.

71. Charnock, *A Treatise,* 369–70.

72. Crane, *Isagoge,* 361.

73. For these reform attempts, see Patrick Curry, *Prophecy and Power: Astrology in Early Modern England* (Princeton, 1989), 64–78.

74. It was not at all clear at the time that the Restoration Church settlement closed the curtains on the prolonged struggle to create a purified English national church. Apart from the activities, legal and illegal, of the Dissenters themselves to undo it, a wing of the established church actively worked to bring back in the moderate Dissenters, and within the church itself many ministers seemed to have carried on a quiet resistance to the suppression of Puritanism, while their godly parishioners moved freely between the Anglican church and Dissenting conventicles in search of satisfying preaching. See John Spurr, *The Restoration Church of England, 1646–1689* (New Haven, 1992), 184–209, and John D. Ramsbottom, "Presbyterians and 'Partial Conformity' in the Restoration Church of England," *Journal of Ecclesiastical History* 43 (1992), 249–70.

75. James Travis Spivey, Jr., "Middle Way Men, Edmund Calamy, and the Crises of Moderate Nonconformity" (Ph.D. diss., Oxford University, 1986).

76. Roger Thomas, "Parties in Nonconformity," in *The English Presbyterians from Elizabethan Puritanism to Modern Unitarianism,* ed. C. G. Bolam, Jeremy Goring, H. L. Short, and Roger Thomas (London, 1968), 95, Richard Ashcraft, *Revolutionary Politics and Locke's Two Treatises of Government* (Princeton, 1986), 54–69, ibid., "Latitudinar-

ianism and Toleration: Historical Myth versus Political History," in *Philosophy, Science, and Religion in England 1640–1700*, ed. Richard Kroll, Richard Ashcraft, and Perez Zagorin (Cambridge, 1992), 151–71. On the deists, see J. A. I. Champion, *The Pillars of Priestcraft Shaken: The Church of England and Its Enemies* (New York, 1991), and on the republicans' earlier religious unorthodoxy, see Blair Worden, "Classical Republicanism and the Puritan Revolution," in *History and the Imagination: Essays in Honor of H. R. Trevor-Roper*, ed. Hugh Lloyd-Jones, Valerie Pearl, and Blair Worden (New York, 1981), 182–200.

77. Edmund Calamy, *An Historical Account of My Own Life*, 2 vols. (London, 1830), Arthur D. Kaledin, "The Mind of John Leverett" (Ph.D. diss., Harvard University, 1965), Edmund Calamy, *A Continuation of the Account of the Ministers . . . Who were Ejected or Silenced After the Restoration in 1660*, 2 vols. (London, 1727), 1:xi, William M. Lamont, *Richard Baxter and the Millennium: Protestant Imperialism, Dissenters and the English Revolution* (London, 1979), 274–80, and James Bennett and David Bogue, *The History of the Dissenters, from the Revolution to the Year 1808*, 2d ed. (London, 1833), 405.

78. Charles Leslie, *Snake in the Grass*, 3d ed. (London, 1698), xxxi. Other parallels between the effects of the Glorious Revolution in England and Massachusetts are noted in Richard P. Gildrie, *The Profane, the Civil, and the Godly: The Reformation of Manners in Orthodox New England, 1679–1749* (University Park, 1994), chap. 8.

79. See, for example, the book by the second-generation latitudinarian (at least until the church crises of Queen Anne's reign) John Sharp, *Sixteen Casuistical Sermons Preached on Several Occasions*, a sustained critique of Puritan piety and Reformed orthodox theology, published in 1729 as volume 3 of John Sharp, *Sermons Preached on Several Occasions*, 4 vols. (London, 1716–29).

80. William Nicholls, quoted in John Waddington, *Congregational History, 1700–1800* (London, 1876), 21.

81. Copies of those journals in the Mather Library at the American Antiquarian Society that have signatures on the flyleaves have Increase's, not Cotton's. For background on the journals, see Norman S. Fiering, "The Transatlantic Republic of Letters: A Note on the Circulation of Learned Periodicals to Early Eighteenth-Century America," *William and Mary Quarterly*, 3d ser., 33 (1976), 642–61.

82. Hall, *Worlds of Wonder*, 107, argues that Mather's *Angelographia* and the treatise bound with it, *A Disquisition Concerning Apparitions* (Boston, 1696), with their rejection of wonder stories from the ancient church historian Eusebius, their argument that the appearance of angels had largely stopped, and their suggestion that many so-called prophets and visionaries were simply unbalanced melancholics, demonstrated a new "mistrust for the lore of wonders" and a questioning of "sources that he [Mather] once took for granted." The stories rejected from Eusebius, however, concerned the appearances of dead saints to the living, a phenomenon Protestants denied was possible. Similarly, it was also Protestant doctrine that the appearance of angels had largely stopped. Mather, *Disquisition*, 17–24, made it clear that satanic as well as natural influences were at work in false prophets. In any event, in a book filled with thoroughly "wonderful" accounts of the appearances and doings of angels and demons, prophetic dreams, and phantom voices drawn from a wide variety of ancient and modern sources, such qualifications are slender evidence for the existence of a new skepticism.

83. Increase Mather, A *Disquisition Concerning the State of the Souls of Men (Especially of Good MEN) When Separated from their Bodies*, 2d ed. (Boston, 1712), sigs. A2r–A2v, ibid., *Several Sermons* (Boston, 1715), 12, ix, ibid., *Five Sermons on Several Subjects* (Boston, 1719), 11, "All sorts of Sins are in the hearts of Men, and those Sins which they may seem to have an Antipathy to . . . *Saul* seemed to have an antipathy against Witches and destroyed them, yet this very *Saul* goes to the Witch of *Endor*," ibid., *Seasonable Meditations Both for the Winter and Summer* (Boston, 1712), I.

Chapter Four. Cotton Mather and the Hand of God

1. Cotton Mather, *Magnalia Christi Americana*, 2 vols. (1702; reprint, Hartford, 1853), 1:28.

2. See the introduction by Kenneth B. Murdock, with the assistance of Elizabeth W. Miller, to Cotton Mather, *Magnalia Christi Americana: Books I and II* (Cambridge, Mass., 1977), 26–30, for an account of the *Magnalia's* conception and original publishing circumstances. Cotton Mather, *The Diary of Cotton Mather*, 2 vols. (New York, n.d.), 1:445.

3. Mather, *Magnalia*, 1:57–58, 283–84, 2:566, 1:84.

4. Mercies and judgments are scattered throughout the *Magnalia*, but see specifically 2:343–403. For epidemics, 1:101, for prodigies, 2:519, 560. Prodigies play a smaller role in the *Magnalia* than one might expect from Mather's earlier work; for reasons for this, see chap. 5.

5. See, for example, *Magnalia*, 1:341, 343, 358, 2:39–40, and for a saint especially given the gifts of the Spirit, the biography of John Wilson, 1:302–21.

6. The references to thunder are 2:361–72. The reference to lightning is on 2:361. The main sections on witchcraft are 1:204–13 and 2:446–79. The reference to Quakers is on 2:528, and to the siege of Cape Anne on 2:621–23.

7. Two fine recent biographies of Mather are David Levin, *Cotton Mather: The Young Life of the Lord's Remembrancer, 1663–1703* (Cambridge, Mass., 1978), and Kenneth Silverman, *The Life and Times of Cotton Mather* (New York, 1984). Perry Miller has a brilliant, if not entirely accurate or impartial, sketch of Mather in *The New England Mind from Colony to Province* (Cambridge, Mass., 1953). Mather's intellectual biography is explored at length in Robert Middlekauff, *The Mathers: Three Generations of Puritan Intellectuals, 1596–1728* (New York, 1971). When possible, Middlekauff should be checked against a study somewhat different in scope, but more accurate, Richard F. Lovelace, *The American Pietism of Cotton Mather: Origins of American Evangelicalism* (Grand Rapids, 1979). For an excellent psychological portrait of Mather, see Mitchell Robert Breitwieser, *Cotton Mather and Benjamin Franklin: The Price of Representative Personality* (New York, 1985). Chapter 4 of James W. Jones, *The Shattered Synthesis: American Puritanism before the Great Awakening* (New Haven, 1973) relies heavily on Miller's framework. Two Ph.D. dissertations worth consulting are Joyce Olson Ransome, "Cotton Mather and the Catholic Spirit" (University of California, Berkeley, 1966) and John S. Erwin, "Like a Thief in the Night: Cotton Mather's Millenniallism" (Indiana University, Bloomington, 1987).

8. For Mather's admiration of Cromwell, see Cotton Mather, *Manuductio ad Ministerium* (Boston, 1726), 63–64, and ibid., *Parentator* (Boston, 1724), 18.

9. Mather, *Manuductio*, 150, 100, ibid., *Observanda* (Boston, 1695), 21, for the Crane quotation. In *Observanda*, Mather took over much of the terminology of Crane's *Isagoge*, as well. In *Providence Asserted and Adored* (Boston, 1719), recently rediscovered by David Levin and printed in facsimile in *Essex Institute Historical Collections* 125 (1989), 209–39, Mather used Flavel's rhetorical device in *Divine Conduct* of making a series of presumed unanswerable "demands" to the scoffer at Providence.

10. Stephen Foster, *The Long Argument: English Puritanism and the Shaping of New England Culture, 1570–1700* (Chapel Hill, 1991), 288.

11. As in his comment neatly tying together the Anglican rejection of predestination and the much-preached Anglican doctrine of passive obedience: "There will be *Great Masters of Reason* (as they would be accounted,) who will allow the most Arbitrary Sovereignty to their Clay Monarchs . . . yett out of their Emnity, and Malignity and Rebellion against the Infinite God, will deny Him this Prerogative." See Romans 9 in Mather's unpublished and unpaginated "Biblia American," MS, Massachusetts Historical Society. I date the comment from internal evidence to have been written in the 1690s.

12. Cotton Mather, *Things for a Distress'd People to Think upon* (Boston, 1696), 50.

13. David D. Hall, *The Faithful Shepherd: A History of the New England Ministry in the Seventeenth Century* (Chapel Hill, 1972), 244–47, has a good discussion of the Mathers' "declension politics" of this period. However, his claim that the above sermon barely mentions the magistrates and that Mather had by this time lost his faith in governmental coercion to bring about reformation hardly seems to agree with the text (247). See *Things*, 54–55, 61–63. Mather, in fact, still had some justification for his faith in rousing the government to action. In 1697, he preached a jeremiad (never printed) to the House of Representatives and stirred them to pass laws against blasphemy and atheism. See Mather, *Diary*, 1:237–38.

14. Mather, *Magnalia* 2:397, 402, 394, 392.

15. Larzer Ziff, "Upon What Pretext?: The Book and Literary History," *American Antiquarian Society Proceedings* 95 (1979), 303. See also D. R. Woolf, "The 'Common Voice': History, Folklore, and Oral Tradition in Early Modern England," *Past and Present* 120 (1988), 26–52.

16. For a general account of the "catholick" party, see John Corrigan, *The Prism of Piety: Catholick Congregational Clergy at the Beginning of the Enlightenment* (New York, 1991). Corrigan presents something of an ideal-type catholick, relying heavily on Colman. For a study of the complex influences on another important, slightly earlier figure, see Michael F. Gibson, "The Ambiguities of Moderation: Influences on the Sermon Theology of William Brattle, 1696–1716" (M.A. thesis, University of Georgia, 1994). On the catholicks' playing down of providential oracularism, see the final chapter of this book. Colman, most prominent of the catholicks, specifically criticized what he saw as excessive providential scrutiny in a rare disapproving comment on another Boston minister, Thomas Bridge, given in his funeral sermon for Bridge, *A Devout and Humble Enquiry* (Boston, 1715). Bridge, raised up in the providentialism of Restoration London Congregationalism, brought that particular brand of experimental piety with him when he arrived in Boston to become minister of the First Church in 1704. He soon became noted in Boston for his observations of Providence. Colman suggested that Bridge observed Providence somewhat obsessively, besides preaching too obscurely

(34, 33). Unsurprisingly, Cotton Mather, in his own funeral sermon on Bridge (*Benedictus* [Boston, 1715], 44, 42), praised both Bridge's providential observations and his preaching. For a sample of what they were reacting to, see Thomas Bridge, *What Faith can Do* (Boston, 1713).

17. John Oldmixon, cited in Cotton Mather, *Parentator* (Boston, 1724), ix, Ebenezer Turrell, *The Life and Character of the Reverend Benjamin Colman* (Boston, 1749), 27, 33. The precise criticism of Colman's preaching was that it was too "legal," in other words, taking after models like Tillotson excessively.

18. For the changes at Harvard in the late 1680s, and Morton's relation to them, see Norman S. Fiering, *Moral Philosophy at Seventeenth-Century Harvard* (Chapel Hill, 1981), chap. 5, ibid., "The First American Enlightenment: Tillotson, Leverett, and Philosophical Anglicanism," *New England Quarterly* 54 (1981), 323–30. Morton is not likely to have approved of the preaching of Tillotson. He advised ministerial candidates in the reign of Charles II to preach Christ and "avoid the unsavoury Way of Moral Philosophy Lectures." The criticism of Tillotson was that he neglected the first for the second. See Edmund Calamy, *A Continuation of the Account of the Ministers . . . Who were Ejected or Silenced After the Restoration in 1660*, 2 vols. (London, 1727) 1:199. On the possible scientific influence of another English immigrant in the 1680s, see Theodore Hornberger, "Samuel Lee (1625–1691): A Clerical Channel for the Flow of New Ideas to Seventeenth-Century New England," *Osiris* 1 (1936), 341–55.

19. See Foster, *Long Argument*, chap. 4, and Francis J. Bremer, *Congregational Communion: Clerical Friendship in the Anglo-American Puritan Community, 1610–1692* (Boston, 1994), 188–89, 198.

20. Richard Baxter, *Reliquae Baxterianae: Or, Mr. Richard Baxter's Narrative of the most Memorable Passages of his Life and Times* (London, 1694), part 2, 297). The passage, neglected by historians of early New England, is worth quoting in full:

> Especially those in France and New England who were yet more remote were far more deceived by these Appearances, and the more ready to bless us in our present State, and almost wish it were their own: Insomuch that there grew on a sudden in *New-England* a great Inclination to Episcopal Government; for many of them saw the Inconveniencies of Separations, and how much their way did tend to Divisions, and they read my Books, and what I said against both the Souldiers and Schismaticks in *England*; and they thought that the Church-Government here would have been such as we were pleased with; so that these and many other Motives made them begin to think of a Conformity: Till at last Mr. *Norton*, with one Mr. *Bradstreet*, a Magistrate, came over and saw how things went, and those in *New-England* heard at last how we were all silenced and cast out: And then they began to remember again that there is something beside Schism to be feared.

For the thinness of Royalist sentiment proper in New England, however, see Paul R. Lucas, "Colony or Commonwealth: Massachusetts Bay, 1661–1666," *William and Mary Quarterly*, 3d ser., 24 (1967), 88–107.

21. On the conjunction of intolerance and a comprehensive church in New England, see E. Brooks Holifield, "On Toleration in Massachusetts," *Church History* 38 (1968), 188–200, and more generally, Hall, *Faithful Shepherd*. For Baxter's attitude to New England ecclesiology, see William M. Lamont, *Richard Baxter and the Millennium:*

Protestant Imperialism and the English Revolution (London, 1979), 227. On the intolerance of the Anglican latitudinarians, see Richard Ashcraft, "Latitudinarianism and Toleration: Historical Myth versus Political History," in *Philosophy, Science, and Religion in England 1640–1700*, ed. Richard Kroll, Richard Ashcraft, and Perez Zagorin (Cambridge, 1992), 151–71.

22. The fellow was Thomas Graves, for whom see Clifford K. Shipton and John L. Silbey, *Biographical Sketches of those Who Attended Harvard College*, 17 vols. (Boston, 1873–1975), 1:480–84, Bernard Bailyn, *The New England Merchants in the Seventeenth Century* (Cambridge, Mass., 1955), 124.

23. The formation of the Brattle Street Church is a set piece of early New England history. The classic account is Perry Miller, *The New England Mind: From Colony to Province* (Cambridge, Mass., 1953), chap. 14. See also Howard C. Adams, "Benjamin Colman: A Critical Biography" (Ph.D. diss., Pennsylvania State University, 1976), 97–130. On the English background to Colman's theology, see Charles Burke Giles, "Benjamin Colman: A Study of the Movement toward Reasonable Religion in the Seventeenth Century" (Ph.D. diss., University of California at Los Angeles, 1963), and Corrigan, *Prism of Piety*, chap. 1. As Foster, *Long Argument*, 281, points out, the other major challenge to the "New England Way," Solomon Stoddard's church innovations, was a variation on a traditional Puritan theme.

24. The popularization of these arguments is usually traced back to Hugo Grotius, although he adopted them surreptitiously in large part from Faustus Socinus (a pedigree that would have presumably appalled most of those who used them). See Jan Paul Heering, "De Veritate Religionis Christiane," in *Hugo Grotius, Theologian: Essays in Honour of G. H. M. Posthumus Meyjes*, ed. Henk J. M. Nellen and Edwin Rabbie (Leiden, 1994), 46–48. For examples of the older method of "proving" the truth of Christianity by Restoration Dissenters, see Samuel Willard, *A Compleat Body of Divinity* (Boston, 1726), 16–20, and *The Works of John Owen*, ed. William H. Goold, 16 vols. (London, 1965), 4:47–55.

25. For Mather's attempts at universality see Breitwieser, *Cotton Mather*, chap. 2. Mather's striving after a representative nature is also a theme of Levin, *Cotton Mather*. For Mather's publications, see Thomas J. Holmes, *Cotton Mather: A Bibliography of His Work*, 3 vols. (Cambridge, 1940).

26. Benjamin Colman, *The Holy Walk of Blessed Enoch* (Boston, 1728), 23.

27. Middlekauff, *The Mathers*, 298–301, Jeffrey Jeske, "Cotton Mather: Physico-Theologian," *Journal of the History of Ideas* 47 (1986), 583–94. The quotation is from Middlekauff (296). Middlekauff also sees a subsequent partial disenchantment with reason on Mather's part, but that disenchantment is based on a questionable interpretation of his initial enthusiasm. Richard F. Lovelace, *The American Pietism of Cotton Mather: Origins of American Evangelicalism* (Grand Rapids, 1979), 41–51, argues that Mather never felt any attraction to Enlightenment rationalism in his religiosity, a reading with which I agree, with the qualifications discussed below.

28. Mather, *Diary*, 1:360–61.

29. Cotton Mather, *Reasonable Religion* (Boston, 1700), 49, 20.

30. The phrase in quotation is from Jeske, "Cotton Mather," 588.

31. Cotton Mather, *The Everlasting Gospel* (Boston, 1700), 4, ibid., *The Great Physician* (Boston, 1700), 7.

32. Mather, *Diary*, 1:389. These were published as *Christianity to the Life* (Boston, 1702).

33. J. Sears McGee, *The Godly Man in Stuart England: Anglicans, Puritans, and the Two Tables, 1620–1670* (New Haven, 1976), 107–13, ibid., "Conversion and The Imitation of Christ," *Journal of British Studies* 15 (1976), 21–39, Mather, *Diary*, 1:120 (recording a series of sermons on the example of Christ preached in 1685). For examples of preaching on the imitation of Christ by Puritans whom Mather admired, see John Cotton, *A Practical Commentary . . . upon the First Epistle General of John* (London, 1656), 72–74, and John Flavel, *The Fountain of Life* (London, 1671), passim.

34. Mather, *Christianity to the Life*, 8, 7.

35. Ibid., 15. Mather had preached on ecumenicism before, most notably in *Blessed Unions* (Boston, 1692), but he had never accompanied such preaching with the use of ecumenical materials. Mather, who, besides dealing with Brattle Street, was also engaged with Solomon Stoddard and his Presbyterian innovations in Northampton and had just finished exposing a very popular but fraudulent preacher from England, also had personal reasons for being attracted to the imitation of Christ at this time. In his diary in 1700, he recorded his first surviving meditation on that imitation. The meditation centered on the theme of being reviled and persecuted by his enemies just as Christ had been. Mather's willingness to be so reviled was an *"infallible Symptome"* that he was among the saved. See Mather, *Diary*, 1:345–46.

36. To imitate Christ in Mather's emotionally wrought fashion, among other practices, one "must *Fast* as well as *Pray*, and spend *whole Dayes* in Cryes unto God." One could expect to wrestle with *"Temptations* from that *Evil Spirit*, whom the *Holy Spirit* called, *The Prince of this World*." One would "*Mourn* for all the *Blindness*, & all the *Hardness*, & and all the *Sins* against God, wherewith you see other men undoing of themselves." Mather, *Christianity*, 39, 42, 50. For later uses of the imitation of Christ by Mather, see *Malachi* (Boston, 1716), 25–27. Mather also incorporated the motif into his private piety; see the series in the *Diary*, 2:552, 555, 556, 557, 558, 559–60, 560–61, 563–64, 565, 566, 568, 569.

37. Richard R. Johnson, *Adjustment to Empire: The New England Colonies 1675–1715* (New Brunswick, 1981), 384–85; Bellomont's first action as governor of New York had been to issue a proclamation forbidding cursing, drunkenness, lewd conduct, and Sabbath-breaking. See Robert C. Ritchie, *Captain Kidd and the War against the Pirates* (Cambridge, Mass., 1986), 169. Bellomont's less than entirely godly relationship with Kidd can be followed in Ritchie's book.

38. Mather might have been particularly concerned to show his urbanity in this sermon because he knew he was not the governor's first choice. See Mather, *Diary*, 1:349.

39. Kenneth Silverman, *The Life and Times of Cotton Mather* (New York, 1984), 193–221.

40. Carl Bridenbaugh, *Cities in the Wilderness: The First Century of Urban Life in America, 1625–1742* (New York, 1960), 259, 226.

41. On Boston's early newspapers within an English context, see Ian K. Steele, *The English Atlantic: An Exploration of Communication and Community* (New York, 1986), 132–58, and Charles E. Clarke, *The Public Prints: The Newspaper in Anglo-American Culture, 1665–1740* (New York, 1994); on the structural nature of the print de-

bates, see Michael Warner, *The Republic of Letters: Publication and the Public Sphere in Eighteenth-Century America* (Cambridge, Mass., 1990), 44–49.

42. Bridenbaugh, *Cities*, 226. In 1692 Mather lashed out at "our Learned *witlings* of the *Coffee-House*" when trying to retain his interpretive control of the convulsions of allegedly possessed Boston adolescents, and in 1724 he growled that the critics of his old-fashioned authority-laden prose style "must not think that the Club at their *Coffee-House* is *All the World*." See Robert Calef, *More Wonders of the Invisible World* (London, 1700), in *The Witchcraft Delusion in New England*, ed. Samuel G. Drake, 3 vols. (Roxbury, Mass., 1866), 2:41, and Cotton Mather, *Manuductio ad Ministerium* (Boston, 1726), 44. Raymond Phineas Stearns, *Science in the British Colonies of North America* (Urbana, 1970), 484–91.

43. For a brilliant portrayal of the shattering of Puritan Massachusetts at this time, see Perry Miller, *The New England Mind: From Colony to Province* (Cambridge, Mass., 1953), book 3. Mather himself in the eighteenth century experienced public derision, physical threats, and even young men gathering under his window at night to sing obscene songs. For a summary of abusive incidents, see Silverman, *Life and Times*, 221.

44. Mather, *Duodecennium*, 5.

45. See, for example, Cotton Mather's *Advice from Taberah* (Boston, 1711), on the Boston fire of 1711, *The Voice of God in a Tempest* (Boston, 1723), preached after a great storm, and *The Terror of the Lord* and *Boanerges* (Boston, 1727), both preached after the earthquake of 1727.

46. Lovelace, *American Pietism*, mentions four "real" jeremiads published after 1700, *Testimony Against Evil Customs* (Boston, 1719), *The Good Old Way* (Boston, 1706), *The Ambassador's Tears*, and *Suspiria Vinctorum* (Boston, 1726). However, if one takes the term "jeremiad" to mean specifically a sermon with a strong emphasis on degeneration from the founding fathers, on a continuing controversy between God and New England, and on threats of terrible judgments if reform does not occur, none of the above resemble Mather's seventeenth-century pronouncements, except fleetingly. Even if the definition is simplified to mean a sermon simply warning of divine judgments if no reformation, these sermons do not display the intensity of Mather's earlier ones. Middlekauff, *The Mathers*, also claims that Mather continued to preach jeremiads until the end of his life, but he cites no examples (407n. 12). Mather's change of tone in the eighteenth century can be demonstrated through the alterations he made in a single document. Mather wrote and sent to London for publication in 1701 a treatise on New England church practices, *Ratio Disciplinae Nov-Anglorum*. The manuscript was not published there, and it was finally printed in 1726, in Boston. Mather ended the 1701 draft (MS, Massachusetts Historical Society, no pag.) with a jeremiad-type caution that New England was declining from the piety of the founders and that some "seers" were afraid that the Lord might soon remove his "golden candlesticks" from the land. The passage remained in the 1726 version (196) but to it, Mather added a few sentences expressing his hopes that this was not to be.

47. Recounting in 1714, in *Duodecennium Luctuosum* (Boston, 1714), for example, the English disasters in the eastern Indian wars, Mather heard the voice of God in each one, saying, *"Thou hast Sinned against my Covenant"* (10). Yet Mather reassured his audience that the voice of God's providences in their entirety was saying "*Ah! My Poor*

People; How shall I give thee up? As yet, I cannot do it; I will not do it!" (26). He ended his sermon with a list of God's favors to New England, including the recent accession of George the First to the throne of England. The following year, in a mostly elegiac sermon, *Successive Generations* (Boston, 1715), 31–39, Mather paraphrased Stoughton's famous phrase from 1668 about God sifting three kingdoms to sow his plantation, and cautioned, as preachers had been doing for fifty years, that the last of the godly generation was almost gone. Mather then predicted destruction for the coming generation if it degenerated. But even so, Mather was far more conditional than he had been twenty years earlier. The emphasis was on potential declension, not the reality thereof: "Beware of *Degenerating* from the Godliness of your *Ancestors*" (quote from 32). Mather's tone could even border on the complacent: "The Body of the People, are a *sober, honest, well-instructed People* . . . there is also . . . a Generation of Serious, Prayerful, Watchfull *Christians* . . . There is likewise a Set of *young Ministers* . . . who are full of Goodness." Cotton Mather, *Thoughts for the Day of Rain* (Boston, 1712), 63–64. See also ibid., *Coelestinus* (Boston, 1723), vi.

48. Mather, *Diary*, 2:71.

49. Cotton Mather, *Compassions Called For* (Boston, 1711), 26–28.

50. Ibid., 30.

51. Ibid., 30–31.

52. Mather, *Boanerges*, 38.

53. Mather himself was the subject of unflattering providential analysis, on the basis of his many misfortunes. For example, in the *Diary*, 2:708, he lamented, "Every Body points at me, and speaks of me, as by far the most afflicted Minister in all *New England*. And many look on me as the *greatest Sinner* because the *greatest Sufferer*: and are pretty Arbitrary in their Conjectures on my punished Miscarriages."

54. Mather, *Boanerges*, 36.

55. Ibid., 25–26.

56. Ibid., 36.

57. Ibid., 32.

58. Ibid., 28.

59. Ibid., 28.

60. Ibid., 41.

61. In 1691, for example, Mather had no difficulty in explaining the knotty question of how God could bring a soul to grace while preserving its free will, a question bound up with that of predestination. Faced with the same question in 1706, Mather replied, "I will make as Learned an Answer to it, as any I have met withal. My answer is, *I cannot tell; I say, I cannot tell* . . . we must Glorify GOD, by Confessing His work to be *Incomprehensible*." In 1724 Mather referred to "a Something within" to explain how the Christian received knowledge of heavenly things. See Cotton Mather, *Little Sheep Guarded against Grievious Wolves* (Boston, 1691), 68, ibid., *A Conquest over the Grand Excuse* (Boston, 1706), 13–14, ibid., *Religious Societies* (Boston, 1724), 11. See also ibid., *Free Grace Maintained and Improved* (Boston, 1706), 22–23, ibid., *Malachi*, 56–57, and ibid., *Utilitia*, 263.

62. Miller, *From Colony to Province*, chap. 25, has a brilliant and still very useful discussion of transformations in the meaning of reason, and Mather's acceptance

thereof, although he misses the historical importance of probabilistic reasoning and its humanist roots.

63. See, for example, Cotton Mather, *Compassions Called For*, 14, ibid., *Bonifacius. Or Essays to Do Good* (Boston, 1710), 25–26. But for an account that stresses the continuities between *Bonifacius* and Mather's earlier pietistic agenda, see David Levin, "Essays to Do Good for the Glory of God: Cotton Mather's *Bonifacius*," in *The American Puritan Imagination: Essays in Revaluation*, ed. Sacvan Bercovitch (New York, 1974), 139–55.

64. See, for example, Cotton Mather, *Reason Satisfied: And Faith Established* (Boston, 1712), ibid., *A Man of Reason* (Boston, 1718), ibid., *Lex Mercatoria, Theopolis Americana* (Boston, 1710), 15–18, ibid., *Bonifacius, Malachi* (Boston, 1716), 38–40, ibid., "The Measure of Equity," in *Piety and Equity United* (Boston, 1717).

65. Mather, *Lex Mercatoria* (Boston, 1705), 6.

66. The only important work of Mather's published in his lifetime not to get printed or reprinted in London was *Ratio Disciplinae Nov-Anglorum* (Boston, 1726). The prominent congregationalist Thomas Bradbury repeatedly reprinted a letter of Mather's supporting Bradbury's refusal to accept the United Brethren's tolerance of non-trinitarians; for the bibliography, see Holmes, *Cotton Mather*, 2:542–43. For positive effects in English disputes, see Francis De la Pilonniere, *The Occasional Paper*, vol. 3, no. 4 (1718), 23. Matthew Mead wrote a preface for the 1689 London edition of *Early Piety Exemplified*; Richard Baxter wrote the preface to the London edition of *Memorable Providences*, titled *Late Memorable Providences* (London, 1690); Nathaniel Mather, Matthew Mead, and John Howe wrote a preface for the 1697 London edition of *Pietas in Patriam*; Daniel Burgess wrote the preface for the 1699 London edition of *Serious Christian*; Daniel Williams, the "Presbyterian bishop," wrote the preface for the London edition in 1713 of *Reasonable Religion*; Thomas Bradbury wrote the preface to *The Christian Philosopher* (London, 1721); Edmund Calamy wrote the preface to the London edition of *Parentator*, abridged by Cotton's brother living in England, Samuel, and published as *Memoirs of the Life of the Late Reverend Increase Mather* (London, 1725).

67. The quotation comes from Walter Wilson, *The History and Antiquities of the Dissenting Churches and Meeting Houses, in London, Westminster, and Southwark*, 4 vols. (London, 1808), 1:230. The last London edition of a work of Mather's for reasons of piety was *Right Thoughts in Sad Hours* in 1831. Thereafter, he was reprinted for antiquarian reasons.

68. Robert Wodrow, *The Correspondence of the Rev. Robert Wodrow, Minister of Eastwood, and Author of the History of the Sufferings of the Church of Scotland*, ed. Thomas M'Crie, 3 vols. (Edinburgh, 1841–1843), 3:396. For a study of Mather emphasizing the complexity of the interaction of his American and English identities, see John Canup, *Out of the Wilderness: The Emergence of an American Identity in Colonial New England* (Middletown, Conn., 1990), 223–35. One difficulty in assessing how formative a sense of provinciality was in Mather's psychology is that it often seems to function as little more than one of a number of handy tools with which to ward off or explain criticism.

69. See Lovelace, *American Pietism*, chap. 7, for the best discussion on Mather and church unity.

70. Cotton Mather, *Things to be More Thought Upon* (Boston, 1713), 86 ff., ibid., *Diary*, 2:196.

71. Mather, *Malachi*, 52, 64.

72. Ibid., 43. The maxims as Mather worded them could cover a broad range of specific theological positions. The second maxim touches on the most controverted issues. For Tillotson's position on dependence on Christ, see *The Works of the Most Reverend Dr. John Tillotson*, 3 vols. (London, 1752), 3:307–17.

73. Cotton Mather, "Letter to F. de la Pilloniere," *The Occasional Paper*, vol. 3, no. 4 (1718), 25–29. The letter was reprinted in Samuel Mather, *An Apology for the Liberty of the Churches in New England* (Boston, 1738), 149–51.

74. Mather, *Malachi*, 56–57, ibid., *Vital Christianity* (Philadelphia, 1725), "Dedication."

75. Thomas Shepard, *The Parable of the Ten Virgins Opened & Applied*, 2d ed. (London, 1695), part 1, 132.

76. William Douglas, *The Abuses and Scandals of Some Late Pamphlets in Favour of Inoculation of the Smallpox* (Boston, 1722), 6, [anon], *A Friendly Debate; Or, A Dialogue Between Rusticus and Academius* (Boston, 1722), 5–6. *Letter-Book of Samuel Sewall*, Massachusetts Historical Society *Collections*, 6th ser., 1 (1886), 407, Mather, *Diary*, 2:775. Mather only identified the maker of the comment on his ecstasies as a "man in black," but this was a nickname for Colman, and the reference comes in a passage in which Mather was struggling to convince himself that he was pleased that Harvard offered its presidency to Colman, rather than him.

77. See Cotton Mather, *The Heavenly Conversation* (Boston, 1710), 31: "A secret Antipathy to a CHRIST . . . is the *Spirit* of the *Wicked One*, in his most undoubted & Apparent *Energy*, I have seen it, ah! I have seen *the horrible Thing*; In my very Neighbourhood I have seen it. One said of a Sermon, *He had not heard of a long while, a sermon that pleas'd him so well; The Name of* CHRIST *was not once mention'd in it.* Another said of a Book, *There was the Name of* CHRIST *so often in it, he could not endure to look upon it.*"

78. Reiner Smolinski, "An Authoritative Edition of Cotton Mather's Unpublished Manuscript 'Triparidisus,'" 3 vols. (Ph.D. diss., Pennsylvania State University, 1987), 2:335.

79. Mather, *Malachi*, 43.

80. Cotton Mather, *Cohelith: A Soul upon Recollection* (Boston, 1720), 2. Mather further swathed this publication in new sources of cultural authority by identifying himself on the title page only as a Fellow of the Royal Society. Elsewhere Mather fervently and conventionally proclaimed that Christianity had mysteries undecipherable by reason (above reason but not against it, the usual formulation went).

81. See the discussion of the prominent English Congregationalist ministers Isaac Watts and Philip Doddridge in Isabel Rivers, *Reason Grace, and Sentiment: A Study of the Language of Religion and Ethics in England, 1660–1780*, vol. 1, *Withcote to Wesley* (Cambridge, 1991), chap. 4.

82. On politeness, see two articles by Lawrence E. Klein, "The Third Earl of Shaftesbury and the Progress of Politeness," *Eighteenth-Century Studies* 18 (1984), 186–214, and "Berkely, Shaftesbury, and the Meaning of Politeness," *Studies in Eighteenth-Century Culture* 16 (1986), 57–68, as well as his book, *Shaftesbury and the Culture of Politeness: Moral Discourse and Cultural Politics in Early Eighteenth-Century England* (Cambridge, 1994). Quotation from "Third Earl of Shaftesbury," 95.

83. Peter Smithers, *The Life of Joseph Addison* (Oxford: Clarendon Press, 1954),

454, Mather, *Diary*, 2:205, 227, 212. On "colonial worship of Addison," see Henry F. May, *The Enlightenment in America* (New York, 1976), 37–38. For a broad discussion on the intersection of Augustan "civility" with traditional Puritan godliness, see Richard P. Gildrie, *The Profane, The Civil, and the Godly: The Reformation of Manners in Ortho-dox New England, 1679–1749* (University Park, Penn., 1994), chap. 9.

84. Mather, *Manuductio*, 30, Silverman, *Selected Letters*, 387. For the lashing out at the new standards, see Mather's well-known diatribe in *Manuductio* against literary criticism (44–46), a form associated with the appearance of the public sphere and its free exchange of opinion. Speaking out of an earlier conception of authority, Mather lamented, "The Blades that set up for *Criticks*, I know not who constituted or commis-sion'd 'em!" (45) But surely Mather reflected the new commercial standards of the eigh-teenth century when he points out in self-defense that his archaic citation-laden style delivered more value for the money! (45). Mather presumably would have agreed with Terry Eagleton's comments on the "juridicial technology" of early-eighteenth-century literary criticism, "revising and adjusting particular phenomena to its implacable mode of discourse . . . in the name of a certain historical emancipation." See Terry Eagleton, *The Function of Criticism: From the "Spectator" to Post-Structuralism* (London, 1984), 12.

85. Those visions are summarized in Middlekauff, *The Mathers*, 239.

86. Cotton Mather, *Une Grande Voix du Ciel a la France* (Boston, 1725), ibid., *Diary*, 2:607, 713, 672.

87. See *Theopolis Americana*, where Mather speculated that Massachusetts might be the site of the New Jerusalem.

88. Cotton Mather, *The Grand Point of Solicitude* (Boston, 1715), 24, ibid., *Stimu-lator* (Boston, 1724), 14, ibid., *The Case of a Troubled Mind* (Boston, 1717), 6.

89. Middlekauff, *The Mathers*, 233–34, claimed that Mather rejected the doctrine of preparation because it obscured God's power. Lovelace, *American Pietism*, 78–80, correctly pointed out that Mather remained all his life a preparationist, although he was aware of the psychological difficulties preparationism could create. Mather's mature opinion about preparation was that "*Converts* do sometimes needlessly *Distress* them-selves . . . by insisting too much on the *Measure* of this *Preparation*. But so much of this work, as will render us *Restless* without a CHRIST . . . Be sure there must be so much in our *Experience*, if we would be *Saved*." See Cotton Mather, *The Greatest Concern in the World* (New London, 1718), 14. His cautions about preparation were traditional ones made by earlier preparationists.

90. Mather underwent a temporary disillusionment with particular faiths after the death of his wife in 1702, but he rebounded fairly quickly; see Cotton Mather, *Parenta-tor* (Boston, 1724), 187–92, for a late defense of them. Scholars always point out that Mather's devotion to the angels, especially his visible communion with them, went be-yond the usual bounds of Puritan restraint. But that devotion was not unprecedented. Richard Baxter called on Protestants to worship angels more fervently in *The Certainty of the World of Spirits* (London, 1691), 221–36, a book Mather admired immensely. While Baxter repeated the usual Reformed caution about avoiding tangible communication with angels, he recommended highly a work by Isaac Ambrose that overlooked such scruples. See Isaac Ambrose, *Ministration of, and Communion with Angels*, especially 135–38, as well as *Looking unto Jesus*, 210–11, both in *The Compleat Works of Isaac Ambrose* (London, 1673–74). Mather cited Ambrose on angels in *Magnalia* (2:367), and

in his handbook for aspiring ministers, *Manuductio ad Ministerium* (100) he praised Ambrose extravagantly. Robert Middlekauff in *The Mathers* has noted the apparent influence of Ambrose on other aspects of Mather's devotional life (399n. 37). A comment John Cotton made in a sermon on Revelation could be read as indicating that seeing angels was a family tradition. See George Selement, "John Cotton's Hidden Antinomianism," *New England Historical and Genealogical Register* 129 (1975), 288.

91. Miller, *From Colony to Province*, 53-67, and passim, argued that Mather was approaching Arminianism. Miller's position was presented even more strongly by Jones, *Shattered Synthesis*, chap. 4. Middlekauff, *The Mathers*, disputed this, claiming that Mather, in a return to Calvinist purity, even rejected the doctrine of preparation because it obscured God's power (233). (But see n. 89 above.)

92. See Mather, *Diary*, 2:358, cautioning against "the commending of Ch[urch] of E[ngland] Authors, without proper Cautions and Antidotes against the corrupt Things, which come with what may be valuable in them." In *Manuductio* (80–89) Mather listed the authors he recommends to aspiring ministers.

Chapter Five. Cotton Mather and the Perils of Natural Philosophy

1. Cotton Mather, "An Appendix Touching Prodigies in New-England," in *The Wonderful Works of God Commemorated* (Boston, 1690), sigs. D–D2iii. Another cabbage root in the shape of a cutlass was observed in New Haven before the outbreak of King Philip's War. See Massachusetts Historical Society *Collections*, 4th ser., 8 (1868), 614. A shorter version of this chapter appeared as "Puritanism, Prodigies, and the Perils of Natural Philosophy: The Case of Cotton Mather," *William and Mary Quarterly*, 3d ser., 51 (1994), 91–105.

2. Good accounts of Mather's involvement with natural philosophy can be found in Raymond Phineas Stearns, *Science in the British Colonies of North America* (Urbana, 1970), 403–43, Robert Middlekauff, *The Mathers: Three Generations of Puritan Intellectuals, 1597–1728* (New York, 1971), chap. 16, and Kenneth Silverman, *The Life and Times of Cotton Mather* (New York, 1984), passim. For a subtle description of the interaction of Mather's scientific and religious interests, see David Levin, "Giants in the Earth: Science and the Occult in Cotton Mather's Letters to the Royal Society," *William and Mary Quarterly*, 3d ser., 45 (1988), 751–70.

3. For Pascalian fright, see Perry Miller, *The New England Mind: From Colony to Province* (Cambridge, Mass., 1953), 440. For dread at the implications of mechanism, see Middlekauff, *Mather*, 284. Middlekauff claims that Mather "must have" been frightened of mechanism (284), but his text gives no example, and the relevant footnote (413n. 16) simply asserts that examples can be found. "Blind" mechanism in Mather's writings was always triumphantly beaten down by properly understood science. Middlekauff makes the subtle argument about Newtonianism that, even if through it Mather consciously no longer perceived science as a threat, he went on to cultivate a religious sensibility that was outside the realm of scientific evaluation. My argument is that Mather never did make his peace with science, Newtonian or otherwise, for all his attraction to it.

4. *Spectator*, 31 May 1712, *The Diary of Cotton Mather*, 2 vols. (New York, n.d.), 2:246.

5. Mather, *Wonderful Works of God,* 24–27, 27–32, 12–13, 19.

6. Mather, "An Appendix," sigs. Dv–D2r. From the totality of Mather's comments about weighing the rest of the skeptics' accomplishments, John Spencer would seem to be the primary target. See note 20 below.

7. For the successful commodification of science in the early eighteenth century, see Larry Stewart, *The Rise of Public Science: Rhetoric, Technology, and Natural Philosophy in Newtonian Britain, 1660–1750* (New York, 1992). For the erasure of its controversial origins, see Robert Markley, *Fallen Languages: Crises of Representation in Newtonian England, 1660–1740* (Ithaca, 1993), chaps. 5 and 6. For its fashionableness, see Michael Hunter, "The Crown, the Public, and the New Science, 1689–1702," *Notes and Records of the Royal Society* 43 (1989), 109–11.

8. Arnold Williams, *The Common Expositor: An Account of the Commentaries on Genesis 1527–1633* (Chapel Hill, 1948), 261. Cotton Mather, "Biblia Americana," MS, Massachusetts Historical Society, Genesis 1 (the "Biblia" is unpaginated, but it follows the sequence of the Bible reasonably closely). The best description of the scientific material in Mather's commentary is Theodore Hornberger, "Cotton Mather's Annotations on the First Chapter of Genesis," *Texas Studies in English* 18 (1938), 112–22. The fullest account is Middlekauff, *The Mathers,* 284–96, but it is not reliable.

9. The manner of legitimizing modern knowledge by reference to ancient and sacred wisdom was not at all unique to Mather. The conception of the *prisca philosophia* was common in seventeenth-century English thought. See Danton B. Sailor, "Moses and Atomism," *Journal of the History of Ideas* 25 (1964), 505–32, J. E. McGuire and P. M. Rattansi, "Newton and the Pipes of Pan," *Notes and Records of the Royal Society of London* 21 (1966), 108–43, Paolo Casini, "Newton: The Classical Scholia," *History of Science* 22 (1984), 1–23, and specifically, if cautiously, for the relationship between the new science, eschatology, and mid-seventeenth-century Puritanism, Charles Webster, *The Great Instauration: Science, Medicine, and Reform, 1626–1660* (London, 1975). Assertions of the Mosaic roots of modern science were made by ministers well into the nineteenth century. See Theodore Dwight Bozeman, *Protestants in an Age of Science: The Baconian Ideal and Antebellum American Religious Thought* (Chapel Hill, 1977), 126–27. Before he had read Dickinson (see text at n. 11), Mather was speculating in his commentary on Genesis that Moses was identical with Hermes Trismegistus, the nonbiblical font of ancient wisdom. See also D. P. Walker, *The Ancient Theology: Studies in Christian Platonism from the Fifteenth to the Eighteenth Centuries* (Ithaca, 1972).

10. The latest possible date for Mather's endorsement of Newtonianism in the "Biblia," from that manuscript's layout, is 1702. Mather's first published praise for Newton did not appear until a decade later, in *Thoughts for the Day of Rain* (Boston, 1712), iii.

11. Mather referred to 1702 as "this present year" when describing Dickinson's book in the "Biblia Americana."

12. Thomas Pyle, *A Paraphrase with Short and Useful Notes on the Books of the Old Testament,* 2d ed., 4 vols. (London, 1738), 1: "Preface."

13. Middlekauff, *The Mathers,* 292–96, gives as an example of synthetic and original thinking by Mather an extended meditation on reconciling the "God of the whirlwind" with Newtonian science. But the meditation, derived from Matthew 12 in the "Biblia Americana," is only a very close, and clearly labeled, paraphrase of Samuel

Clarke, *A Discourse Concerning the Unchangeable Obligations of Natural Religion* (London, 1706), 349–67.

14. Cotton Mather, *Manuductio ad Ministerium* (Boston, 1726), 49.

15. Cotton Mather, *The Day and the Work of the Day* (Boston, 1692), 62.

16. Cotton Mather, *Magnalia Christi Americana*, 2 vols. (1702; reprint, Hartford, 1853), 2:519, 560.

17. See Cotton Mather, *Shaking Dispensations* (Boston, 1715), 7, ibid., *The Voice of God in a Tempest* (Boston, 1723), 9, ibid., *A Voice from Heaven* (Boston, 1719), 7–10.

18. Mather, *Day*, 66. The quotation, slightly changed, is from John Spencer, *A Discourse Concerning Prodigies*, 2d ed. (London, 1665), 227.

19. Colonial Society of Massachusetts *Collections* 33 (1940), 93, Massachusetts Historical Society *Collections*, 4th ser., 8 (1868), 354.

20. Cotton Mather, inscription dated 1692 on flyleaf of Increase Mather's copy of Spencer, *Discourse*, Mather Collection, American Antiquarian Society.

21. Mather, *Voice from Heaven*, 9, ibid., *Manuductio*, 28. Spencer is best remembered today for *De Legibus Hebraeorum* (London, 1685), an attempt to explain the Jews' ritual laws not as divine edicts but as adaptations from their pagan neighbors. While the book is regarded as a pathbreaking work of anthropology, one of Spencer's incentives (10–12) in naturalizing the Mosaic code was to prevent its appropriation by "Jews, Papists, and Fanatics," the last of whom bore more than a passing resemblance to Puritans. Unsurprisingly, Mather in Leviticus in "Biblia Americana" denounced Spencer's project as "a *Fine*, and perhaps the *Last*, Essay of Satan, to introduce Irreligion into the world." In this instance, Mather's unease about the direction of Spencer's scholarship was widely shared, as he knew. See J. A. I. Champion, *The Pillars of Priestcraft Shaken: The Church of England and its Enemies, 1660–1730* (Cambridge, 1992), 155–58, Mather, "Historia Apostelica" (preceding the Acts of the Apostles), 26, in "Biblia Americana."

22. Mather, *Shaking Dispensations*, 7, ibid., *Voice from Heaven*, 9.

23. The Mather quotation on the parhelion is from David Levin, *Cotton Mather: The Life of the Lord's Remembrancer, 1663–1703* (Cambridge, Mass., 1978), 92–93, Mather, *Manuductio*, 54–55, 50.

24. Mather, *Magnalia*, 2:560.

25. Cotton Mather, drafts of letters to the Royal Society, 15 October 1713, and 3 July 1716, Massachusetts Historical Society. "Reasonable Philosophers" by this time had stopped considering monsters to be ominous. See Lorraine J. Daston and Katherine Park, "Unnatural Conceptions: The Study of Monsters in Sixteenth- and Seventeenth-Century France and England," *Past and Present* 92 (1981), 20–64.

26. Thomas Milner, *The Life, Times, and Correspondence of the Rev. Isaac Watts, D.D.* (London, 1834), 372, R.G., in *Nature* 3 (1870), 46, Alexander Pope, *God's Revenge against Punning* (London, 1716), in *The Prose Works of Alexander Pope, 1711–1720*, ed. Norman Ault, 2 vols. (Oxford, 1936), 1:270, Robert H. Eather, *The Majestic Lights: The Aurora in Science, History, and the Arts* (Washington, D.C., 1980), 52.

27. Samuel A. Green, "Appearances of the Aurora Borealis in New England during the Last Century," *Massachusetts Historical Society Proceedings*, 2d ser., 2 (1885–86), 102–5. Green cited the 18 January 1643 entry in John Winthrop's journal and the

22 December 1692 entry in Samuel Sewall's diary as earlier observations of the aurora borealis; Mather, *Diary*, 2:596, ibid., *Voice from Heaven*, 2.

28. Stearns, *Science in the British Colonies*, 484–91.

29. Thomas Robie, *A Letter to a Certain Gentleman, &c.* (Boston, 1719), 8. On Robie's connections to Mather, see Stearns, *Science*, 427, 433.

30. Thomas Prince, *An Account of a Strange Appearance in the Heavens on Tuesday-Night, March 16, 1716* (Boston, 1719), 1–3, 11–12. Prince did not specifically offer an interpretation of the phenomenon, but the scripture verses at the end of the pamphlet and on the title page refer to the signs that would be seen in the heavens before the Second Coming of Christ.

31. Mather, *Diary*, 2:596. Prince's reaction to the pamphlet is unrecoverable, but he surely knew his older friend well enough not to take him seriously when he claimed that "If you incline to suppress it, I shall in that also be entirely satisfied."

32. Mather, *Voice from Heaven*, 6.

33. Ibid., 6–7. The defensiveness Mather showed in his approach to nature demonstrates a radically different sensibility than that of an earlier generation. Increase Mather, for example, in a digressive chapters in his *An Essay for the Recording of Illustrious Providences* (Boston, 1684; reprint, London, 1856, as *Remarkable Providences Illustrative of The Earlier Days of American Colonisation*), simply noted as self-evident that there existed wonders of nature that mortal man could not comprehend (70) before he went on to discuss these wonders at length. When he wished to bring up the subject of evil angels and lightning, rather than defend himself against charges of enthusiasm, as Cotton felt he must (see below), Increase defended himself against charges of heresy (88). Middlekauff, asserting that Increase was trying to "undermine the authority of scientific explanation" and restore the "ancient sense of divine mystery in life," posits a crisis of authority which there is no evidence that Increase felt (*The Mathers*, 144). Increase's nature was wondrous, not mysterious; any lacunae were effortlessly filled up by God. The crisis came one generation later. Maxine Van de Wetering, "Moralizing in Puritan Natural Science: Mysteriousness in Earthquake Sermons," *Journal of the History of Ideas* 43 (1982), 417–38, confutes Middlekauff by demonstrating that New England preachers up to 1727 and beyond found nothing mysterious in earthquakes; they were the rational communications of a rational God. But by limiting the scope of her inquiry, Van de Wetering misses the genuine dilemma felt by someone as alert and pious as Cotton Mather.

34. Mather, *Voice from Heaven*, 7–10.

35. Spencer, *Discourse*, sig. A3r.

36. See Simon Schaffer, "Newton's Comets and the Transformation of Astrology," in *Astrology, Science and Society: Historical Essays*, ed. Patrick Curry (Woodbridge, 1987), 219–44.

37. Mather, *Voice from Heaven*, 8, 10, 12.

38. Ibid., 13, 15, 14.

39. George Lyman Kittredge, "Cotton Mather's Scientific Communications to the Royal Society," American Antiquarian Society *Proceedings*, n.s., 26 (1916), 35.

40. Cotton Mather, *Christian Philosopher* (London, 1721), 1.

41. While many books mention English physico-theology in passing, the closest we have to a survey is Richard S. Westfall, *Science and Religion in Seventeenth-Century*

England (New Haven, 1958), a book very much showing its age. See also Robert H. Hurlbutt III, *Hume, Newton, and the Design Argument*, rev. ed. (Lincoln, 1985).

42. John Ray, *The Wisdom of God Manifested in the Works of Creation* (London, 1691), William Derham, *Physico-Theology, or a Demonstration of the Being and Attributes of God from His Works of Creation* (London, 1713). I used the edition of Ray edited by John H. Maddendorf (Oceanside, N.Y., 1976) and the second edition of Derham (London, 1714). For an intensive examination of the sources of *The Christian Philosopher*, as well as its composition, see Winton Solberg's introduction and notes to his edition of *The Christian Philosopher* (Urbana, 1993). See also ibid., "Science and Religion in Early America: Cotton Mather's *Christian Philosopher*," *Church History* 56 (1987), 73–92, ibid., "Cotton Mather, *The Christian Philosopher*, and the Classics," *American Antiquarian Society Proceedings* 96 (1986), 323–35.

43. Mather, *Christian Philosopher*, 293.

44. For Pershing Vartanian, "Cotton Mather and the Puritan Transition into the Enlightenment," *Early American Literature* 7 (1973), 220, *The Christian Philosopher's* "thought conform[s] to the beliefs of the early Enlightenment." For Kenneth Silverman, *The Life and Times of Cotton Mather* (New York, 1984), 249, its deity is "the smiling Deity of eighteenth-century liberal Protestantism." For Jeffrey Jeske, "Cotton Mather: Physico-Theologian," *Journal of the History of Ideas* 47 (1986), 588, 592, it has an "Enlightenment-like regard for reason" and displays "essential secularity." For Solberg, "Science and Religion," 90, it is "the herald of the Enlightenment in America" and is "in accord with the best scientific knowledge of the times." Middlekauff, *The Mathers*, 302–3, builds his analysis of *The Christian Philosopher* around a discussion of the Trinity that he attributes to Mather, but which Mather himself attributed quite properly to the Newtonian mystic George Cheyne. The passage itself in its effort to trace natural signs of the Trinity hardly demonstrates the conservative reservations about reason that Middlekauff claims for it. For more nuanced readings, see Perry Miller, *The New England Mind: From Colony to Province* (Cambridge, Mass., 1953), 441–43, and the very different analysis in Mitchell Robert Breitwieser, *Cotton Mather and Benjamin Franklin: The Price of Representative Personality* (New York, 1985), 101–16.

45. Mather, *Christian Philosopher*, 232, 295, 291, 114. Mather made his condemnation of reason after recounting the various puzzles the human mind had been unable to fathom. It was common for physico-theologians to claim that science demonstrated the limits of human reason (Mather had cited Boyle to that purpose a few pages earlier), as well as its capacities, but Mather's emphasis was his own. He may have been inspired in drawing up his list of puzzles by a similar sequence in Derham, for example, but Derham, instead of denouncing reason as a result, serenely concluded that the "infinitely wise Creator of the World" had kept those puzzles hidden either for unknown reasons or because people might misuse them. See Derham, *Physico-Theology*, 279.

46. Mather, *Christian Philosopher*, 53.

47. Ibid., 88, 8–9, 53, 101, 169, 162, 172, 197, 301. Mather presented the story of the raven with some diffidence. A few scholars note one or two of these supernatural interferences, usually the withholding of rain; none of them have commented on the extent and variety of the list. John Ray mentioned in *Wisdom of God* the withholding of rain as punishment (89). Both Ray (374–75) and Derham (83–84) stumbled trying to explain the benevolence of poisonous snakes and other venomous creatures; while

noting that their venom had some positive uses, they concluded that they existed as the rods and scourges of God. Derham consoled himself with the observation that such creatures were more prevalent in heathen lands, and Mather quoted that cheery thought (169). Mather was unique in credulously repeating in the best manner of the wonder tradition, stories from ancient authors about extraordinarily colossal snakes (167–68).

48. Mather, *Christian Philosopher*, 282.

49. Ibid., 292. For charms and witchcraft, see Cotton Mather, *The Angel of Bethesda*, ed. Gordon W. Jones (Barre, Mass., 1972), 294, 34. For prodigies, see ibid., *Shaking Dispensations*, 7–8, ibid., *Voice from Heaven*, 7–10. On meteorological operations by spirits, see ibid., *Voice from Heaven*, 7, ibid., *The Voice of God in a Tempest* (Boston, 1723), 5.

50. Mather, *Manuductio*, 51, ibid., *Christian Philosopher*, 2. On the significance of 1716, see Richard F. Lovelace, *The American Pietism of Cotton Mather: Origins of American Evangelicalism* (Grand Rapids, 1979), 64–72, and Middlekauff, *The Mathers*, 343–46. On Mather's attempts at Christian union, see Lovelace, *American Pietism*, chap. 7.

51. Mather, *Christian Philosopher*, 2.

52. Stearns, *Science in the British Colonies*, 426, Silverman, *Life and Times*, 252.

Chapter Six. Cotton Mather and the True Power of Devils

1. "Mather-Calef Paper on Witchcraft," ed. Worthington Chauncey Ford, Massachusetts Historical Society *Proceedings* 98 (1914), 251–52.

2. For extended discussions of Mather's relationships with the powers of darkness, see Richard H. Werking, "'Reformation is Our only Preservation': Cotton Mather and Salem Witchcraft," *William and Mary Quarterly*, 3d ser., 29 (1972), 281–90, Kenneth Silverman, *The Life and Times of Cotton Mather* (New York, 1984), chap. 4 and passim., David Levin, *Cotton Mather: The Young Life of the Lord's Remembrancer, 1663–1703* (Cambridge, Mass., 1978), passim, Perry Miller, *The New England Mind: From Colony to Province* (Cambridge, Mass., 1952), chap. 13.

3. Cotton Mather, *Memorable Possessions, Relating to Witchcraft and Possession* (Boston, 1689), 3d pag., 27. Divinatory practices in seventeenth-century New England are extensively discussed in Richard Godbeer, *The Devil's Dominion: Magic and Religion in Early New England* (New York, 1992), chap. 1.

4. Puritan writers generally made a sharp distinction between the predictive science of astrology, which they mostly considered impious, as well as conceptual nonsense, and the reality of astral influence upon earthly affairs. For a striking expression of this attitude, see William Perkins, *A Resolution to the Countrey-Man*, in *The Workes of that Famous and Worthy Minister of Christ in the University of Cambridge, Mr. William Perkins*, 3 vols. (London, 1613–18), 3:653–67. Perkins, in the course of an intense denunciation of the follies of astrologers and the meaninglessness of much of their terminology, gave spectacular examples of the causal power of celestial happenings on earthly mortal affairs. For example, the power of a conjunction of Saturn and Jupiter together with an eclipse of the sun in 1524 led to dramatic earthly results: "*Charles* King of *France* driven forth of his country, warre betweene the *Danes* and the men of *Sleswicke*. There was a great plague in *Germanie*, Civill dissention amongst the Princes of the Empire and

them which took the part of *John Huss*" (664). However, to actually make specific civic predictions on the basis of planetary movements was to skirt the edge of impiety, as well as illogicality. For a good overview of the use of astrology in New England, see Richard Godbeer, *Devil's Dominion*, chap. 4.

5. David D. Hall, *Worlds of Wonder, Days of Judgment: Popular Religious Belief in Early New England* (New York, 1989), 99.

6. Jonathan Mitchel, "A Continuation of the Body of Divinitie (lib. 4)," Massachusetts Historical Society, 31. For Cotton Mather's interest in astrology, see Michael P. Winship, "Cotton Mather, Astrologer," *New England Quarterly* 63 (1990), 308–14. The great Puritan William Perkins had an impressive knowledge of the rules of astrology and warned his readers that "this study [is] so pleasant, that it can hardly be left, when it is once begun." See Perkins, *Workes*, 3:622. A story about Samuel Lee is particularly interesting in its display of the mixture of fascination and dread with which the godly could approach astrology. Lee studied astrology when young, but then drew off in horror and burnt "near an Hundred Books" on the subject. However, he continued to keep a nervous eye on the heavens. When about to embark from Boston back to England in 1691, "he told his Wife he had view'd a Star, which according to the Rules of Astrology presag'd captivity." Lee tried to get the ship's captain to postpone the trip, without giving a reason, but failed. Off the coast of Ireland, the ship was captured by French privateers, and Lee died in a French prison. See Edmund Calamy, *A Continuation of the Account of the Ministers . . . Who were Ejected or Silenced After the Restoration in 1660*, 2 vols. (London, 1727), 1:55–56. For a fascinating attempt by an English Restoration Dissenter to both pursue his interest in astrology and remain within the bounds of orthodoxy, see *An Astrological Diary of the Seventeenth Century; Samuel Jeake of Rye (1652–1699)*, ed. Michael Hunter and Annabel Gregory (Oxford, 1988).

7. Keith Thomas, *Religion and the Decline of Magic: Studies in Popular Beliefs in Sixteenth- and Seventeenth-Century England* (London, 1971), 435–36. Secondary discussions of seventeenth-century astrology tend to get somewhat murky through the difficulty of dealing with a set of technical terms murky enough to start with. The outstanding exception is Patrick Curry, *Prophecy and Power: Astrology in Early Modern England* (Princeton, 1989).

8. Cotton Mather, *Wonders of the Invisible World* (Boston, 1692), 48, ibid., *Magnalia Christi Americana*, 2 vols. (1702; reprint, Hartford, 1853), 1:223, 222. It was common for hostile commentators to claim that successful predictions by astrologers too difficult to explain as lucky guesses were done with the aid of devils.

9. Cotton Mather, *Wonders*, 48, ibid., *The Short History of New England* (Boston, 1694), 30.

10. See Godbeer, *Devil's Dominion*, 139–51, for an overview of the almanacs' astrological material.

11. John Tully, *An Almanack for . . . 1694* (Boston, 1694), C. Lodowick, *The New England Almanack for . . . 1695* (Boston, 1695), and Tully, *An Almanack for . . . 1696* (Boston, 1696). Tully had been working civic predictions into his almanacs since *An Almanack for . . . 1692* (Boston, 1692). In 1694 he positively reveled in astrological terminology and predictions. There were some general predictions in the 1695 almanac, but following Lodowick's blast, there was no astrology in the 1696 almanac. Tully worked some predictions into the first issue of *An Almanack for . . . 1697* (Boston, 1697), but

left them out of the second issue of that almanac, presumably after a further uproar. In
An Almanack for . . . 1700 (Boston, 1700), Tully mentioned a forthcoming conjunction
of Mars and Saturn and remarked, in a wistful but perhaps gun-shy fashion, "much might
be inserted about these things according to Astrologie, but I will leave it to time to manifest the Effects." See Richard Godbeer, *Devil's Dominion*, 144–51, for a fuller and somewhat different account of reactions to Tully.

12. Hall, *Worlds of Wonder*, 58–60, suggests that the appearance of the Man of
Signs (a medical figure) in the New England almanacs in the last quarter of the century
was an indication of impiety, or a relaxation of Puritan vigor. However, Calvin himself,
in *An Admonicion against Astrology Judiciall* (London, 1561), sig. Di, sanctioned the use
of astrology for healing, and Jonathan Mitchel, "A Continuation," 28, seconded him in
New England. Godbeer, *Devil's Dominion*, while not regarding the appearance of the
Man of Signs as itself indicating a change in attitudes does see a loosening of astrological restraints in the almanacs of the late 1680s and early 1690s. He speculates that clerical expressions of hostility to astrology might have been fueled by those almanacs
(147). However, none of the almanacs until Tully's of 1694 actually trespassed into the
forbidden territory of judicial astrology. In fact, none of them skirted as close to judicial
astrology as Israel Chauncy's *An Almanac of the Coelestial Motions for the Year of the
Christian Aera 1663* (Cambridge, Mass., 1663).

13. On the decline of astrology in English learned culture, see Patrick Curry,
Prophecy and Power, chaps. 3 and 6. For a Dissenting divine's late-seventeenth-century
fulmination against astrology, see Francis Crow, *The Vanity and Impiety of Judicial Astrology* (London, 1690).

14. Clive Holmes, "Popular Culture? Witches, Magistrates, and Divines in Early
Modern England," in *Understanding Popular Culture: Europe from the Middle Ages to the
Nineteenth Century*, ed. Steven L. Kaplan (Ithaca, 1984), 85–111, has an excellent discussion of the interplay between popular and theological concerns in the development
of English witchcraft beliefs. Thomas, *Religion*, 444, points out that Puritans never
managed to get the laws of England regarding witchcraft rewritten to fully reflect their
spiritual priorities, and it was not until the beginning of the seventeenth century and
the passing of the most intense period of witchcraft persecution that their chief obsession, the contract with the Devil, began to figure in witch trials. He discusses the general difficulty of making a correlation between "strong Protestantism" and witch-hunting zeal (499–502). Similarly, there was no orgy of witch prosecutions during the brief
period of Puritan control in England in the mid seventeenth century, nor during the
Jacobean period when, if Patrick Collinson is to be believed, the Church of England
had finally achieved a certain amount of live-and-let-live tolerance between Puritans
and others. See Patrick Collinson, *The Religion of Protestants: The Church in English Society 1559–1625* (Oxford, 1982).

15. William Perkins, in the midst of a ferocious attack on the "damned art of
witchcraft," stressed that the common law requirements for conviction in a capital
crime, a free confession or two eyewitnesses, applied to witchcraft. He recognized that
some would object that those requirements would make it impossible to kill witches,
but juries had to be careful not to shed innocent blood. Richard Bernard and George
Gifford emphasized that the Devil could inflict afflictions without the aid of witches
and indeed often stirred up unjust witch prosecutions. John Gaule also noted the com-

mon people's quickness to make accusations of witchcraft, and he complained that "to advise them to prudence and Conscience in such a case; is to be reputed and reported, a Patron, a Pleader, a Favourer and a Flesher of Witches." Henry Holland, while not specifically sounding a note of caution regarding accusations, emphasized the need for the preaching of a regenerate minister, sound parish and family discipline, and the spiritual counselling of suspected witches before invoking the civil arm. William Perkins, *A Discourse of the Damned Art of Witchcraft*, in *Workes*, 3:644–45, Richard Bernard, *A Guide to Grand Jury Men* (London, 1627), 84–85, George Gifford, *A Dialogue Concerning Witches and Witchcraftes* (London, 1593), sig. G2r, John Gaule, *Select Cases of Conscience Touching Witches and Witchcrafts* (London, 1646), 86–87, Henry Holland, *A Treatise Against Witchcraft* (Cambridge, 1590), sigs. H1r–H3v, 13–18. The one exception to the generalizations above is Thomas Cooper's *The Mystery of Witchcraft* (London, 1617), which displays both a marked Puritan sensibility and a zeal to harry witches out of the land.

16. New England's exceptionalism might also be explained by the destruction of most of Virginia's colonial records during the burning of Richmond in 1864. The last recorded colonial trial for witchcraft, that of Grace Sherwood in 1706, took place in Virginia.

17. Carol F. Karlsen, *The Devil in the Shape of a Woman: Witchcraft in Colonial New England* (New York, 1988), suggests that the first generation of ministers helped to mount a witch hunt, spurred by a Puritanism that had a misogynist woman-as-witch bias. But her evidence, admittedly slender, vanishes almost to nothing upon examination. She claims that the Hartford minister Samuel Stone "extracted" and "pressured" a "confession" from an accused witch (21, 31); her source, however, only says that Stone tried to bring about the conversion of that alleged witch while imprisoned and says nothing about him extracting a confession. See *Narratives of the Witchcraft Cases, 1688–1706*, ed. Charles Lincoln Burr (New York, 1906), 135–36. Karlsen also cites a brief trial reference to what might have been a zealous sermon against witchcraft preached by John Davenport, but the reference might also only indicate a passing aside in a sermon on a different topic, "improved" by Davenport's listeners. Karlsen later cites (173–77) as evidence for her thesis the Massachusetts minister Samuel Willard's account of the Fall in his *A Compleat Body of Divinitie* (Boston, 1727). That account, according to her, dramatically demonstrates a witchlike Eve and a "blameless" Adam. As her citations in her summary demonstrate (176–77), she makes her case for extreme misogyny by taking quotations out of context and misreading others, while ignoring numerous passages that assert the exact opposite of what she claims Willard was arguing. Willard, for example, emphatically dismissed Adam's attempt to shuffle off his blame onto Eve (186–87) and lambasted Adam, clearly conceptualized as male, for violating all ten commandments (193–94).

18. Bernard, *Guide*, sig. A5v, Gaule, *Select Cases*, 68–69, John Cotton, *The Way of Life* (London, 1641), 5. Stuart Clark, "Inversion, Misrule and the Meaning of Witchcraft," *Past and Present* 87 (1980), 98–127, sees in the portrayal of witchcraft as an inversion of godliness a characteristic operation not just of theological thought of the period but of Renaissance thinking in general.

19. Bernard, *Guide*, 9–10. A non-Puritan dealing with the theme of malefic afflictions could strike a very different note. James I wrote in *Daemonologie* (1597; reprint,

1924), 48–49, that the afflicted could be helped "onlie by earnest prayer to GOD, by amendment of their lives, and by sharp persewing everie one, according to his calling of these instruments of Sathan, whose punishment to the death will be a salutarie sacrifice for the patient." See also Alan MacFarlane, "A Tudor Anthropologist: George Gifford's *Discourse* and *Dialogue*," in *The Damned Art: Essays in the Literature of Witchcraft*, ed. Sydney Anglo (London, 1977), 146–47.

20. Possessions were frequently thought to have been brought about through the actions of a witch. In seventeenth-century England, the epithets 'possessed' and 'bewitched' were almost synonymous. Thomas, *Religion*, 570, 583–84.

21. For studies of the ways in which the meanings of possessions were negotiated between the possessed person and attending ministers and other authority figures, see *Witchcraft and Hysteria in Elizabethan London: Edward Jordan and the Mary Glover Case*, ed. Michael MacDonald (London, 1991), xxxvi–xxxviii, and Karlsen, *Devil in the Shape of a Woman*, 231–48.

22. For discussion of the Darrell case, see Thomas, *Religion*, 576–83, Paul H. Kocher, *Science and Religion in Elizabethan England* (San Marino, Calif., 1953), 127–45, D. P. Walker, *Unclean Spirits: Possession and Exorcism in France and England in the Late Sixteenth and Early Seventeenth Centuries* (Philadelphia, 1981), 52–73.

23. Samuel Willard, *Useful Instructions for a Professing People in a Time of Great Security and Degeneracy* (Boston, 1673), 33, [John Carrington], *The Surey Demoniack* (London, 1697), sig. A2iiir. English Dissenter activities are summed up in Thomas, *Religion*, 487.

24. For Jollie and Petto, see A. G. Matthews, *Calamy Revised* (Oxford, 1934), 301, 338. On Jollie, see Richard L. Greaves, *Deliver Us from Evil: The Radical Underground in Britain, 1660–1663* (New York, 1986), 25, 31, 178, 197, 199. Massachusetts Historical Society *Collections*, 4th ser., 8 (1868), 350, 320, 315. Jollie's diary, *The Note Book of the Rev. Thomas Jolly A.D. 1671–1693*, ed. Henry Fishwick, Chetham Society, n.s., 33 (1894), shows an acute providential sensibility.

25. Cotton Mather, in Obadiah Gill et al., *Some Few Remarks Upon a Scandalous Book* (Boston, 1701), 43, 44.

26. Samuel Petto, *A Faithful Narrative of the Wonderful Extraordinary Fits Which Mr Tho. Sprachet (Late of Dunwich and Cookly) was under by Witchcraft* (London, 1693), 2.

27. Ibid., 13.

28. Ibid., sig. Aiiv.

29. On Jollie's reputation, see Edmund Calamy, *The Nonconformist's Memorial*, ed. Samuel Palmer, 2 vols. (London, 1775), 1:v. The fullest modern account of the Surey Demoniack is in Wallace Notestein, *A History of Witchcraft in England from 1558 to 1718* (Washington, D.C., 1911), 315–19.

30. The following account of Dugdale's possession is taken from Carrington, *Surey Demoniack*, and Thomas Jollie, *A Vindication of the Surey Demoniack as no Imposter* (London, 1698). According to Zachary Taylor, *The Surey Imposter: Being an Answer to a Late Fanatical Pamphlet, Entitled the Surey Demoniack* (London, 1697), 6, Carrington was said to have written the account, Jollie to have compiled it. The pamphlet was presented as a collective venture. Thomas Jollie signed his name to the defense of it, *A Vindication of the Surey Demoniack as no Imposter* (London, 1698).

31. Jollie, *Vindication* 48.

32. *The Diary of Abraham De La Pryme, The Yorkshire Antiquary*, ed. Charles Jackson, Publications of the Surtees Society, vol. 59 (London, 1870), 189.

33. Jollie, *Vindication*, 73.

34. Ibid., 76, Carrington, *Surey Demoniack*, sig. A2iiir, 39.

35. Thomas Hutchinson, *The History of the Colony and Province of Massachusetts-Bay*, ed. Lawrence Shaw Mayo, 3 vols. (Cambridge, Mass., 1936),· 2:15.

36. Charles Morton, James Allen, Joshua Moody, Samuel Willard, in Cotton Mather, *Memorable Providences*, sigs. Air, Aiv.

37. Mather, *Memorable Providences*, 3d pag., 10, 34.

38. Cotton Mather, *Unum Necessarium* (Boston, 1693), 130, ibid., *Addresses to Old Men, Young Men, and Little Children* (Boston, 1690), 88.

39. Mather, *Memorable Providences*, 135.

40. Ibid., 52, Hutchinson, *History*, 2:16.

41. Mather's other dispossessions were those of Mercy Short and Margaret Rule in 1692 and 1693. In the first instance, the young woman joined Mather's church, along with "many others, even some scores, of young People, awakened by the Picture of Hell, exhibited in her Sufferings." Mather, *The Diary of Cotton Mather*, 2 vols. (New York, n.d.) 1:161. The second episode similarly drew in converts, again mostly young, so that Mather could exclaim "the Devil got just nothing; but God got praises, Christ got Subjects, the Holy Spirit got *Temples*, the Church got *Additions*, and the Souls of Men got everlasting *Benefits*." Cotton Mather, *Another Brand Pluckt out of the Burning*, in Robert Calef, *More Wonders of the Invisible World*, in *The Witchcraft Delusion in New England*, ed. Samuel G. Drake, 3 vols. (Roxbury, Mass., 1866), 3:47.

42. Cotton Mather, *Late Memorable Providences Relating to Witchcrafts and Possessions* (London, 1691). Baxter, of course, had less than smooth relations with other Dissenters because of his theological innovations, and it could be argued that the label of "Puritan" falls more problematically on him than it does on figures like Jollie and the young Cotton Mather. See Cotton Mather's assessment of him in the *Magnalia*, 1:292–93.

43. Richard Baxter, *The Certainty of the World of Spirits* (London, 1691), sig. A4r.

44. On the various English editions of the Mathers' accounts of Salem, and their less than scrupulous editing by the publisher, John Dunton, see Albert B. Cook, "Damaging the Mathers: London Receives the News from Salem," *New England Quarterly* 65 (1992), 302–8, Samuel Petto, *A Faithful Narrative*, sig. Aiiv.

45. Baxter wanted an account of the Surey Demoniack for his *World of Spirits*, but his death ended that plan. The attempt to add it to Increase Mather's account of Salem failed when London ministers wanted more proofs and affidavits. Thereafter strange providences affected the project. After midnight on 18 November 1693, one of the ministers lying in his bed heard melodious sounds and indistinct sentences that seemed to threaten him with death if the manuscript were not published. On 16 September 1695, armed men stole the manuscript from one of the ministers while he was walking with it down the Strand in London to the publisher. A scornful reference to the case in a pamphlet by a local Anglican minister published in 1696, finally spurred John Carrington to publish his own version of the narrative, evidently without first clearing that particular draft with the other ministers involved, although it came with a preface signed by most of the attending ministers. See [Carrington], *Surey Demoniack*, sigs. A2v–A3r.

The reference to Mather is in a fragment of a letter to Jollie from Oliver Heywood, Jollie Papers, MS 12.78, Dr. Williams Library, London.

46. Charles Webster, *From Paracelsus to Newton: Magic and the Making of Modern Science* (Cambridge, 1982), 92. See also Moody E. Prior, "Joseph Glanvill, Witchcraft, and Seventeenth-Century Science," *Modern Philology* 30 (1932), 167–92, Allison Coudert, "Henry More and Witchcraft," *Henry More (1914–1687): Tercentenary Studies*, ed. Sarah Hutton (Dordrecht, 1990), 115–36, and Michael Hunter, "Alchemy, Magic and Moralism in the Thought of Robert Boyle," *British Journal for the History of Science* 23 (1990), 387–410.

47. Even when Anglicans had to wrestle with the Devil's work directly, they were little inclined to "improve" it, to draw religious lessons out of it. Consider, for example, the last conviction for witchcraft in England, that of Jane Wenham in 1712. She was indicted on the basis of a complaint from an Anglican clergyman, whose serving girl she had caused to run seven miles with a lame leg. The conviction and subsequent pardon produced a flurry of pamphlets. Most interesting for the present purpose is the pamphlet that both defended the prosecution and the existence of witches. The account was entirely matter of fact. The only attempt to "improve" upon present circumstances of the case came in the opening paragraph: "It often falls out, that by the overriding Providence of Almighty God, the most Hidden and Private Wickednesses are discovered by the very means us'd to conceal them, and so it happened to *Jane Wenham*." [Anon.], *A Full and Impartial Account of the Discovery of Sorcery and Witchcraft, Practis'd by Jane Wenham* (London, 1712), 1. The most thorough modern account of the affair can be found in Phylis J. Guskin, "The Context of Witchcraft: The Case of Jane Wenham (1712)," *Eighteenth Century Studies* 15 (1981–82), 48–71. See also the matter-of-fact encounter of an Anglican minister, J. Boys, with an old professed witch, *The Case of Witchcraft at Coggeshall, Essex, in the Year 1699, Being the Narrative of the Rev. J. Boys, Minister of That Parish* (London, 1901).

48. Cited in Norman Fiering, *Moral Philosophy at Seventeenth-Century Harvard* (Chapel Hill, 1981), 219.

49. Joseph Glanvill, *A Blow at Modern Sadducism*, 4th ed. (London, 1668), "Epistle Dedicatory," Joseph Glanvill (with additions by Henry More), *Saducismus Triumphatus*, 2d ed. (London, 1682), 216–17, 58–67. For the way in which More and Glanvill used their arguments about witches and evil spirits to combat radical sectarianism, see Thomas Harmon Jobe, "The Devil in Restoration Science: The Glanvill-Webster Witchcraft Debate," *Isis* 72 (1981), 343–56. An obscure book, Richard Bovet, *Pandaemonium* (1684; reprint, Aldington, Kent, 1951, ed. Montague Summers), appeared in the 1680s, combining "hot" Protestantism and an intensely intrusive, partisan supernatural realm. *Pandaemonium* assimilates stories of witchcraft to the witchcraft of the Catholic Church, an appropriate enough theme at the time. Bovet was a staunch Whig, and if he was not a Dissenter, he was at least a sympathizer, considering the surplice the Devil's work (72), and perhaps regarding recent theological trends in the Church of England in the same light (6). *Pandaemonium* includes what reads like an account of a recent Dissenting dispossession in Bristol (101–3), and it asserts the reality of prodigies and divinely assisted foreknowledge (56–57).

50. Richard Baxter, "To the Reader," in Cotton Mather, *Late Memorable Providences*, sigs. A4iiir–A4iiv. Baxter, true to his attempt always to locate himself as steer-

ing a middle course in religious matters, also attributed devilish influence to antinomianism.

51. Baxter, *Certainty*, 53.

52. Ibid., 239.

53. Jollie, *Vindication*, 43, Mather, *Memorable Providences*, 24. The devils also seemed to favor Quaker books, jest books, and books disproving the existence of witches, although Mather did insist that this "was no Test for Truth to be determin'd by."

54. MacDonald, *Witchcraft and Hysteria*, xlix–l.

55. Forrester Kent, "Decay of the Literary Supernatural During the Age of Dryden," *Enlightenment Essays* 5 (1974), 57–64, D. P. Walker, *The Decline of Hell* (Chicago, 1964).

56. Michael MacDonald, "Religion, Social Change, and Psychological Healing," in W. G. Shiels, ed., *The Church of Healing* (Oxford, 1982), 101–25, Thomas, *Religion*, 452–53. Only one of the early Restoration treatises attacking belief in witches, N. Orchard, *The Doctrine of Devils, Proved to be the Grand Apostacy of these later Times* (London, 1676), 67, 123, made even a passing slam at Dissenters, a situation to change dramatically later. Ian Bostridge, "Debates about Witchcraft in England, 1650–1756" (Ph.D. diss., Oxford University, 1991), has argued that Robert Filmer's *An Advertisement to the Jury-men of England* (London, 1653) was affected by his anticalvinism (32–55), but if it was a conscious polemic, it was at the least an extremely subtle one.

Chapter Seven. Cotton Mather and the Decline of the Demonic

1. *New England Weekly Journal*, 10 April 1727. The identification of Byles is based on the key given by C. Lennart Carlson in "John Adams, Matthew Adams, Mather Byles, and the *New England Weekly Journal*," *American Literature* 12 (1940–41), 347–48. Concern about 1666 stretched across Europe all the way to Russia and included Jews as well as Christians. See B. S. Capp, *The Fifth Monarchy Men: A Study in Seventeenth-Century Millenarianism* (London, 1972), 213–14. On the *New England Weekly Journal* itself, see Charles E. Clark, *The Public Prints: The Newspaper in Anglo-American Culture, 1665–1740* (New York, 1994), 143–57, who aptly describes its ethos as "polite Puritanism." Cotton Mather's friend Thomas Prince took an active editorial role in the journal, and the journal printed extracts from Mather's writings.

2. For expressions of bewilderment about Salem, see Cotton Mather, *The Day and the Work of the Day* (Boston, 1693), 65, ibid., *A Short History of New England* (Boston, 1694), 56, ibid., *The Diary of Cotton Mather*, 2 vols. (New York, n.d.) 1:215–16, ibid., *Magnalia Christi Americana*, 2 vols. (1702; reprint, Hartford, 1853), 2:446–71, 519.

3. Increase Mather, *Cases of Conscience Concerning Evil Spirits Personating Men* (Boston, 1693), 65–66, John Hale, *A Modest Enquiry Into the Nature of Witchcraft, and How Persons Guilty of that Crime May be Convicted* (Boston, 1702, written in 1697), Thomas Brattle, "Mr. Brattle's Account of the Witchcraft, in the county of Essex, 1692," *Massachusetts Historical Society Collections* 5 (1798; reprint, 1816), 64, 67, 73, 77, 78. See also David Levin, "Did the Mathers Disagree about the Salem Witchcraft Trials?" *American Antiquarian Society Proceedings* 95 (1985), 19–37. For interpretations claiming Salem did have a large intellectual impact, see Richard Weisman's conclusion in *Witchcraft, Magic, and Religion in Seventeenth-Century Massachusetts* (Amherst, Mass.,

1984), 181, and David D. Hall, *Worlds of Wonder, Days of Judgment: Popular Religious Beliefs in Early New England* (New York, 1989), 108, and 277n. 108.

4. Zachary Taylor, *The Surey Imposter* (London, 1697). The reference to the whoring is on p. 62. Taylor's surmise of Jesuit interference is based upon extremely circumstantial evidence and hardly accounts for the intricacies of the case (the theory is outlined on 58–69). The Surey Demoniack represented Taylor's second go at the exposure of exorcisers. Taylor had claimed in 1696, in *The Devil Turned Casuist* (London, 1696), to have exposed an attempted exorcism by Jesuits as similarly fraudulent. The Jesuits, he surmised, coached the possessed person in how to act convincingly, but then, by his own account, they were unable to fully exorcise him.

5. Taylor, *Surey Impostor*, sig. A2ir.

6. Ibid., sig. A2iiir.

7. John Deacon and John Walker, *Dialogicall Discourses of Spirits and Divels* (London, 1601), 106, 230. Deacon and Walker argued that the age of miracles ended in the New Testament, and therefore there could be neither possessions nor dispossessions. Their stand was an uncommon one for the time, but they still affirmed that the Devil vexed people bodily and circumstantially (61, 229), as well as mentally.

8. Taylor, *Surey Impostor*, 19.

9. For earlier examples of guilt by association with astrologers, alchemists, and Rosicrucians, see Thomas Sprat, *History of the Royal Society* (London, 1665), 364, John Spencer, *A Discourse Concerning Prodigies*, 2d ed. (London, 1665), 46. The classic assimilation of Puritanism to occultism and of both to enthusiasm is Jonathan Swift's *A Tale of a Tub*, written around 1696.

10. Taylor, *Surey Imposter*, sig. A2ir.

11. Jollie, *A Vindication of the Surey Demoniack* (London, 1698), 7.

12. The excerpts from letters are found in *The Surey Imposter*, 10–16, 33. The reference to Alsop is in Zachary Taylor, *Popery, Superstition, Ignorance, and Knavery, very Unjustly by a Letter in the General Pretended* (London, 1698), 17. Jollie was to claim in *A Vindication*, sig. A2v, that Alsop's initial skepticism about the Surey Demoniack was overcome when he examined all the affidavits attesting to it. [N.N.], *The Lancashire Levite Rebuk'd* (London, 1698), 2.

13. N.N. is occasionally identified in the secondary literature as John Carrington, but there is no positive evidence for this attribution, his style does not resemble that of *The Surey Demoniack*, and the author makes it clear that he does not approve of Carrington's text.

14. [N.N.], *The Lancashire Levite Rebuk'd*, 22–23, ibid., *The Lancashire Levite Rebuk'd: or a Farther Vindication* (London, 1698), passim.

15. "I concealed [my name] to avoid the blows of the contending Parties. For it's often the Fate of them that interpose as Friends to both . . . to disoblige both . . . And this I find too true from both Parties." N.N., *The Lancashire Levite Rebuk'd: or a Farther Vindication*, sigs. A2r–A2v.

16. Anne Calef Boardman, "Robert Calef and Some of his Descendants," *Essex Institute Historical Collections* 74 (1938), 255, 261.

17. The usual assumption, drawn from Calef, *More Wonders*, is that Calef's discussions with Mather began with the Margaret Rule possession in 1693. My speculation is built upon an admittedly weak chain of "perhapses." In "Mather-Calef Paper on

Witchcraft," ed. Worthington Chauncey Ford, *Massachusetts Historical Society Proceedings* 98 (1914), 265, Calef made the curious marginal note on a reference to Goody Glover, the convicted witch in the Goodwin children possession, "I remember you once told me you did not then understand the wiles of Satan, and how much of it you will now abide by I know not." Calef's quotation sounds like it came from a relatively leisurely and open conversation, somewhat removed from the pressures of Salem. In *More Wonders*, Calef mentioned being even in the same room with Mather only once, at the possession of Margaret Rule, in a crowd of some thirty people. Immediately thereafter, Calef circulated his salacious account of Mather's conduct at that scene, and their relationship became hostile. Given Calef's indignation at the proceedings at Salem, the conversation cited above might have preceded Salem and might have been contemporaneous with the Goodwin case. Another argument for Calef's beliefs not being indigenous is their singularity. The most Calef could say in *More Wonders* about public opinion in Massachusetts five years after Salem was that "most People were convinced of the Evil of some, if not most of those Actions" (93), hardly a popular vindication of his thorough skepticism regarding witchcraft.

18. Calef, *More Wonders*, 187–89. Calef's reluctance to acknowledge the corporeal reality of biblical devils and angels indicates that he was far from the "stark Biblical literalism" that was claimed for him by Perry Miller in *The New England Mind: From Colony to Province* (Cambridge, Mass., 1953), 250.

19. Calef, *More Wonders*, 106–7.

20. Ibid., 108–9.

21. Ibid., 86. The incident to which Calef was referring came when Mather was inspired "by a strong *impression* upon his mind" to abandon a prepared sermon and speak upon the glorious voice of God in the thunder. What made this "remarkable" was that at that very moment his house was struck by lightning. See Mather, *Magnalia*, 2:363.

22. Cotton Mather, in John Gill et al., eds., *Some Few Remarks*, 42, 54.

23. *A Collection of Tracts. By the Late John Trenchard, Esq; and Thomas Gordon, Esq.*, 2 vols. (London, 1751), 1:387. For the French Prophets, see Hillel Schwartz, *The French Prophets: The History of a Millennarian Group in Eighteenth-Century England* (Berkeley, 1980). For a discussion of Trenchard's *Natural History of Superstition*, see Frank E. Manuel, *The Eighteenth Century Confronts the Gods* (Cambridge, Mass., 1959), 71–78.

24. Trenchard, *Collection of Tracts*, 1:386.

25. *New-England Courant*, 11 September 1721, 2 February 1722.

26. For Hutchinson's background, and a speculative reconstruction of the prehistory of his *Historical Essay*, see Ian Bostridge, "Debates about Witchcraft in England, 1650–1756" (Ph.D. diss., Oxford University, 1991), 228–42.

27. Hutchinson, *Historical Essay*, xiii, xiv. That statement, besides being a hit at a certain kind of Dissenter, presumably reflects Hutchinson's desire to wish the High Church party out of the Anglican communion, not the first time he rewrote the realities of his church to fit his vision of it. See Bostridge, *Witchcraft Debates*, 239n. 45.

28. Hutchinson's vigorous attack on belief in witchcraft drew only one learned response, Richard Boulton, *The Possibility and Reality of Magick, Sorcery, and Witchcraft, Demonstrated* (London, 1722), a feeble and badly printed effort. Henceforth, witchcraft was left to popular culture.

29. Hutchinson, *Historical Essay*, 149–50.

30. Ibid., 101.

31. Mather could quite effortlessly explain the opposition to him in the smallpox crisis of 1721 as the result of satanic influences. To the end of his life, he was experiencing Satan's continual revenges upon him for his efforts to glorify God, revenges that included the stirring up of his considerable anger. Mather, *Diary*, 613, 632, 664, *The Diary of Cotton Mather D.D., F.R.S., for the year 1712*, ed. William R. Manierre II (Charlottesville, 1964), 39.

32. See Reginald Scot, *The Discoverie of Witchcraft* (London, 1584), 126, Thomas Ady, *A Perfect Discovery of Witches* (London, 1661), 68–69, Robert Filmer, *The Freeholders Grand Inquest* (London, 1669), 337–39, John Wagstaffe, *The Question of Witchcraft Debated* (London, 1669), 14–18, John Webster, *The Displaying of Supposed Witchcraft* (London, 1677), 127–31.

33. Cotton Mather, "Mather-Calef Paper," 256.

34. I thank Constance J. Post for help in puzzling out Mather's orthography in this passage. See also Mather's commentary on Deuteronomy 18 in the "Biblia Americana," Massachusetts Historical Society, for the traditional translation of "ob."

35. George Lyman Kittredge, "Cotton Mather's Scientific Communications to the Royal Society," American Antiquarian Society *Proceedings*, n.s., 26 (1916), 29.

36. In 1707 Mather published a tract in which he cautioned cursers that "Sometimes the *Daemons*, which are Invisibly and Generally about us," get permission to execute those curses on their objects, and "Sometimes no less than a Suspicion of their *Confederacy* with Daemons has been thus raised upon them." The sentence leaves it unclear whether such a suspicion would be warranted. See Cotton Mather, *A Golden Curb for the Mouth* (1707; reprint, Boston, 1709), 11–12. When Mather returned to the subject of cursing some years later, he made no mention of demons doing harm or of the danger of being identified as a witch. See ibid., *The Religion of an Oath* (Boston, 1719).

37. Isaac Watts's less than ringing endorsement of the Salem trials came in a letter to Mather sympathizing with him about Daniel Neal's history of New England: "I am much persuaded that there was much immediate agency of the devil in those affairs, and perhaps there were some real witches too." See Massachusetts Historical Society *Collections* 5 (1798; reprint, 1835), 202. In the 14 July 1711 issue, the *Spectator* made its famous pronouncement about believing in witchcraft without believing in a single recorded instance of it. My statement about Mather's reputation among London Dissenting ministers is based on an account of a dinner conversation in London at the beginning of 1710 in "The Autobiography of John Barnard," Massachusetts Historical Society *Collections* 3d ser., 5 (1836), 207, in which prominent ministers assimilated his account of the giant bones found at Claverack, New York, to a previously established opinion of him as credulous. Barnard returned to Massachusetts later that year.

38. Cotton Mather, *Parentator* (Boston, 1724), 167–69.

39. Bostridge, "Debates about Witchcraft," 183–98.

40. Mather, *Parentator*, 169.

41. Ibid., 164–65. For a similar interpretation of Salem at the end of the eighteenth century, see James Sullivan, *The History of the District of Maine* (Boston, 1795), 212. Sullivan, one of the founders of the Massachusetts Historical Society, fellow of the American Academy of Arts and Sciences, and future Republican governor of Massa-

chusetts, thought that atmospheric conditions might have contributed along with the evil spirits to the general irrationality.

42. Cotton Mather, *The Christian Philosopher* (London, 1721), 24.

43. In *Kalendarium Nov-Anglicanum . . . for . . . 1705* (Boston, 1705), Samuel Clough made general comments on the astrological import of eclipses and conjunctions but avoided specific astrological comments on stellar events, noting that "the practice thereof has not been usual in this country and the Lawfulness of it doubted by many Divines." Evidently, he drew no significant protest for doing so, and in his almanacs of the same title for the next two years, he was expansive in his use of astrology for civic predictions. Clough died in 1707, and no almanac writer followed up on his interest in the subject with anything like the same enthusiasm.

44. *Spectator*, 9 October 1712.

45. Cotton Mather, *Menachem* (Boston, 1716), 15, ibid., *Diary*, 2:401.

46. Cotton Mather, *The Angel of Bethesda*, ed. Gordon W. Jones (Barre, Mass., 1972), 294, 34, ibid., *Ignorantia Scientifica* (Boston, 1726), 15.

47. For comments on possessions, see Cotton Mather, *Reason Satisfied: And Faith Established* (Boston, 1712), 29, ibid., *The Christian Temple* (Boston, 1706), 24, Kittredge, "Cotton Mather's Communications," 32. On the continuing acceptance of the reality of the Goodwin possessions into the mid eighteenth century, see Thomas Hutchinson, "The Witchcraft Delusion of 1692," *New England Historical and Genealogical Register* 26 (1870), 389, evidence the more convincing because this continued acceptance disturbed Hutchinson.

48. Cotton Mather, *Angel of Bethesda*, 28–34. In this section, Mather was expounding his derivative idea of the "Nishmath-Chajim,"a vital spirit linking the body and the rational soul which regulated the body's health and could survive death. Mather had hopes that this entity could be used to explain witchcrafts and possessions, as well as apparitions and psychic phenomena.

49. Mather, *Ignorantia*, 16.

50. Increase Mather, *Five Sermons on Several Subjects* (Boston, 1719), 11. Edward Taylor in the 1710s pronounced that "God by his law ordered that such as dealt with familiar spirits should not live," and he claimed that "in the shape of a fly he [the Devil] is the Familiar of his Hags." See Edward Taylor, *Harmony of the Gospels*, ed. Thomas M. and Virginia L. Davis with Betty L. Parks, 3 vols. (Delmar, N.Y., 1983), 4:534–35. The editors date the writing of this massive manuscript from the 1680s to c. 1715–18 (4:iii–iv). The quotations occur on the sixth and fifth leaves from the end. See also Jonathan Edwards, *Religious Affections*, ed. John E. Smith, *The Works of Jonathan Edwards*, vol. 2 (New Haven, 1959), 310, and the extraordinary remark by a Salem minister, Peter Clark, drawing parallels between Baptists and witches in *A Defence of the Divine Right of Infant-Baptism* (Boston, 1752), 33.

51. *New England Weekly Journal*, 17 April 1727.

52. Ebenezer Turrell, "Detection of Witchcraft," *Collections of the Massachusetts Historical Society*, 2d ser., 10 (1822), 6–7. Turell acknowledged the reality of witchcraft, 19–20, but it is hard to imagine from his document a specific incident of it he would believe. Turell's attitude was typical of pious educated people in the eighteenth-century Anglo-American world. See Herbert Leventhal, *In the Shadow of the Enlightenment: Occultism and Renaissance Science in Eighteenth-Century America* (New York, 1976),

92–94. Turrell specifically took a swipe at Glanvill in *The Life and Character of the Reverend Benjamin Colman D. D.* (Boston, 1749), 33–35, contrasting favorably an encounter of Colman's with a ghost with Glanvill's stories.

53. Turell, quoted above, was reacting to a dramatic hoax staged by two young girls in 1720 in Littleton, Massachusetts. At the time, people argued only about whether it was a case simply of possession or whether it was witchcraft, similar to Salem. See Turell, "Detection of Witchcraft," 7–22. Thomas Hutchinson in the mid eighteenth century reported that the Salem outbreak was still widely considered to be the result of demonic activity, with the debate centering only around whether the afflicted or the accused were the center of that activity. Hutchinson, *History*, 2:19, and ibid., "Witchcraft Delusion," 393. For survival of witchcraft beliefs, see also Leventhal, *Shadow of the Enlightenment*, 85–91, 95–96, 99–107, and John Greenleaf Whittier, *The Supernaturalism of New England*, ed. Edward Wagenknecht (Norman, Okla., 1969), chap. 8. Perry Miller, *Colony to Province*, 357, implies that there was a mass revulsion against Mather expressed during the smallpox inoculation controversy for his role at Salem. The only evidence he gives for this is a mild quote from James Franklin in his preface to William Douglas, *Inoculation of the Small Pox as Practised in Boston* (Boston, 1722) (the charge was repeated in the *New England Courant*, 15 May 1722, and by John Williams, *An Answer to a Late Pamphlet* [Boston, 1722], 4), stating that there had been three infatuations in Massachusetts's history, the Quaker persecutions, Salem, and inoculation, with Mather's involvement censorable in the last two. Mather, at least in private, would not necessarily have disagreed with that characterization of Salem, and the characterization says nothing about witchcraft per se. The anti-inoculators had far heavier ammunition to fling at Mather, which they did frequently and with great gusto.

Chapter Eight. A Farewell to Wonders

1. Cotton Mather, *Providence Asserted and Adored* (Boston, 1719), 28, Samuel Mather, *The Life of the Very Reverend and Learned Cotton Mather, D.D. & F.R.S.* (Boston, 1729), 23.

2. Perry Miller, *The New England Mind: From Colony to Province* (Cambridge, Mass., 1953), 403, first made this argument, using as evidence Mather's "particular faiths," which he seemed to regard as Mather's own innovation. Robert Middlekauff, *The Mathers: Three Generations of Puritan Intellectuals* (New York, 1971), used the progression within a more complicated framework of the privatization of religious experience in the eighteenth century, alluding to Mather's growing "obsession with the Spirit and with subjectivity" and to "stories told of witchcraft and possessions" during this period that "offer no criticism of superstitious folklore," and "suggest the depths of Mather's growing anti-rationalism" (318–19). Richard F. Lovelace, *The American Pietism of Cotton Mather: Origins of American Evangelism* (Grand Rapids, 1979), 96, points out, without referring to Middlekauff directly, that much of what Middlekauff advanced as evidence for this obsession (*The Mathers*, 315–17) was Mather's propounding of the traditional doctrine of assurance by direct witness of the Spirit, and that Mather never abandoned "objective" methods of finding assurance. Michael J. Crawford, *Seasons of Grace: Colonial New England's Revival Tradition in its British Context* (New York, 1991), chap. 1, has shown that many Dissenting ministers in the late seventeenth and early

eighteenth century had a fervent interest in the coming approach of the Holy Spirit. All that stories of witchcraft and possession demonstrate is that Mather was out of sympathy with the direction of a natural philosophy whose parameters of legitimate knowledge were rapidly contracting.

3. Cotton Mather, *Utilitia* (Boston, 1716), 282. The comment comes at the end of a woeful list (275–82) demonstrating the inscrutability of Providence, long and fully elaborated: the godly afflicted, the wicked prosperous, the death of infants, wicked children of good parents, bad marriages, prayers of the Saints unanswered, the Reformation failing in Europe, evangelical attempts in America mostly unsuccessful, and a God who says, "*I desire not the Death of a Sinner, but had rather have him turn and live*" (281), while putting the vast majority of humanity out of reach of the only means by which a sinner could avoid eternal death, the Gospel.

4. On the cultural differences between Boston and its hinterland, see Richard R. Johnson, *Adjustment to Empire: The New England Colonies 1675–1715* (New Brunswick, N.J., 1981), 272–73.

5. A. W. Plumstead, *The Wall and the Garden: Selected Massachusetts Election Sermons 1670–1775* (Minneapolis, 1968), 10–11, Richard D. Brown, *Knowledge is Power: The Diffusion of Information in Early America, 1700–1865* (New York, 1989), 33. The other sources for background on the election sermons are Lindsay Swift, "The Massachusetts Election Sermons," *Proceedings of the Colonial Society of Massachusetts* 1 (1895) 388–451, Timothy H. Breen, *The Character of a Good Ruler: A Study of Puritan Political Ideas in New England 1630–1730* (New Haven, 1970), Perry Miller, "Declension in a Bible Commonwealth," *Proceedings of the American Antiquarian Society* 51 (1942), 67, ibid., *The New England Mind: From Colony to Province* (Cambridge, Mass., 1953), 375–84, and Harry S. Stout, *The New England Soul: Preaching and Religious Culture in Colonial New England* (New York, 1986), 140–41.

6. Biographical information on the preachers of the election sermons is taken from Clifford K. Shipton and John L. Silbey, *Biographical Sketches of those Who Attended Harvard College*, 17 vols. (Boston, 1873–1975).

7. This summary is based on my reading of the published seventeenth-century election sermons.

8. Increase Mather (b. 1639), *The Excellency of a Public Spirit Discoursed* (Boston, 1702), Solomon Stoddard (b. 1643), *The Way for a People to Live Long in the Land that God hath Given Them* (Boston, 1703), Jonathan Russell (b. 1655), *A Plea for the Righteousness of God* (Boston, 1704), Joseph Estabrooks (b. 1640), *Abraham the Passenger His Privilege and Duty Described* (Boston, 1705), John Norton (b. 1651), *An Essay Tending to Promote Reformation* (Boston, 1708), Grindall Rawson (b. 1659), *The Necessity of a Speedy and Thorough Reformation* (Boston, 1709), Samuel Cheever (b. 1639), *Gods Sovereign Government Among the Nations Asserted* (Boston, 1712), Peter Thatcher (b. 1651), *The Alsufficient Physician Tending to Heal the Political and Spiritual Wounds & Sicknesses of a Distressed Province* (Boston, 1711), Jeremiah Shepard (b. 1648), *God's Conduct of His Church Through the Wilderness, with His Glorious Arm, to Make Himself an Everlasting Name* (Boston, 1715), Samuel Belcher (b. 1640), *An Essay Tending to Promote the Kingdom of Our Lord Jesus Christ* (Boston, 1707).

9. Russell, *Plea*, 11.

10. Ibid., 10.

11. Ibid., 11, 13.

12. See, for example, Stoddard, *Way*, 7, 8, Estabrooks, *Abraham*, 16, Norton, *Essay*, 18, Rawson, *Necessity*, 26. Belcher had little time to concern himself with questions of declension, he was preparing his audience for the arrival of Christ's kingdom.

13. Shepard, *God's Conduct*, sig. A3r, 17, 28.

14. Ibid., 23–24. For Shepard's father's sermon, see, "Thomas Shepard's Election Sermon, in 1638," *New England Historical and Genealogical Register* 24 (1870), 366.

15. Benjamin Colman, *David's dying Charge to the Rulers and People of Israel* (Boston, 1723), 29.

16. Peter Thatcher (nephew to the Peter Thatcher cited above), *Wise and Good Civil Rulers, to be Duely Acknowledged before God's People as a Great Favour* (Boston, 1726), 14, Ebenezer Pemberton, *The Divine Original and Dignity of Government Asserted* (Boston, 1710), 29, Shepard, *Gods Conduct*, 12, Russell, *A Plea for the Righteousness*, 1.

17. The sermons are Pemberton, *Divine Original*, Benjamin Wadsworth, *Rulers Feeding and Guiding Their People with Integrity and Skillfulness* (Boston, 1716), Benjamin Colman, *The Religious Regards We Owe our Country, and the Blessing of Heaven Assured thereunto* (Boston, 1718), William Williams, *A Plea for God, and an Appeal to the Consciences of a People Declining in Religion* (Boston, 1719), Nathaniel Stone, *Rulers are not a Terror to Good Works, but to the Evil* (Boston, 1720), John Hancock, *Rulers should be Benefactors* (Boston, 1722), Colman, *David's Dying Charge to the Rulers and People of Israel* (Boston, 1723), Thatcher, *Wise and Good Civil Rulers*, and Robert Breck, *The Only Method to Promote the Happiness of a People and Their Posterity* (Boston, 1728).

18. Colman, *Religious Regards*, 20, Stone, *Rulers*, 14.

19. Breck, *Only Way*, 1–2, 2–3.

20. Wadsworth, *Rulers Feeding and Guiding Their People*, 10–11, Williams, *A Plea for God*, 37, Hancock, *Rulers should be Benefactors*, 12, Breck, *Only Method*, 31.

21. Norton, *Essay*, 2, Stoddard, *Way* 25. For an excellent discussion of how the concepts of reason, nature, and self-interest changed the quality of early-eighteenth-century Massachusetts preaching, see Edward Bruce Tucker, "The Founders Remembered: The Anglicization of the Puritan Tradition in New England, 1690–1760" (Ph.D. diss., Brown University, 1979), chap. 3.

22. Samuel Danforth, *An Exhortation to All: To use Utmost Endeavours to obtain a Visit of the God of Hosts, for the Preservation of Religion, and the Church, upon Earth* (Boston, 1714), Joseph Sewall, *Rulers Must be Just, Ruling in the Fear of God* (Boston, 1724), Samuel Moodey, *A Sermon Preached before his Excellency Samuel Shute Esq.* (Boston, 1721), Ebenezer Thayer, *Jerusalem Instructed and Warned* (Boston, 1725).

23. For example, Wadsworth, *Rulers*, 19: "A People are expos'd to heavy Judgment, by abusing and profaning Gods holy day"; Colman, *David's Dying Charge*, 35: "God threatned his People of old, if they were disobedient & impenitent . . . that they and their posterity should perish quickly from the good land which he gave unto them"; Hancock, 12: "Religion tends to prevent and divert Divine Judgments, and the Judgments of GOD are wasting and breaking things." The identification of the catholicks is taken from John Corrigan, *The Prism of Piety: Catholick Congregational Clergy at the Beginning of the Enlightenment* (New York, 1991), 4, 8.

24. Danforth, *Exhortation*, 7, Thayer, *Jerusalem Instructed*.

25. Thatcher, *Wise*, 15.

26. Williams, *Plea*, 10, 11, 12, 15, 34, 43.

27. John Rogers, *A Sermon Preached before his Excellency the Governour* (Boston, 1706), 29–30. The passage Rogers cites can be found in *The Works of the Most Reverend Dr. John Tillotson, Late Lord Archbishop of Canterbury*, 3 vols. (London, 1752), 1:36.

28. Breck, *Only Way*, 27–28.

29. Ibid., 28.

30. Rogers, *Sermon*, 50. The jeremiad passage runs from 49 to 53.

31. A good account of ministerial reactions to the earthquake is found in James West Davidson, *The Logic of Millennial Thought: Eighteenth-Century New England* (New Haven, 1977), chap. 3. English Anglican ministers at this time did not doubt that earthquakes were divine warnings, although others in English society were more skeptical. See T. D. Kendrick, *The Lisbon Earthquake* (London, 1956), chaps. 1 and 8.

32. Ebenezer Parkman, *The Diary of Ebenezer Parkman, 1703–1782*, ed. Francis G. Walett, with a foreword by Clifford K. Shipton (Worcester, Mass., 1974), 4, Breck, *Only Way*, 40.

33. Plumstead, *Wall*, 145, 225n. 2, Stout, *New England Soul*, 140, 141.

34. My definition of secularization is adapted from Michael MacDonald and Terence R. Murphy, *Sleepless Souls: Suicide in Early Modern Europe* (Oxford, 1990), 6. Stout's own masterful analysis of eighteenth-century election preachers' discussions of "Israel's constitution" in *New England Soul*, 166–72, supports the application of this definition to Massachusetts ministers.

35. Two of the three general surveys of Massachusetts orthodoxy of this period use a dialectical model. Perry Miller created a Puritan intellectual world so loaded with contradictions as to make its arrival at the Enlightenment all but inevitable. The only other attempt to describe the general development of New England orthodoxy over this period, James Jones, *Shattered Synthesis: New England Puritanism before the Great Awakening* (New Haven, 1973), presents the same picture of an unstable dynamic. Stout in *The New England Soul* turns the formula on its head by denying that significant change took place.

36. Mary Rowlandson, *The Sovereignty and Goodness of God, Together with the Faithfulness of His Promises Displayed* (Cambridge, Mass., 1682), William Okeley, *Ebenezer: Or, A Small Monument of Great Mercy* (London, 1675). Okeley's account was published by a printer for the Congregationalists, and in his preface Okeley claimed to have published his account at the importuning of several ministers in order to display the wonders of God's Providence.

37. The characterization is, of course, implicit in the concept of declension, a mode of analyzing the history of Puritanism that has been in continuous use from the seventeenth century to the end of the twentieth.

38. For the "Anglicanization" of Massachusetts sermonic imagery, see "Behold the Bridegroom Cometh! Marital Imagery in Massachusetts Preaching, 1630–1730," *Early American Literature* 27 (1992), 170–84. For the fissures in early-eighteenth-century English Congregationalism over the issue of Calvinism and Reformed orthodoxy, see Jeremy Goring, "The Breakup of the Old Dissent," in *The English Presbyterians from Elizabethan Puritanism to Modern Unitarianism*, ed. C. G. Bolam, Jeremy Goring, H. L. Short, and Roger Thomas (London, 1968), 175–218.

39. The characterization of some ministers' Calvinism is from Stephen Foster, *The*

Long Argument: English Puritanism and the Shaping of New England Culture, 1570–1700 (Chapel Hill, 1991), 308.

40. On the development of Arminianism in New England, see Conrad Wright, *The Beginnings of Unitarianism in America* (Boston, 1955).

41. *Jonathan Edwards: The Great Awakening*, in *The Works of Jonathan Edwards*, ed. C. C. Goen, vol. 4 (New Haven: Yale University Press, 1972), 294–95, 419, 427, 486, 420, 480, 468-69, for alarm about social disruptions, 431–32, for revelations being the root cause. Edwards used the term "revelations" in a contemporary sense, to mean "immediate significations from heaven . . . of something that should come to pass, or something that it was the mind and will of God . . . [to] do, which was not signified or revealed anywhere in the Bible without these impulses," a definition that if taken strictly, which Edwards did, eliminated a vast array of acceptable seventeenth-century practices (278).

42. Ibid., 432–39, ibid., *Religious Affections*, in *The Works of Jonathan Edwards*, ed. John E. Smith, vol. 2 (New Haven, 1959), 206–7. The dating of the *Religious Affections* sermons comes from Sereno E. Dwight, *The Life of President Edwards* (New York, 1830), 223.

43. Jonathan Edwards, *The Life of David Brainerd*, ed. Norman Pettit, in *The Works of Jonathan Edwards*, vol. 7 (New Haven, 1985), 504, 520. See also 450, 458, 502, 503, 518. On Edwards's editing of Brainerd's experiences, see ibid., 81. Edwards's 1743 example was his wife (presented anonymously). See ibid., *Great Awakening*, 432–39. Edwards stressed, not entirely accurately, that her "transporting views and rapturous affections are not attended with any enthusiastic disposition, to follow impulses, or any supposed prophetic revelations." He toned down her account of her spiritual experiences and made no mention of her occasional forays into prophecy (331–41). For Sarah Edwards's own account of her experiences, see *The Works of President Edwards: With a Memoir of His Life*, 10 vols. (New York, 1829), 1:171–86. For her prophetic capacities, see *Sketches of the Life of the Late Rev. Samuel Hopkins, D.D.* (Hartford, 1805), 41.

44. Edwards never repudiated the substitutionary atonement in print, but he wrote a preface to Joseph Bellamy's *True Religion Delineated* (Boston, 1750), a book that did just that and claimed on its title page to have found a middle ground between antinomianism and Arminianism. In the preface, Edwards praised Bellamy's work for having discovered the "distinguishing Nature of saving Religion" and, more sweepingly, the "Truth" (vii).

45. Joseph A. Conforti, "Jonathan Edwards' Most Popular Work: 'The Life of David Brainerd' and Nineteenth-Century Evangelical Culture," *Church History* 54 (1985), 188–201. Richard Rabinowitz, *The Spiritual Self in Everyday Life: The Transformation of Religious Experience in Nineteenth-Century New England* (Boston, 1989), 61–62, claims that New England orthodoxy by 1800 had stripped the conversion process of its nature of contact with a deity, turning it into consent to the "distant logic of the gospel plan," with God more or less the rational order of the universe. For the extent to which Edwards's followers altered Puritan conceptions of Providence, see Mark Valeri, "The New Divinity and the American Revolution," *William and Mary Quarterly*, 3d ser., 46 (1989), 741–69, and *Law and Providence in Joseph Bellamy's New England: The Origins of the New Divinity in Revolutionary America* (New York, 1994), passim.

46. *The Diary of Isaac Backus*, ed. William G. McLaughlin, 3 vols. (Providence,

1979) 1:4, 12, 21, for verses, 1:112, for judgments, and 1:79, for remarkable providences.

47. John Brooke, *The Heart of the Commonwealth: Society and Political Culture in Worcester County, Massachusetts, 1713–1861* (New York, 1989), 82–83, Isaac Backus, *A History of New England, with Particular Reference to the Denomination of Christians called Baptists,* 2 vols. (1777, 1784, 1796; reprint, Newton, Mass., 1879), 1:vi. By plotting his history in the language of civic humanism, Backus followed in the path of contemporary New England learned ministers. For discussions of the adoption of Whig themes into their providentialism, see Nathan O. Hatch, *The Sacred Cause of Liberty: Republican Thought and the Millennium in Revolutionary New England* (New Haven, 1977), and John F. Berens, *Providence and Patriotism in Early America: 1640–1815* (Charlottesville, 1978), 32–80. See also the interpretive essay by Mark A. Noll, "The American Revolution and Protestant Evangelism," *Journal of Interdisciplinary History* 23 (1993), 615–38. For brief discussions of how in ways besides the adoption of Whig themes the providentialism of learned ministers during the revolutionary struggle differed from earlier forms, see Hatch, *Sacred Cause of Liberty,* 163, and Lester S. Cohen, *The Revolutionary Histories: Contemporary Narratives of the American Revolution* (Ithaca, 1980), 15.

48. For a good introduction to the "Dark Day," now believed to have been caused by the combined effects of massive forest fires and a thermal inversion, see Peter Eisenstadt, "The Weather and Weather Forecasting in Colonial America" (Ph.D. diss., New York University, 1990), 184–88, Samuel Ellsworth, *There Shall be Wars and Rumors of Wars before the Last Day cometh* (Bennington, 1787), 7–11. Ellsworth is especially interesting in that he portrayed himself as a stalwart defender of New England orthodoxy while relying heavily on astrological predictions; Nardi Reeder Campion, *Mother Ann Lee: Morning Star of the Shakers* (Hanover, N.H., 1990), 92, 116, 123, Alan Taylor, *Liberty Men and Great Proprietors: The Revolutionary Settlement and the Maine Frontier, 1760–1820* (Chapel Hill, 1990), 2, John Dane, "John Dane's Narrative," *New England Historical and Genealogical Record* 5 (1854), 151. For survival of signs and wonders in popular religion, see Taylor, *Liberty Men,* chap. 5, D. Michael Quinn, *Early Mormonism and the Magic World View* (Salt Lake City, 1987), Nathan O. Hatch, *The Democratization of American Christianity* (New Haven, 1989), Stephen A. Marini, *Radical Sects of Revolutionary New England* (Cambridge, 1982), Jon Butler, *Awash in a Sea of Faith: Christianizing the American People* (Cambridge, 1990), 236–47, and John H. Wigger, "Taking Heaven by Storm: Enthusiasm and Early American Methodism, 1770–1820," *Journal of the Early Republic* 14 (1994), 653–70.

49. Horace Bushnell, *Nature and the Supernatural* (New York, 1858), chap. 14, has a wistful discussion of the affective and cognitive gulf between the learned providentialism of the seventeenth century and the learned providentialism of the nineteenth. For a general introduction to providentialism before the Civil War in the nineteenth century, see Lewis O. Saum, *The Popular Mood of Pre–Civil War America* (Westport, Conn., 1980), chap. 1. For civic providentialism through the Civil War, see Berens, *Providence and Patriotism,* 81–170.

50. On the disappearance of Providence as a learned doctrine, see Charles D. Cashdollar, *The Transformation of Theology, 1830–1890: Positivism and Protestant Thought in Britain and America* (Princeton, 1989), 346–63, and his earlier article, "The Social

Implications of the Doctrine of Divine Providence: A Nineteenth-Century Debate in American Theology," *Harvard Theological Review* 71 (1978), 265–89. For a general introduction to the decline of popular providentialism in the late nineteenth century, see Lewis O. Saum, *The Popular Mood of America, 1860–1890* (Lincoln, 1990), chaps. 1 and 2. In those segments of the evangelical and fundamentalist world not overly concerned about measuring themselves by extrinsic standards, the doctrine of special Providence is alive and well, as is the hermeneutic associated with it; a writer in the 20 June 1994 issue of *Christianity Today*, 29, praised John Flavel's treatise on Providence as "the classic on the subject."

Index

✶

Adams, Matthew, 136
Addison, Joseph, 90. See also Spectator;
    Tillotson, John
Afflictions, 10, 17, 47, 58, 59
Alchemy, 41
Allen, Thomas, 10
Allin, John, 54
Alsop, Vincent, 127
Anabaptists, 32, 72
Angel Gabriel, 22
Angels, 91, 126, 184n. 82, 194n. 90
Anglicans, 29, 32, 54, 60; apologetics of, 79;
    in Boston, 82; and Christ, uses of imita-
    tion of, 81; and Dissenters, concern about,
    71–72; High Church, 71, 209n. 27; in
    Restoration Massachusetts, 78. See also
    Church of England; Dissenters; Dissenters,
    Massachusetts; Israel; Judgments; Mather,
    Cotton; Possessions; Providence; Reason;
    Theology; Tillotson, John; Witchcraft
Anticalvinism, 31–32
Antinomianism, 32, 60, 216n. 44
Arianism, 69, 134
Arminianism, 30–31, 88–89, 150, 165n. 10,
    216n. 44
Assurance, doctrine of, 12, 13, 212n. 2
Astrology, 29, 31, 41; ministerial opinions
    on, 112–13, 202n. 12; Mather, Cotton,
    on, 113, 135; New England almanacs and,
    113–14, 135, 211n. 43; and reading Provi-
    dence, 38, 42, 51, 76; and weather, 67
Atheism, 42–43, 55
Atonement, 34, 151
Aubrey, John, 51
Aurora borealis, 101–5

Bacon, Francis, 31, 61
Backus, Isaac, 151
Baptism, 32

Baptists, 21, 24, 151, 162n. 65, 211n. 50
Batman, Stephen, 66
Battle of Worcester, 41
Baxter, Richard, 37, 121; Certainty of the
    World of Spirits, 119, 121, 205n. 66
Beard, Thomas, A Theatre of Gods Judgments,
    30, 68
Belcher, Samuel, 142
Bellamy, Joseph, True Religion Deliniated,
    216n. 44
Bellomont, Earl of, 82, 189n. 37
Bentley, Richard, 44, 96
Bercovitch, Sacvan, 8
Bible, 54; interpreting Providence, 10, 17–
    18, 57, 86, 141–42
Birds: demons or damned souls as, 72; talk-
    ing, 107, 108
Births, monstrous, 100, 182n. 55; Hutchin-
    son, Anne, and Mary Dyer's, 18, 22, 38,
    98, 133, 160n. 57, 170n. 57
Blake, William, 71
Blount, Charles, Miracles no Violation of the
    Laws of Nature, 173n. 81
Book of Common Prayer, 115, 122
Boston, 1676 fire, 26
Boulton, Richard, The Possibility and Reality
    of Magic, 209n. 28
Bovet, Richard, Pandaemonium, 206n. 49
Boyle, Robert, 72, 120, 173n. 79; discursive
    techniques, 64; as emblematic figure, 64;
    and Providence, 43, 64
Bozeman, Theodore Dwight, 8
Bradford, William, 21, 26
Bradstreet, Simon, 187n. 20
Brainerd, David, 151
Brattle, Thomas, 77, 125
Brattle, William, 45
Brattle Street Church, 71, 78–81
Breck, Robert, 145–47

Bridge, Thomas, *What Faith Can Do*,
  186n. 16
Bunyan, John, *The Life and Death of Mr.
  Badman*, 178n. 24
Burke, Peter, 6
Burnet, Thomas, *Sacred Theory of the Earth*,
  43
Burton, Robert, *Anatomy of Melancholy*,
  167n. 31
Bushnell, Horace, *Nature and the Super-
  natural*, 217n. 49
Byles, Mather, 124, 126

Calamy, Benjamin, 39
Calamy, Edmund, 71, 192n. 66
Calef, Robert, 128, 209n. 17; *More Wonders
  of the Invisible World*, 128–29
Calvin, John, 21, 27, 44; Providence, con-
  ception of, 11–15, 157n. 18. *See also*
  Astrology
Calvinism: in Church of England, 30, 32,
  35, 36, 165n. 10; and melancholy, 39, 51,
  167n. 10; and Providence, abuse of, 38–9,
  51. *See also* Enthusiasm; Presbyterians;
  Theology
Carrington, John, 117, 205n. 45
Catholicism, 29, 53, 117
Catholicks, 77–78, 144, 186n. 16. *See also*
  Colman, Benjamin; Dissenters,
  Massachusetts
Certainty, moral, 35, 79
Charles I, 41
Charles II, 37, 41, 55
Charnock, Stephen, 54–60, 70
Chauncy, Charles, *Seasonable Thoughts*,
  150
Chemists, 42
Cheyne, William, 106
Chiswell, Richard, 25
Christ, 20, 24, 31, 54, 107, 108
Christianity Today, 218
Church, true, 16, 24, 25, 53–54, 57–58
Church of England, 30, 32, 36, 37; High, 71,
  130, 209n. 27; Low, 134. *See also*
  Anglicans
Civil War (American), 152
Civil Wars, 64, 71, 150
Clarendon Code, 36
Clark, Peter, 211n. 50
Clarke, Samuel, 44
Clough, Samuel, 211n. 43

Coffeehouses, 50, 51, 83
Collinges, John, 53–60, 178n. 21
Colman, Benjamin, 77, 140, 142–43,
  193n. 76; and judgments, use of, 144,
  186n. 16
Comets, 63, 98; as omens, 18, 22, 163n. 8;
  predictability, 180n. 44; and weather, 67,
  98
Congregationalists, 78, 162n. 65
Contingency, 10–12, 44
Conversion, 16, 17, 47, 87
Cooper, Thomas, 203n. 15
Cotton, John, 75, 115, 161n. 60, 181n. 31.
  See also Comets
Council of Trent, 15
Covenant, of Grace, 86, 115
Covenant, national, 140, 146
Covenant renewal, 76, 86
Covenant, witch's, 115, 119, 129, 132–34
Crane, Thomas, 54–60
Cromwell, Oliver, 75
Cudworth, Ralph, 43

Dane, John, 9, 13, 15, 152
Dark Day, 151
Darrell, John, 115, 126
Darwinism, 43
Davenport, John, 18, 37, 63
Declension, 23, 24, 149
Dee, John, 31, 42
Deism, 71
Delbanco, Andrew, 8
Depravity, 35
Derham, William, 97, 105, 199n. 45
Descartes, René, 42
Devil, 14, 20, 24, 30, 47, 202n. 15; and
  Christ, imitation of, 81; and Great Awak-
  ening, 150; in Massachusetts, 74–75; pro-
  digies caused by, 38, 99. *See also*
  Astrology; Possessions; Salem witchcraft;
  Storms; Witchcraft
Dickinson, Edmund, *Physica vetus et vera*,
  97
Dissenter Providence treatises: on afflictions,
  58–59; interpretive assumptions of, 56, 70;
  on judgments, 58; on the Last Days; 59;
  on prayer, 57; on the true Church, 57–58
Dissenters, 22, 25, 35–37, 64, 68, 134. *See
  also* Anglicans; Calvinism; Dissenter Providence treatises; Enthusiasm; Providence;
  Reason; Surey Demoniack; Tillotson, John

Dissenters, Massachusetts: and Anglican Church, 78, 187n. 20; international perspective, 53–54; provincialization of, 149. *See also* Catholicks; Congregationalism; Dissenter Providence treatises; Sermons, election

Divination: Calvinist interpretation of Providence as, 15; ministerial attitudes toward, 112, 113, 135; popular New England attitudes toward, 112; Renaissance learned knowledge as, 10, 135. *See also* Astrology

Dreams, 10, 18

Drummer of Tedworth, 65

Dudley, Joseph, 82

Dugdale, Richard. *See* Surey Demoniack

Duncalf, John, 40

Dyer, Mary. *See* Births, monstrous

Earthquakes, 18, 85, 147, 215n. 31

Echo, Proteus. *See* Adams, Matthew; Byles, Mather

Eclipses, 181n. 44

Economic change, in Restoration England, 50

Edwards, John, 44, 92

Edwards, Jonathan, 150–51; *Life of Brainerd*, 151

Edwards, Sarah, 216n. 43

Election, 32, 33

Eliot, John, 49, 161n. 60

Enlightenment, early, 45, 148; definition, 7; discursive patterns, 50–51; Mather, Cotton, reaction to, 138–39

Enthusiasm, 33; and Calvinism, 34, 51, 60; and Mather, Cotton, 89, 129; and Puritans, 34, 131, 167n. 31. *See also* Mechanical philosophy

Epicurus, 172n. 76

Estabrooks, Jonathan, 140

Eusibius, 184n. 82

Fasts, 54

Filmer, Robert, 207n. 56

Fiske, John, 19

Flavel, John, 54–60, 70, 218n. 50

Ford, Simon, 40

Foster, Stephen, 75

Francis II, 14

Franklin, Benjamin, 45

Franklin, James, 212n. 53

French Prophets, 51, 130

Gale, Theophilus, *Anatomie of Infidelitie*, 178n. 78

Gaule, John, 115, 202n. 15

Gearing, William, *The Eye and Wheel of Providence*, 177n. 6

General Court, Massachusetts, 19, 25, 161n. 60

Ghosts, 51, 62, 182n. 55

Gifford, George, 202n. 15

Glanvill, Joseph, 65, 120, 121

Glorious Revolution, 49, 71

Glover, Jane, 128, 209n. 17

God, governance of world, 9–11, 38, 43–44. *See also* Afflictions; Church, true; Dissenter Providence treatises; Judgments; Providence; Theology

Goodwin, John, 118; children of, 119, 128, 136, 211n. 47

Goodwin, Thomas, 164n. 97

Gordon, Thomas, 130

Grace, 32, 34, 46, 60, 107

Great Awakening, 150

Great Tew circle, 31

Greece, 14

Greenham, Richard, 168n. 31

Grotius, Hugo, 188n. 24

Habermas, Jürgen, 50, 51

Hale, John, *A Modest Inquiry*, 125

Hale, Matthew, 96

Halfway Covenant, 162n. 65

Hall, David D., 3, 5

Hall, Joseph, 30

Hall, Michael G., 25

Halley, Edmund, 102

Hammond, Henry, 32

Hancock, John, 144

Hartlib, Samuel, 63

Harvard College, 45, 77, 78, 82

Hawkins, Jane, 98, 133

Hesketh, Henry, 41

Heydon, Christopher, 29

Hibbins, Anne, 22

Higginson, John, 181n. 46

History of the Works of the Learned, The, 72

Holy Spirit, 12, 32, 47; and assurance, 212n. 2; Providence illuminated by, 18, 20, 33, 42, 160n. 55

Holy Trinity, 35

Hobbes, Thomas, *Leviathan*, 43

Hooke, Robert, 180n. 44

Hooker, Thomas, 16, 18, 19
Hubbard, William, 164n. 98; and Providence, conception of, 20–24; on tolerance, 21, 162n. 65. Works: *General History of New England*, 20–22, 162n. 65; *Happiness of a People*, 22, 162n. 5; *History of the Indian Warrs*, 22–23. *See also* King Philip's War
Hutchinson, Anne: and revelations, 19, 33, 83, 150, 161n. 60; and witchcraft, 151, 167n. 27. *See also* Births, monstrous
Hutchinson, Francis, *An Historical Essay Concerning Witchcraft*, 130–32
Hutchinsonianism, 174n. 83

Independents. *See* Congregationalists
Indians, 24, 25, 93, 149
Interregnum, 39, 60, 61
Israel: Anglican ministers on, 40, 53; Massachusetts, compared with, 141, 151. *See also* Church, true

Jackson, Thomas, 31, 170n. 59
Jacob, Margaret C., 50
James II, 54
Jeremiad, 76, 141–42, 145, 146, 190n. 46
Jollie, Thomas, 116, 118–22, 127. *See also* Surey Demoniack
Judgments, 14, 20–21, 25, 72; Anglican association of, with Puritans, 37; Anglican depoliticization of, 40; Catholick de-emphasis of, 144; against drinking, 20, 72, 84; Mather, Cotton, use of, 76–77, 82–86, 107; national, 40, 49, 146, 178n. 28; natural phenomena as, 67; partisan nature of, 62; against persecutors, 14, 58, 151, 178n. 24, 182n. 62; against Quakers, 65, 68, 150, 182n. 62; against Sabbath abuse, 14, 86; vindicating social hierarchy, 21, 76–77. *See also* Tillotson, John
Judicial astrology. *See* Astrology
Jurieau, Pierre, 133
Justification, 34, 46, 168n. 36

Keith, George, 182n. 62
King Philip's War: causes of, 23–24; and other Church disasters, 53; prayer, role in, 25; prodigies foreshadowing, 22, 98, 100. *See also* Hubbard, William; Mather, Increase

Klein, Lawrence E., 90
Knapp, Elizabeth, 116

Last Days, 25, 26, 51, 59, 69; and *The Christian Philosopher*, 108; Dissenter disagreements about, 59, 164n. 89
Laud, William, 31
Lawson, Deodat, 120
Lee, Samuel, 151
Leverett, John, 45, 71, 77, 82
Lightning, striking churches, 27
Licensing Act of 1662, 36
Locusts, 24
London, 1666 fire, 26
Long Parliament, 37
Lots, 30
Louis XIV, 114

Magic, 31, 41
Mason, John, 51–52
Mather, Cotton, 27, 44, 49, 54, 130; and Anglican apologetics, 79; and Brattle Street Church, 79, 80, 81; on Genesis I, 95–98; international reputation, 87–88, 134; in Massachusetts community, 76, 82–89, 129; particular faiths, 91; piety, maxims of, 88; politeness, accommodation to, 89–90; and Providence, 74–75, 138–39; and Puritanism, 75; and theology, 87–89, 91, 194n. 89; and universality, aspiration to, 79–80. Works: *Angel of Bethesda*, 136; *Armour of Christianity*, 133; "Biblia Americana," 95–98, 132–33, 197n. 21; *Boangeres*, 85–86; *The Christian Philosopher*, 105–9; *Late Memorable Providences*, 119, 121; *Magnalia Christi Americana*, 74–75, 77, 98, 100, 124, 148; *Memorable Providences*, 118, 119; *Reasonable Religion*, 79; *Terriblia Dei*, 76–77, 84; *Things for a Distress'd People to Think upon*, 76. *See also* Angels; Astrology; Enthusiasm; Judgments; Natural philosophy; Possessions; Prodigies; Reason; Salem witchcraft; Spencer, John; Witchcraft; Witch of Endor
Mather, Increase, 49, 72, 99, 100, 140, 184n. 82; on Providence, 24–27; and Salem witch trials, blame for, 131, 134; on witchcraft, 72, 125. Works: *A Brief History of the Warr with the Indians*, 26; *Cases of Conscience*, 125; *The Doctrine of Divine*

Providence, 53, 66–67; *An Essay for the Recording of Illustrious Providences*, 63–69, 148; *A Further Account of the Salem Trials*, 120; *Wo to Drunkards*, 66. See also Dissenter Providence treatises; Natural philosophy; Spencer, John
Mather, Nathaniel, 192n. 66
Mather, Richard, 26, 75
Mather, Samuel, 192n. 66
Maule, Thomas, *Truth Set Forth and Maintained*, 128
Mead, Matthew, 192n. 66
Mechanical philosophy, 42–44, 70, 172n. 77
Melancholy, 38, 39, 86, 170n. 59, 184n. 82. See also Calvinism
Millennium. See Last Days
Miller, Perry, 8, 26
Mirabilis Annis, 37, 38
Mixon, John, 133
Montague, Richard, 35
Moodey, Samuel, 140
More, Henry, 43, 120, 121
Morse, William, 65
Morton, Charles, 27, 78, 99, 187n. 18
Morton, Nathaniel, 21
Moses, 96, 97, 196n. 9

N.N., 127–28
Natural philosophy: Restoration reconfiguration of, 42–43, 59, 83; and Mather, Cotton, 93–110; and Mather, Increase, 63, 72–73. See also Boyle, Robert; Reason; Royal Society
Nature, 143–47
Neal, Daniel: *The History of New England*, 133, 210n. 37; *The History of the Puritans*, 178n. 24
New England Courant, 83, 212n. 53
New England Weekly Journal, 124, 136
New Haven, 21
New Model Army, 32
Newspapers, Boston, 83
Newton, Isaac, 51; on gravity and Providence, 44, 93, 96; and High Church, 173n. 83
Nonconformists. See Dissenters
Norton, John, 9, 13, 16, 21, 187n. 20

Occultism, 15; Puritan divinity compared to, 42

Okeley, William, 215n. 36
Old Testament, 33, 141–42; witches of, 131. See also Witch of Endor
Omens, 22, 30, 182n. 55
Orchard, N., *The Doctrine of Devils*, 207n. 56
Original sin, 118
Owen, John, 52

Paré, Ambrose, 29
Parhelia, 19, 100
Parker, Samuel, 36; *Disputationes Deo, et Providentia Divina*, 177n. 6
Patrick, Simon, 41, 178n. 28
Paul, Saint, 46, 47
Perkins, William, 201n. 6; and astrology, 113, 168n. 31, 200n. 4; and witchcraft, 125, 202n. 15
Philosophical Transactions, 72
Pilonniere, Francis De la, 192n. 66
Plymouth Plantation, 21
Politeness: cultural ascendency of, 90; and Mather, Cotton, 89–90, 108–9; and Puritanism, opposite of, 90
Poole, Matthew, 60–63
Pope, Alexander, *Gods Revenge against Punning*, 69, 101
Pope-ass, 14
Popish Plot, 54
Possessions, 29; belief in, 122; Church of England attitude toward, 115–16; Dissenter publications on, 119–20, 131–32; Mather, Cotton, use of, 118–19, 122, 135, 136, 205n. 45, 209n. 17; Puritan and Dissenter attitude toward, 115–16. See also Goodwin, John; Sprachet, Thomas; Surey Demoniack
Prayer, answers to, 25, 54, 57, 74
Predestination, 12, 32, 36, 46, 157n. 18
Presbyterians, 32, 49, 62; and Calvinism moderated, 71; and Church of England, reunion with, 71
Preston, John, 32
Prince, Thomas, 102, 207n. 1
Prodigies, 36, 51; cabbage roots as, 93, 195n. 1; and Hubbard, William, 22, 28; Jackson, Thomas, treatise on, 31; and Mather, Cotton, 94–95, 98–105. See also King Philip's War; Spencer, John
Prophecy, 15, 51, 74. See also Providence

Providence: Anglican reformulation of, 36–
    41; Dissenters' political interpretation,
    36–41; Enlightenment conception of, 51,
    105; Norton, John, definition of, 9; Puri-
    tan use, 13–15, 17–20, 141–42. *See also*
    Calvin, John; Comets; Dissenter Provi-
    dence treatises; Hubbard, William; Judg-
    ments; Mather, Cotton; Mather, Increase;
    Natural philosophy; Possessions; Prodigies;
    Tillotson, John; Turner, William;
    Witchcraft
Public sphere, 50–51, 83, 176n. 114
Puritanism, 19, 148; definitions, 7, 75. *See
    also* Calvinism; Congregationalists; Dis-
    senters; Dissenters, Massachusetts; Enthu-
    siasm; Melancholy; Possessions;
    Presbyterians; Providence; Witchcraft
Pyle, Thomas, 97

Quakers, 21, 24, 72, 88; and revelations,
    160n. 55. *See also* Judgments

Ray, John, 105
Reason: Dissenters, attraction to, 71; Massa-
    chusetts election sermons use of, 143–47;
    Mather, Cotton, use of, 80; and natural
    philosophy, 42; Restoration Anglican use
    of, 35–36, 42, 45
Reprobation, 33, 34, 51
Restoration Church Settlement, 22, 36,
    183n. 74
Revelation, Book of, 27
Revelations: fatal example of, 179n. 37; Pu-
    ritan use of, 18, 19–20, 150–51, 160n. 55
Robie, Thomas, 101–2
Rogers, John, 145–46
Rosecrucians, 42
Rowlandson, Mary, 149
Royal Society: foundation of, 42; Mather,
    Cotton, communications to, 100, 105,
    133; members, 49, 51, 94, 101; norms,
    methodological and discursive, 42, 61–62,
    64–65; and witchcraft, decline in, 131
Rule, Margaret, 205n. 41, 209n. 17
Russell, John (Baptist), 21
Russell, John (Congregational minister),
    141–42

Salem witchcraft: Mather, Cotton, on, 119,
    124, 134; New England reactions to, 125,
    209n. 17, 212n. 53; satires on, 124; Sul-

livan, James, on, 210n. 41. *See also*
    Hutchinson, Francis; Mather, Increase;
    Mixon, John; Neal, Daniel; Watts, Isaac
Sanctification, 46
Satan. *See* Devil
Saul, King, 72
Science. *See* Natural philosophy
Scripture verses, as revelations, 8, 19, 127
Sectaries, 32, 60, 61, 62
Secularization, 148
Sermons, election, 140–47
Shepard, Jeremiah, 140, 142
Shepard, Thomas, 17, 18, 89
Sherlock, William, *A Discourse Concerning
    the Knowledge of Jesus Christ*, 168n. 36
Sherwood, Grace, 203n. 16
Short, Mercy, 205n. 41
Sibbes, Richard, 32
Sion College, 62, 63
Society for the Propagation of the Gospel,
    82
Socinianism, 134
Socinus, Faustus, 188n. 24
Sommerville, C. John, 34
Spectator, 51, 90, 94, 135, 147, 210n. 37
Spencer, John: *De Legibus Hebraeorum*,
    197n. 21; Mather, Cotton, attitude to-
    ward, 99, 197n. 21; and Mather, Increase,
    visits by, 99, 105; and prodigies desig-
    nified, 38
Sprachet, Thomas, 116
Sprat, Thomas, *History of the Royal Society*,
    38
Standish, John, 41
Steele, Richard, 90
Stoddard, Solomon, 140, 144
Stone, Nathaniel, 143–44
Stone, Samuel, 203n. 17
Storms, 67, 74; Devil's role in, 74–75, 107,
    152
Stout, Harry, 148
Surey Demoniack, 117–18, 120; controver-
    sies over, 126–28, 131; Dissenting re-
    sponses to, 127
Synod of 1679, 116

Taylor, Edward, 20, 68, 211n. 50
Taylor, Zachary, 126–27
Thatcher, Peter (1651–1727), 143
Thatcher, Peter (1678–1739), 146
Theology, 32, 34–36. *See also specific doctrines*

Thomas, Keith, 6, 50, 61; *Religion and the Decline of Magic*, 6

Tillotson, John: and Addison, Joseph, 51; and Dissenters, influence on, 45, 49–50, 71, 146; influence, general, 45; on judgments, 47–49; Providence, concept of, 46–49. *See also* Afflictions; Conversion; Devil; Grace; Holy Spirit; Justification; Predestination; Regeneration

Toleration, 62, 71, 88–89

Toleration Act, 71

Trenchard, John: *Cato's Letters*, 130; *Natural History of Superstition*, 130

Trinity College, 27

Turks, 14

Turner, William, *A Compleat History of the Most Remarkable Providences*, 68–69

Turrell, Ebenezer, 137

Ussher, James, 92

Wadsworth, Benjamin, 140, 141

Watts, Isaac, 210n. 36

Weber, Max, 148

Wenham, Jane, 206n. 47

Wheelright, John, 20, 161n. 61

Whigs, 71, 130, 134, 151

Whiston, William, 69; *A New Theory of the Earth*, 43, 44, 96

Whole Duty of Man, The, 175n. 99

Willard, Samuel, 29, 54, 116, 164n. 89

Williams, Daniel, 192n. 66

Williams, John, *An Answer to a Late Pamphlet*, 212n. 53

Williams, William, 144, 145

Wilson, John, 18, 25

Witchcraft, 22, 62, 72, 211n. 50; and astrology, 112; belief in, 122; Anglican interest in, 120–21, 206n. 47; Dissenter publications on, 119–20, 132; Mather, Cotton, attitude toward, 118–19, 133, 210n. 36; Puritan attitude toward, 114, 202n. 14, 202n. 15. *See also* Calef, Robert; Hutchinson, Anne; Hutchinson, Francis; Mather, Increase; Royal Society; Salem witchcraft; Sprachet, Thomas; Surey Demoniack; Witch of Endor

Witch of Endor, Cotton Mather's interpretations of, 129, 132–33

Winter, Samuel, 27

Winthrop, John, 26, 100, 161n. 60; and Hutchinson, Anne, 19, 160n. 57

Wonders, 14, 20, 29

Woodbridge, Timothy, 54

Worship, William, 168n. 31

Ziff, Larzer, 77

Library of Congress Cataloging-in-Publication Data

Winship, Michael.
Seers of God : Puritan providentialism in the Restoration and
early Enlightenment / Michael P. Winship.
p.   cm. — (Early America)
Includes bibliographical references and index.
ISBN 0-8018-5137-8 (hc : alk. paper)
1. Providence and government of God—History of doctrines—17th
century.   2. Providence and government of God—History of
doctrines—18th century.   3. Divination—History—17th century.
4. Divination—History—18th century.   5. Mather, Cotton, 1663–1728—
Contributions in doctrine of providence and government of God.
6. Massachusetts—Church history.   7. Puritans—Massachusetts—
Doctrines—History—17th century.   8. Puritans—Massachusetts—
Doctrines—History—18th century.   9. Reformed Church—Doctrines—
History—17th century.   10. Reformed Church—Doctrines—
History—18th century.   I. Title.   II. Series
BT135.W57   1996
231'.5'0974409032—dc20   95-32346
                                                        CIP

Printed in the United States
137139LV00003B/7/A